{ The Designer's Graphic Stew }

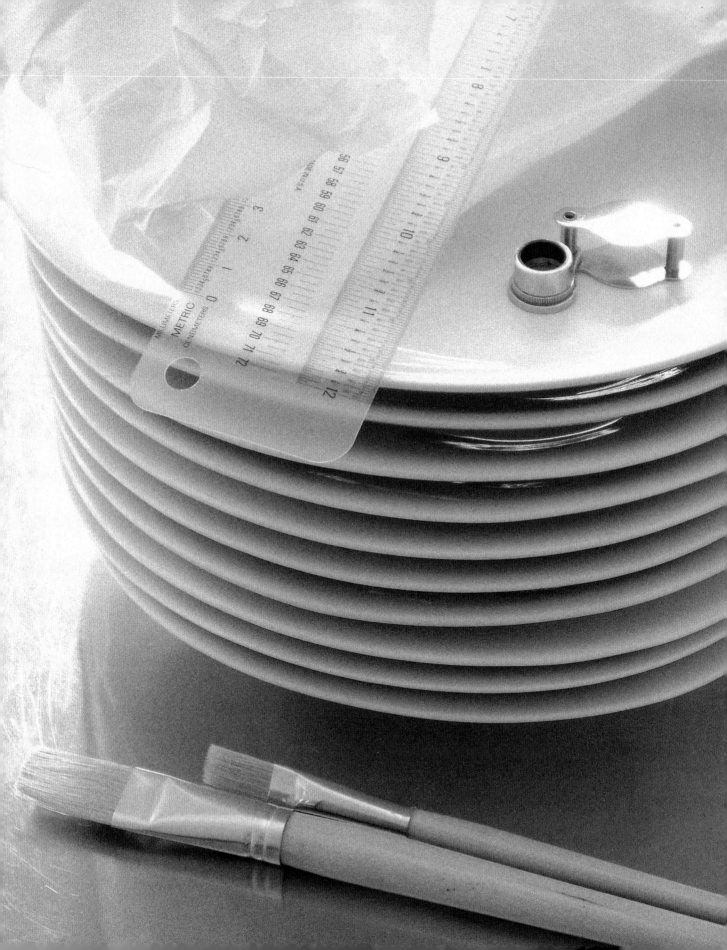

The Designer's
Graphic
Stew

Visual Ingredients, Techniques, and
Layout Recipes for Graphic Designers

Chef de Cuisine Graphique

Timothy Samara

BEVERLY MASSACHUSETTS

ROCKPORT PUBLISHERS

First published in the United States of America by
Rockport Publishers
A member of Quayside Publishing Group
100 Cummings Center
Suite 406-L
Beverly, Massachusetts 01915-6101
Telephone: (978) 282-9590
Fax: (978) 283-2742
www.rockpub.com

Library of Congress Cataloging-in-Publication Data

Samara, Timothy.
 The designer's graphic stew : visual ingredients, techniques, and layout recipes for graphic designers / Timothy Samara.
   p. cm.
 Includes index.
 ISBN-13: 978-1-59253-547-7
 ISBN-10: 1-59253-547-X
 1. Graphic arts--Handbooks, manuals, etc. I. Title.
 NC997.S23 2009
 741.6--dc22

                          2009017566
                           CIP

Cover and book design, book photography, and illustrations by Timothy Samara.

Photographic components of some illustrations in the Ingredients and Recipes sections are stock photographs, © Jupiter Images; such photographs are reproduced under license to the author/designer and used in accordance with the terms of that licensing agreement.

Printed in China

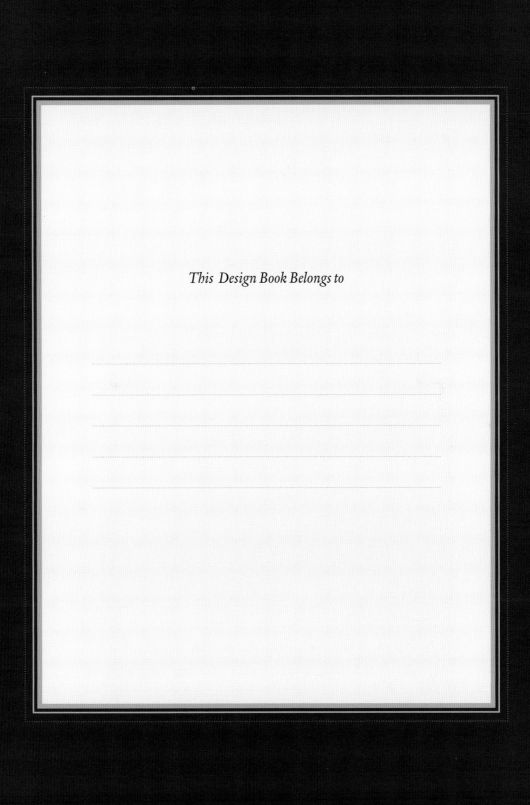

This Design Book Belongs to

....

....

....

....

....

CONTENTS

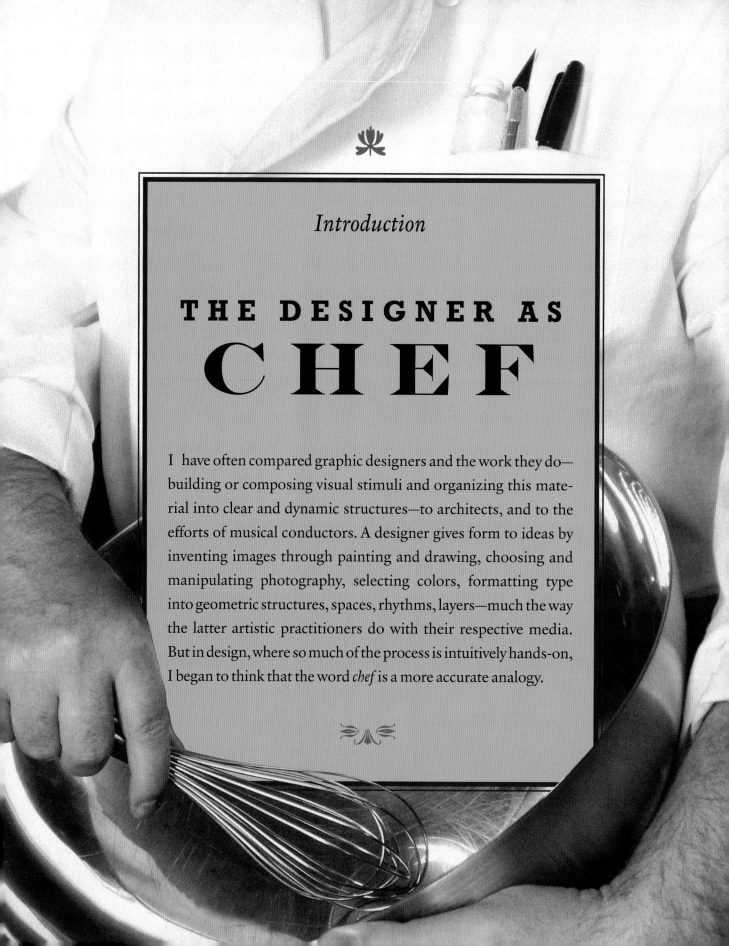

Introduction

THE DESIGNER AS
CHEF

I have often compared graphic designers and the work they do—
building or composing visual stimuli and organizing this material into clear and dynamic structures—to architects, and to the
efforts of musical conductors. A designer gives form to ideas by
inventing images through painting and drawing, choosing and
manipulating photography, selecting colors, formatting type
into geometric structures, spaces, rhythms, layers—much the way
the latter artistic practitioners do with their respective media.
But in design, where so much of the process is intuitively hands-on,
I began to think that the word *chef* is a more accurate analogy.

What is it, after all, that a designer does which is so different from what a chef does?

Each confronts an empty space—the page or the platter—charged with the task of producing a memorable, meaningful, and hopefully enjoyable experience. Each peruses his or her catalog of content, styles, methods, and details to envision a concoction that will speak to his or her audience with depth, drawing on the history of his or her cuisine (culinary or visual) and interpreting it with distinction.

The design process mirrors that of cooking. A chef tests various cuts of meat, combinations of vegetables, and preparation methods to create a basic culinary concoction. On the stove and on the fly, he or she adds more of this or that spice, changes the consistency of a sauce, turns the heat up or down ... fine-tuning the dish as it develops toward its savory conclusion. The same is true of designing. Testing conventions of page structure, differing column grids, and pictorial options, the designer comes to a vision for conceptualizing the content he or she must convey—and proceeds, through iterative experimentation, with the precise drawing technique, cooler or warmer color palettes, sharper or softer serif typefaces, textural fields or blocks of pattern, the larger or smaller instance of a photograph, to arrive at a visual meal that is, hopefully, just

as savory. A good designer, like a good chef, is aware not only of how each kind of ingredient is similar or different, but also of which delivers one message in contrast to another, and which will combine to create experiences that are harmonious or jarring, neutral or metaphorical, financial or medical.

You, as a designer, are the master chef in the kitchen that is your studio. Your bookshelves and paints and paper are your pantry; your worktable and your computer are your gas-fired grill and your convection oven. Your project—be it cosmetics packaging, a website, or a brochure—is the stew pot into which you'll toss the pictures, shapes, and symbols that make the meat of the project; the typography is your soup stock, the base on which the stew's flavor profile will ride; you'll flavor the melange with colors, both bold and nuanced, and braise the whole brew in a provocative composition that is satisfying in its messaging and delicious to the eyes.

How to Use This Book

The majority of this book catalogs a varied smorgasbord of graphical elements to which a graphic designer can turn in developing unique, engaging visual solutions on behalf of his or her clients—a breadth of compositional devices that can be used as is, or combined as needed for more intriguing flavors. This section, "Graphic Ingredients," presents fifty-seven categories of such elements, divided into four distinct groups: "Pictorial Staples" (icons, abstract languages, textures, and patterns); "Chromatic Flavors" (formal and conceptual color palettes); "Typographic Confections" (typeface combinations, form manipulations, editorial configurations, and ornamental devices); and "Spatial Presentations" (methods for dividing pages, cropping, and grid structures).

Each ingredient category fills two pages and has been assigned a number; within those pages, the individual ingredients are also numbered. The category number, plus the individual ingredient number, create a reference code for that particular ingredient. For example, the pictorial ingredient category *Textures: Representational* is numbered **10**. The last ingredient in that category (in the lower-right corner) is numbered **072**, so that ingredient's reference code is **10072**.

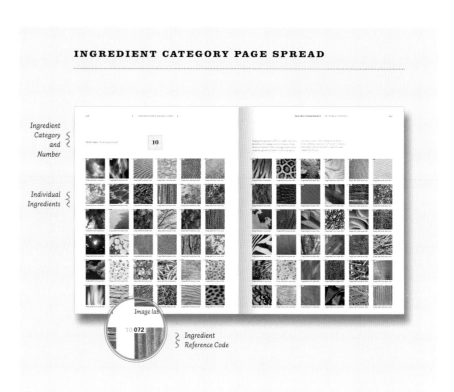

Once a designer has established the ingredients to be mixed, he or she must then be able to consider what possibilities exist for these ingredients in practical application— and how different ingredients may combine to create appropriate communications. In the second major section, "Project Recipes," the ingredients are used in hypothetical layouts for a range of project types—design recipes formulated to illustrate specific compositional and conceptual goals. Each project recipe begins with a *Messaging Menu*—a design brief that outlines the project's conceptual and visual communication goals to provide readers a context for the approaches being demonstrated. Translation of the English language typography that appears in the recipe design solutions is also provided in this introduction. All of the ingredients used in a given recipe are listed by their reference codes and a brief *Flavor Profile* describes how those ingredients interact, both visually and with regard to the meanings they evoke. Furthermore, the effect of substituting one or more ingredients in the same recipe is shown as a series of variations, so designers may understand both the visual and the evocative results of mixing different ingredients in similar kinds of layouts. Sprinkled among the recipe pages are real-world examples of related projects—tastefully prepared by some of the world's *chefs de cuisine graphiques*.

While the catalog of ingredients is comprehensive, and the recipes offer broad approaches that will help a designer start conceptualizing a project, it's important to note that no formula is offered here, only a mindset—an entrée into some of the limitless possibilities of bringing image, type, and layout together. It will always be the designer's task to determine not just which ingredients go together, but also what modifications an ingredient will need to work best. It's the idea of using an archetypal icon, rather than a photograph, embodied in that ingredient; what the icon shows, and its specific drawing quality, are other questions to be pondered.

Similarly, the recipes present methodologies, rather than set procedures, for using the graphic ingredients—just as cooking recipes do for the chef. A good cook knows that *Chicken Milanese* is a recipe for a breaded

PROJECT RECIPE OPENING PAGE SPREAD

~~
Each recipe is accompanied by a
Messaging Menu *that describes the
reasoning behind ingredient selection
and layout decisions.*

~~
*Ingredients used in a given recipe
are listed by their reference codes,
categorized by section, and
supplemented by their respective
page numbers.*

cutlet in a white wine and butter sauce; but the thickness of the cutlet, the amount of flour and egg, the proportion of wine to butter, and the duration of cooking are all variables the cook is free to change to accomplish his or her own vision of the dish. So, too, graphic designers must look beyond the hard-and-fast recipe presentation to determine which aspects of the recipe are most appropriate, which need modification for his or her particular purposes, and which must be discarded or combined with other recipe concepts to resolve the project in the most compelling and satisfying manner.

BASIC TECHNIQUES

Essential Visual Strategies

IN COOKING, MANY RECIPES OF a similar nature require common, underlying processes to realize the final dish—poaching a chicken breast, for instance, or preparing puffed pastry dough. Similarly, nearly all design problems share some fundamental aspects: Typefaces will need to be selected or photographs arranged in an interesting way across a layout. Regardless of specific concerns that may need to be addressed in a particular project, there are general strategies most designers will use as foundations for more complex visual concepts, or to ensure common notions of quality (e.g., that a layout is dynamic) are met in the final presentation.

In this preliminary section, you'll find a sampling of such essential visual techniques: developing rich color palettes; reliably mixing typefaces for contrast and style; using abstract forms to support other imagery and customize visual experiences; achieving dynamic picture placement within a column grid; and many more. Consider these strategies as building blocks—work from them with the ingredients and recipes that follow, and you're sure to become the *chef de cuisine* in your studio.

Preliminary Prep

Being able to conceptualize and compose seamlessly, efficiently working among various media to explore different ideas, means having all the tools you need—and the best ones for the job—on hand at all times. Here are the items no well-appointed studio can do without.

GUI Computer It's the six-burner cooktop, the studio workhorse. When comparison shopping, realize that there are few apples among the lemons—choose the best you can afford.

Spot- and Process-Color Swatch Books Don't trust the computer screen for color: See the real thing. They're an expensive, but ultimately indispensable, investment.

Precision Rulers The master design chef measures in 1/64" (0.396 mm) increments, and it's even better when the mea-suring device is transparent and flexible`   .

White and Kneaded Erasers White is for serious erasing from tough stocks. The kneaded version is best for delicate papers, or for slight tonal adjustments.

Lucite Brayer Unlike a rubber brayer, whose porous surface may stain or encourage peel-up, this rolls hard and fast, and cleans up spotlessly.

Steel Straightedge and Triangle Avoid aluminum for these tools—knife blades shred aluminum and, after a short while, a true edge is no longer a given. The triangle, archaic as it may seem, helps ensure 90° angles.

Bone Folder At some point, you'll need to make mock-ups to show clients. This is what you'll use to fold pages and covers.

Studio Knife Get a good knife with a textured gripping surface, and an array of interchangeable blades. Replace the blade every 6 to 8 cuts to keep the slicing sharp and clean.

Sable Brushes There's nothing like Kolinsky hair for precise handling. Two sizes—No. 4 and No. 6—are sufficient, but have three of each size on hand: one for black, one for white, and one for color.

Designer's Gouache Rich, opaque finish in both color and black and white; for the old-school virtuoso.

High-Resolution Loupe For examining serifs up close or supervising registration on a press sheet, 10X magnification or higher is best.

Cutting Mat Self-healing is best, to prevent making grooves that will misdirect your blade in the future.

Stainless Steel Whisk This tool is most useful for beating air into colors and rapidly combining visual elements into flawless layouts. Just kidding, actually.

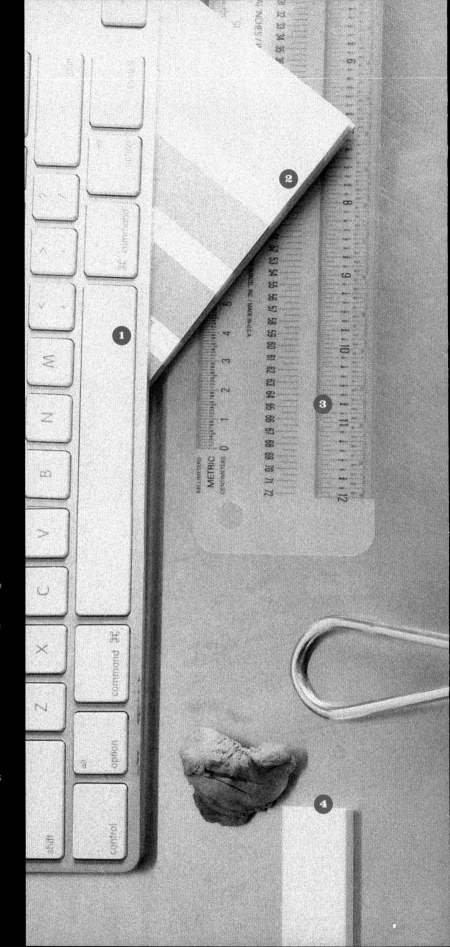

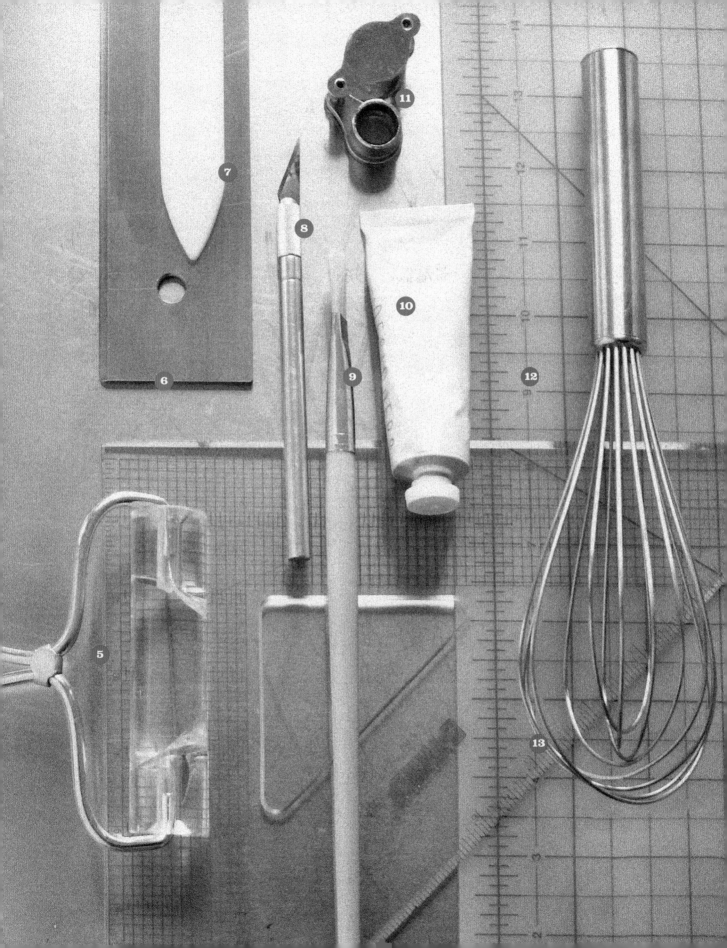

The Basics of Building a Strong Composition

Seeing Form and Space

The first step in composing a dynamic layout is being able to decipher what, exactly, a visual element really is—to understand the visual element in the simplest way possible. A silhouetted image of a teapot, for instance, is really a dot: radial, enclosed, curvilinear; a spoon, seen on edge, is a line. As far as composition is concerned, the meaning or content of a visual form is unimportant; its true identity is what determines how it will behave when juxtaposed with other forms.

FORM IDENTITY CONVERSION TABLE

DOT *The fundamental building block of visual form: a fixed point. Simultaneously radiates and contracts.*

LINE *A dot in motion. Describes direction, separates elements, defines spaces; may be solid or broken.*

PLANE *A dot large enough for its outer contour to become important; also referred to as* **shape**. *Geometric forms are mathematical and often angular, while organic forms are irregular, soft, or "natural" in appearance.*

SURFACE ACTIVITY *Also called* **texture** *or* **pattern**, *which are themselves distinct: texture [A] is irregular, random, or organic; a pattern [B] is repetitive and/or geometric—hence, artificial or invented.*

A   **B**

DESIGN CHEF'S TIP

1

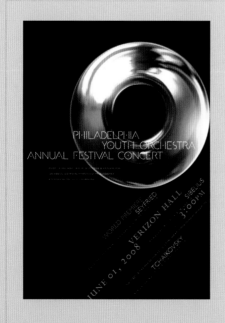

MAKE NEGATIVE SPACE AS INTERESTING AS FORM

Consider negative space as shapes that are created by the material you place within a format, not as a background simply to be filled up. Those shapes are exceedingly important in a composition—they help direct the eye, they enhance the perception of movement, and they provide places for the eye to rest while navigating the composition. Analyze the shapes of negative space above, below, and in between forms: What are those shapes and how many are there? Are they tight or expansive? Do they run parallel around the forms or in opposing directions? How different are they? Compare the negative spaces and their distribution around the format in this example, noting the system of repetition and contrast they set up as a counterpoint to positive forms.

Paone Design Associates: Philadelphia, PA: USA

Scale, Contrast, and Organization

After identifying the essential forms being considered, the next step is to look at how they're going to behave when they're mixed together. Form, or figure, is considered a positive element, or the ingredients of the layout; while space, or ground, is considered the negative, or opposite, of form—it's the pot the ingredients are being mixed in, or the plate on which they'll be arranged and served. Because page or screen space is intrinsically flat, as are the forms within them, viewers are predisposed to taking them for granted (much the way bored gourmands do with oatmeal).

To ensure a rich, engaging optical experience, the designer must compose form in space in such a way that the viewer perceives not only that the forms are interacting three dimensionally, but also that there is a kind of harmonic rhythm among all the layout's aspects. This harmonic rhythm is often called *tension*—it's a perceived vibrancy or liveliness that one experiences in layouts where all the parts are relating to each other. But as the term itself implies, tension isn't only about formal and spatial relationships being the same. Just as must be in a successful culinary creation, some elements must oppose each other in some way, or create contrast, in order to appreciate each of the parts more clearly. A strong composition consists of visual relationships that support and restate each other, as well as some that conflict with the expectations that those mutually supportive relationships create.

Every successful composition organizes a variety of compositional characteristics, held in a state of tension, to impart a sense of resolution. This property of a composition is called its *gestalt*, meaning "totality"; the viewer senses an underlying logic that unifies individual relationships into a whole. Individual relationships among forms and, therefore, the gestalt, will change each time a single element is altered; be aware of these changes as the design process leads you from rough iterations through the eventual solution.

While forms of the same size appear flat, making forms different sizes creates the perception of three-dimensional space: Larger forms appear closer, and smaller forms appear farther away.

Play unique properties or proportions against each other by bringing them into close proximity: angle against curve, line against mass, vertical against horizontal.

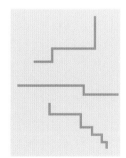

Creating repetitions of, or variations on, a particular kind of form or spatial area invites the eye to compare and re-examine its understanding of a visual idea.

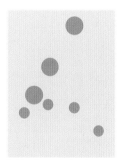

Position elements so that there is a sense of movement and, ideally, a recognizable rhythm. Organize the elements across an invisible superstructure, such as a triangle, curve, or grid.

Create clear, purposeful relationships that appear intentional: If you mean for two elements to align or to appear the same size, make sure these attributes are unquestionable.

Defining Clear Visual Hierarchy

Strong composition depends not only on the compositional states of the various elements, but also on how those states contribute to the viewer being able to navigate, or understand, the content, and in what order the content should be "read" (whether in terms of type or purely pictorial content). Defining this order, or *hierarchy*, and controlling the sequence in which viewers will perceive and assimilate each level of information is an unavoidable process in every design project, no matter how straightforward it is.

In coming to determine the most important element (whether pictorial or typographic), the designer most often relies on common sense by answering the simple question: What do I need to look at first? Beyond simply establishing this entry point into a sequence, the designer must also

ensure that elements don't compete with each other. This often means making some formal attributes—such as relative sizes, densities, or spatial intervals—subtler or more nuanced, while exaggerating others so that the viewer can process the material more efficiently without sacrificing vitality and tension.

General Methods for Ordering Material
Focusing attention on one form within a composition most often results from two primary strategies: differentiating that element from all others (by means of exaggerated scale, density, or color distinction), and/or arranging surrounding elements so that the orientation of their angles, curves, or interstitial spaces directs the eye toward it. With the first strategy, viewers tend to perceive a special emphasis on a form or

space that separates itself in some way from the gestalt of the composition: While all other forms share similar relationships, the most important form has unique attributes. To create a more complex hierarchy using this approach—establishing decreasing levels of importance in a sequence of elements—the unique attribute applied to the top element may be applied in diminishing degrees to each subsequent form.

Under the second general strategy, known as *continuity*, the relative proximity of surrounding forms creates an emphasis on the primary form and then directs the eye to a secondary location. Designers may use each strategy individually or in tandem.

HIERARCHICAL STRATEGIES

DIFFERENTIATION

  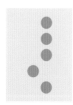   

| Scale | Weight or Density | Alignment | Direction | Rhythm | Proximity | Identity or Proportion | Orientation |

CONTINUITY

      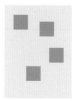

| Rotational Alignment | Axial Alignment | Spatial Progression: Interval | Spatial Progression: Scale/Depth | Structural Focus | Triangulation | Spiraling | Stepping |

Symmetry and Asymmetry

Two basic kinds of gestalt logic govern composition in every layout: symmetry and asymmetry. Symmetry is a compositional state in which the arrangement of forms responds to the central axis of the format (either the vertical or the horizontal axis); forms also may be oriented relative to their individual central axes. Symmetrical arrangements create a "mirroring" effect—spaces or contours on either side of the orga-nizational axis are the same. Asymmetry is an opposing logic: The arrangement of every form defies relationship with any central axis or among the forms themselves. The result is a collection of spatial proportions that are inherently different from each other.

Visual and Metaphorical Differences in Compositional Logic

Symmetry and asymmetry produce very different visual experiences in a viewer. The similarity of spaces or shapes in a symmetrical configuration is very direct and efficient, but can be too simple or static, causing viewers to hastily gloss over information. Asymmetrical arrangements provoke rigorous involvement—they require continual assessment of differences in space, stimulating the eye to greater movement. From the standpoint of communication, asymmetry improves the ability to differentiate, catalog, and recall content because the viewer's investigation of spatial difference becomes tied to the ordering, or cognition, of the content itself.

On another level, symmetry and asymmetry come with cultural and conceptual baggage. Prior to the early twentieth century, all design was ordered symmetrically. As a result, symmetrical, or centered, layouts tend to be perceived as traditional or historical; because design prior to the Industrial Revolution was primarily created by religious, governmental, and academic institutions, symmetrical layouts also are generally perceived as formal, careful, decorative, or institutional. Choosing the best gestalt logic for a given project depends on which association will be most appropriate for the target audience—compositional logic itself is a message to be conveyed.

DESIGN CHEF'S TIP

2 COUNTERACT THE STATIC QUALITIES OF SYMMETRY

Scale the symmetrical configuration overall so that it is confrontational within the format.

Force the spatial intervals between elements aligned on the axis to be as different as possible.

Disturb the overall symmetrical layout with an asymmetrical element.

Exaggerate the variation in widths of elements across the axis.

Distribute color or density among symmetrically configured elements to create an asymmetrical emphasis in weight or intensity.

COMPARING ATTRIBUTES

SYMMETRY	ASYMMETRY
Static	Dynamic
Quiet	Loud
Formal	Casual
Studied	Spontaneous
Historical	Contemporary
Conservative	Innovative
Decorative	Essential
Solid	Fragmented
Simple	Complex

Working with Imagery

Every pictorial element falls on a continuum between the literal, or representational, and the abstract. The method of making the pictorial element is referred to as its *mode*, and the degree of stylization and, therefore, interpretation, imposed by the designer is defined as *mediation*. A photograph of a figure and a stylized, geometric drawing of a figure are both representational—but if the photograph is lit dramatically and the figure's position highly contrived (in contrast to the neutral presentation of the drawing), the photograph may be considered more mediated than the drawing. Still, photographic images tend to be perceived as "real," or "believable," simply because they depict an empirical experience. Illustrative images, even if extremely naturalistic, will always be perceived as inventions and, therefore, less credible than photos. Choose the degree of abstraction, the image mode, and mediate it according to the conceptual and informational necessities of the project.

Mixing Image Treatments
As with all compositional strategies, creating contrast among visual elements is key—and this is no less true for imagery. Along with overall compositional contrast (achieved through scale, spacing, and positioning changes), combining different image modes is effective in creating tension and liveliness in a layout. It's important, however, that while the different image modes being combined contrast each other decisively, they also share some visual qualities so as to clearly relate.

All three images depict the same subject, an apple, but using different modes. In this example, the "pure" photograph is the least mediated; while the two illustrative images are inherently more mediated than the photograph, the paper collage is more mediated than the charcoal drawing.

Although the semantic content of the images is the same (seeing any of them establishes the same factual knowledge), the mode of representation has consequences for our perception of meaning that may be associated with the image. The photograph's clarity alludes to the apple's freshness and organicism; the charcoal drawing skews its allusion toward the act of creation, and may be read with a somber overlay; the collage of cut paper in primary colors suggests a childlike, or educational, metaphor.

Sharpened, stylized plant images drive the identity for a design studio, above. Grow Creative: Portland, OR: United States

Important elements in the book cover, right, are colorized in the production process. DesignLiga: Munich, Germany

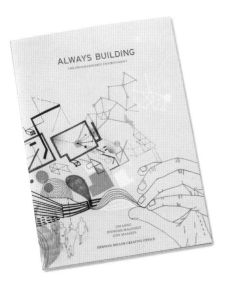

Combining different kinds of images adds interest and contrast to the overall visual language of a project. (top) People Design: Grand Rapids, MI: USA (bottom) Stein Øvre: Oslo: Norway

Using Abstract Form

All pictorial form carries meaning—and that includes abstraction, or form that doesn't represent anything we actually experience in real life. However, abstract form has the potential to convey stronger, more direct, and more universally understood messages, because it is a distilled representation of something that is real, so it can transcend cultural and linguistic barriers. Abstract images are also more open to interpretation, involving the audience and helping them to make deeper, richer connections; for this reason, abstraction can easily take on the role of symbol or metaphor more fluidly than representational images. Finally, the uniqueness and simplicity of abstraction deliver a powerfully memorable experience, building recall and equity in designed messages.

The power of abstraction to communicate universally— and to evoke greater interpretation or association beyond simple depiction— is demonstrated in this comparison of two simple, elemental geometric forms.

Organic · Totality · Continuum · Biology · Water · Planet · Cell · Cycle · Endless · Unity · Fluidity

Logic · Mathematics · Artificial · Order · Intellectual · Finite · Rational · Architectural · Partitioned · Solid

DESIGN CHEF'S TIP

4

How to Develop Abstract Form That Communicates

1 Distill the essential idea of a message as an emotion: What is the feeling to be communicated, in one word? What kinds of forms feel that way?

2 Consider the idea as an action word: What should the form appear to be doing? What kinds of forms will appear to perform that action?

3 Translate the visual structure of an elemental force or a kind of place or object into its basic geometry: What kinds of shapes—dots, lines, curves, and so on— make up that thing's physical structure? How many marks or shapes are needed to recognize what it is?

Creating Visually Dynamic Color Relationships

Understanding how to use color effectively depends first on understanding its visual attributes—how colors are identified, how they can be varied, and the optical effects they have on each other in juxtaposition. Every color has a core identity, or hue; a color is first generally recognized as blue or green or orange. Any hue, however, may be intense or dull (degrees of saturation); it may also be dark or light (degrees of value); and it may be perceived as cool or warm (degrees of temperature).

Palettes Based on Chromatic Interaction

The first direction a designer may pursue in developing a color palette for a project is that of optical interaction. Creating a rich palette depends on combining colors that can be clearly distinguished from each other, but that also share some unifying optical relationships. Because of the strong opposition of complements, palettes based on this relationship tend to be the most optically dynamic—that is, cells in the eye are stimulated more aggressively, and the brain is provoked into greater activity as a result. Analogous colors, by their very similarity, create more complex, but less varied, palettes.

Using such a basic relationship as a starting point guarantees a viewer's clear perception of a color idea; the designer may opt to maintain that simplicity, using the hues of that relationship in purer form, or introduce complexity—adjusting the value or intensity differences between the base colors, or adding colors that support and expand the relationship between the base colors.

Color identity is often mapped on a color wheel, a diagrammatic model developed by British artist and scientist Albert Munsell. The relative positions of the hues around the wheel help describe their relationships to each other.

Hues that are adjacent are made of similar wavelengths, and are referred to as being **analogous.**

Hues that lie opposite each other are made up of wavelengths that stimulate opposing cells in the eye and optically negate each other; these pairs are called **complements.**

*Hues positioned at 120° to each other (in a triangular relationship) are called **triads**, or **split complements**.*

Neutral ········ ⚹ **SATURATION** ⚹ ········ Intense

Warmer ⚹ ········ TEMPERATURE ⚹ ········ Cooler

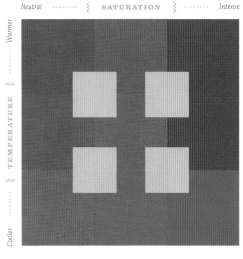

This matrix helps visualize the complexity resulting from variations in saturation, temperature, and value that are possible for a single hue—in this case, violet. Swatches increase in saturation left to right while progressing from warm at the top to cool at the bottom—all at the same relatively dark value. Smaller, light-value swatches of each variant are positioned in the corners for comparison across their respective boundaries.

*Color identity is relative—the perception of hue, saturation, value, and temperature of a color changes depending on the colors around it and how much of each is present. This effect, called **simultaneous contrast**, is demonstrated by the change in apparent color of the central swatch as it appears in different contexts.*

The process of defining a palette can begin very simply: choosing two complementary colors, for example, because their interaction is so strong.

Adjusting the relative values of the complements creates greater contrast without disturbing the clarity of the relationship.

Seeking a richer experience, the designer may shift the temperature of the complements, maintaining the relationship but skewing it slightly.

Altering the intensities of one or both introduces yet greater complexity.

The addition of a neutral version of one of the complements expands the palette; a second version of the neutral, lighter in value, introduces greater variation.

To this already complex mix, the designer lastly adds the analog of one of the base complements, adjusting its value and intensity to correspond more closely to one of the neutrals.

Using Color to Enhance Messaging

Selecting Color for Meaningful Effect
Color, of course, can also mean something. Very often, that meaning is tied to associations we make between colors and objects or environments—water is blue, vegetation is green, and so on. But colors also evoke intangible feelings, whether by association or by the biological effects resulting from their perception. Red, for example, connotes hunger and violence (because of the color of blood), but provokes arousal and even anger, because it takes more energy to process red lightwaves—resulting in increased metabolic activity. Further, colors carry cultural or social meanings, related to their use in religious ceremonies or iconography, or in heraldry, in flags, or historically in clothing or art. For Westerners, violet and gold signify nobility; among Hindus, white signifies death. Select colors wisely with regard to specific cultural and psychological associations to ensure the messages they carry are appropriate.

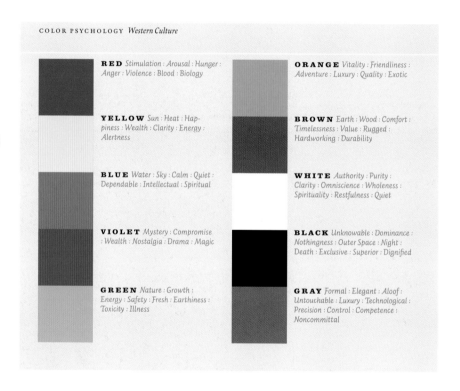

COLOR PSYCHOLOGY *Western Culture*

RED *Stimulation : Arousal : Hunger : Anger : Violence : Blood : Biology*

YELLOW *Sun : Heat : Happiness : Wealth : Clarity : Energy : Alertness*

BLUE *Water : Sky : Calm : Quiet : Dependable : Intellectual : Spiritual*

VIOLET *Mystery : Compromise : Wealth : Nostalgia : Drama : Magic*

GREEN *Nature : Growth : Energy : Safety : Fresh : Earthiness : Toxicity : Illness*

ORANGE *Vitality : Friendliness : Adventure : Luxury : Quality : Exotic*

BROWN *Earth : Wood : Comfort : Timelessness : Value : Rugged : Hardworking : Durability*

WHITE *Authority : Purity : Clarity : Omniscience : Wholeness : Spirituality : Restfulness : Quiet*

BLACK *Unknowable : Dominance : Nothingness : Outer Space : Night : Death : Exclusive : Superior : Dignified*

GRAY *Formal : Elegant : Aloof : Untouchable : Luxury : Technological : Precision : Control : Competence : Noncommittal*

Be careful when assigning unusual coloration to images of people or food. While the hue shift toward the warm end of the spectrum (left) may convey fun or vitality, a shift toward yellow or green (right) conveys a sense of illness or toxicity.

Exploiting Color to Enhance Hierarchy

Our optical system (the eyes and brain) allows us to perceive colors as occupying different spatial depths. Red appears stationary at a middle distance; yellow appears to advance toward us; blue appears to recede. In general, cool colors appear to recede, while warm colors advance.

Consider the spatial property of color carefully with regard to hierarchy, whether visual or typographic. Clearly, form elements colored in red, orange, and yellow are likely to capture attention easily because they will appear to advance toward the viewer; in a field of neutrals, a more saturated color will draw attention. But the degree of value contrast between elements, or between elements and background—tends to trump temperature or saturation with respect to establishing hierarchy. A very light element will appear to advance forward of any element whose value is relatively dark when both are situated on an even darker background—no matter how cool or warm, dull or saturated, any of the hues involved may be, and no matter how small the light element is. Conversely, a very dark element situated within a light field will advance forward of any other form that is also of light value.

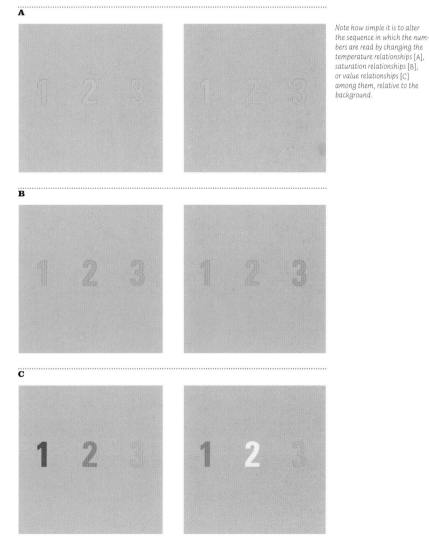

Note how simple it is to alter the sequence in which the numbers are read by changing the temperature relationships [A], saturation relationships [B], or value relationships [C] among them, relative to the background.

Limiting (and Maximizing) the Palette

Designers very often make the mistake of using too many colors, especially in process-color projects—simply because they can. While full-color imagery is always dynamic and engaging, too many hues being present dilutes the color experience. Even when all colors are possible, limiting the palette creates a more focused, and therefore, more memorable color experience. This is especially important to consider in branded communications, where the color story of the client—first established by the color(s) of its logo—must always reinforce its identity, building recognition and recall of the brand. Working with only two or three colors can be challenging, but also extremely rewarding.

A

B

C

D

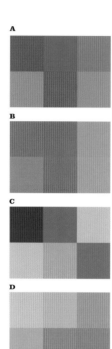

If the lightness and darkness, dullness and brilliance, coolness and warmth of every color all are allowed to change, the specificity of the color idea is radically diminished—the viewer can't tell what the color idea may be. But if the hues are relatively analogous in temperature and are all of the same value—with shifts only in saturation—the constraint in variables allows the viewer to more clearly understand the color idea by focusing their attention on the variable that does change. Palette A: Analogous hue, value, and saturation / Palette B: Analogous temperature, value, and saturation / Palette C: Analogous hue, temperature, and saturation / Palette D: Analogous temperature and value only.

In a spot-color job, the trick is to build in as much flexibility for combining the two or three ink colors as possible. Printing a job with two complements as counterparts, for example, is an intuitive first possibility. The complements need not be exact, that is, as with blue and orange; skewing the relationship can create more interesting combinations that retain the complements' inherent contrast: a blue-violet and orange, for example. Because most printing inks are translucent, a designer has the option of surprinting just two inks, as solids or tints, on top of each other to create a vast array of interrelated tones.

DESIGN CHEF'S TIP 5

Use Black with Caution

Because of the ubiquity of black, its somewhat default nature, and its lack of chromatic stimulus, try to avoid using this color, especially in a limited palette.

First, black is everywhere, so it's not easy for an audience to retain black with regard to identifying its relationship to communication. Second, it's a dead zone with regard to other colors. Used as a large field to ground and illuminate intense, deep-value colors, it can be highly effective; but if the color palette overall is relatively subtle, light, or desaturated, black may seem weak or empty—or, worse yet, may appear to suck the life out of the colors surrounding it.

For projects in which only two colors (or only one) are possible, using black is like throwing a color away. Choose a very deep-value color, instead of black, that can interact dynamically with the second color. In a single-color job, simply replacing black with another color will make the project infinitely more memorable. Even type need not be black: Explore how much more interesting words can be when set in other colors. Just be sure the color has enough contrast with the background on which it's situated to remain legible.

Quick, Easy Coding Strategies

Color is very effective for coding—using different colors to identify parts of a system, sections in publications, or counterparts in a line of products. When using color this way, the designer's first concern must be what the needs of the audience might be in terms of understanding how the coding relates the parts to each other. If the project is a packaging system, for instance, are all the products being packaged remarkably different or does each represent a grade or level? Is there one family of products, or are there several related lines, each with its own subproducts? The answers to questions such as these will help determine the complexity that the color coding must address and, therefore, how much variation in hue (or combinations of hues) will be useful to the audience. Although each component within a coded system must be clearly distinguishable, the colors used to distinguish them must bear some relation to support an understanding that the components are a family. Carefully controlling the aspects of hue, value, saturation, and relationships created with accent or secondary colors becomes critical.

To distinguish components by grade or level, select a single hue and, for each grade, change the saturation or value, or both.

For components that are more closely related and equivalent to each other in their quality or grade, choose a single base hue and create analogous counterparts for the components by shifting the temperature. As an alternative, choose a single unifying hue and then combine it with secondary hues that communicate each component's difference, but still under some limitation (all still analogous, or of the same value).

To code a system of three or more components that are remarkably different from each other, choose very different hues—but create a sense of family by constraining their values and intensities.

In a system of multiple families, try to first establish a limited palette to distinguish each family—perhaps hues that are analogous—clearly projecting the fundamental relationship between the families as parts of a greater whole. One might also choose a highly differentiated hue for each family, such as those in a triad, or sets of complements, and then unify the families with a single hue. The components within each family could be coded as grades (using the value or intensity of the family color) or themselves differentiated through subtle analogous relationships.

Choosing and Combining Typefaces

Many designers are baffled by the prospect of selecting a typeface for a project—where to begin? A text's intended use is the best starting point for narrowing down the many options: Is it for display or extended reading? For display, the imagelike quality of the face, and its personality, are of utmost concern. If it's continuous reading, eschew dramatically styled faces in favor of simplicity. Next, consider the subject or ideas to be communicated in the project. If the text is formal, for example, perhaps a serif is appropriate; but if the subject is technology, a sharply cut sans serif may be better. The feeling the typeface's texture generates—tight, dark, open, light, romantic, organic, fresh, fluid, chunky, and so on—should reflect both the subject itself and the tone of the language used. Designers must be familiar with the stylistic classes of type and be able to analyze and compare the internal attributes of various styles.

TIME-TESTED TYPEFACE FLAVORS *A Go-To List to Get You Started*

AB
Archaic Capitals Roman
Titles, headlines, subheads, callouts. *Formal, dramatic, authoritarian, dramatic, elegant, classical, cultured*

AaB
Blackletter Germanic
Titles, initials, very short callouts. *Medieval, sinister, formal, aggressive, Old-World, superstitious, dangerous, magical, exotic, punk*

Aab
Gothic Oldstyle Serif German, Dutch
Titles, headlines, decks, short to mid-length texts, subheads, callouts, captions. *Austere, authoritarian, formal, quirky, elegant*

AaB
Humanist (Rounded) Oldstyle *French, Italian* Titles, headlines, decks, extensive texts, subheads, callouts, captions. *Formal, soft, classical, academic, elegant, poetic, organic, friendly, fluid*

AaB
Transitional Serif English
Titles, headlines, decks, extensive texts, subheads, callouts, captions. *Formal, academic, refined, sharp, delicate, elegant, poetic, cultured, prestigious, well-bred*

AaB
Neoclassical (Modern) Serif *French, Italian* Titles, headlines, decks, shorter texts, subheads, callouts, captions. *Precise, vibrant, sharp, elegant, mechanical, strong, progressive, scientific, corporate*

AaB
Slab Serif *American* Titles, headlines, subheads, callouts, initials. *Strong, heavy, promotional, industrial, mechanical, chunky, informal, aggressive, loud, dark*

AaB
Art Nouveau Types *French, Austrian, English* Titles, subheads, short callouts, initials. *Fanciful, elegant, organic, informal, fluid, artistic, exotic, handcrafted*

AaB
Grotesk Sans Serif English, German, Belgian, Dutch Titles, headlines, decks, short to mid-length texts, subheads, callouts, captions. *Strong, authoritarian, stiff, industrial, scientific, mechanical, journalistic*

AaB
Geometric Sans Serif German, English Titles, headlines, decks, extensive texts, subheads, callouts, captions. *Sharp, vibrant, rhythmic, industrial, mechanical, avant-garde, scientific, mathematical, informal, aggressive, elegant, strong*

AaB
Transitional Sans Serif Swiss Titles, headlines, decks, extensive texts, subheads, callouts, captions. *Neutral, international, minimal, cold, authoritarian, accessible, precise, corporate, progressive, calculated, scientific, aloof, direct, clean*

AaB
Humanistic Sans Serif Dutch, German, Swiss Titles, headlines, decks, extensive texts, subheads, callouts, captions. *International, accessible, friendly, corporate, progressive, inclusive, honest*

AaB
Serif/Sans Hybrids *German* Titles, headlines, decks, extensive texts, subheads, callouts, captions. *Multicultural, inclusive, corporate, respect for history, inventive, competent, academic, sharp, elegant*

AaB
Florid Scripts Dutch, French Titles, headlines, decks, callouts. *Formal, romantic, elegant, feminine, exotic, magical, fluid, organic, poetic, fanciful, idiosyncratic*

AaB
Italic/Script Hybrids English, French, Italian, German Titles, headlines, decks, subheads, callouts. *Formal, romantic, elegant, stately, rhythmic, steady, academic*

Ab Ab Ab *Ab* Ab *Ab*
Ab Ab *Ab* Ab *Ab* Ab
Ab ***Ab*** **Ab** ***Ab*** **Ab**
Ab ***Ab*** **Ab**
Ab

The Single Family Theory
Choosing a type family with enough variants in weight, width, and posture ensures great flexibility in typographic texture while respecting a certain level of restraint.

For Modernists, this option is the best expression of the "do less with more" tenet of their cooking philosophy. The classic face that demonstrates this technique most admirably is Univers. Each

variant offers a different cadence, rhythm, value, and mass that not only offers rich visual experience, but also will address the most complex typesetting demands.

Typeface Combinations

More daunting still is contemplating how to pair type styles—or, worse yet, combine three or four. Conventional wisdom suggests first that designers limit themselves to two type families and, if possible, to only two specific weights or styles in each. The point of this constraint focuses solely on making it easier for a reader to recognize and catalog different treatments among editorial components such as heads, decks, subheads, captions, and so on; the more styles applied, the easier it is to lose one's way. From an aesthetic standpoint, a bit of restraint makes the visual language that much clearer. But by all means, if fifteen faces are needed, use them—but choose wisely. The essential issue in combining faces is that of visual texture relative to function (function, here, also including supporting metaphor or enriching visual language overall). Each of the typefaces added to the mix must be different enough to bring some noticeable change to the page, and it must fulfill some function. There are myriad possibilities with which to approach combinations.

Quae coelis
Duis autem vi
lorem ipsum t

The classic serif/sans serif combination is often the first combination strategy that designers will turn to when looking for something a little more flavorful. Conventionally, a serif makes up the text and a sans serif is used for subheads, callouts, or large titling elements; but feel free to reverse this relationship.

AaGgRr
AaGgRr

Select counterparts with enough stylistic contrast, but be aware of their similarities—overall width; tightness or shape of curves; degree of contrast among strokes; heights of joints; shapes of similar elements, such as the leg on the uppercase R; angle at which the terminals are cut; angle of axis in the curved forms; and so on.

LOREM IPSUM
Duis autem velure ai
summa laude lorem
quae coelis nunc eta

Mixing within a single style is usually not a good idea, unless the textural difference is unmistakable. Combining two transitional serifs in text, for instance—or even a Venetian oldstyle and a transitional—is indecisive. Combining the small caps of the Venetian with the transitional text—that's another story altogether.

Duis autem
Duis **autem**

On a functional level, sometimes the bold weight of a serif, relative to its Roman counterpart, isn't quite bold enough to be easily distinguished, as in this example. It's perfectly acceptable to substitute an alternative bold face, as long as the substitute is credibly similar in detail and structure.

Lorem ipsum
Lorem ipsum
Lorem ipsum

Riffing off a single idea can create interesting combinations. For instance, finding a variety of slab-serif faces that all vary in weight, contrast, and width could be very dynamic, yet clearly unified by overall style.

LOREM IPSUM
Duis autem velure summa nunc etui
quae coelis inversus consectitur ad
vulputate ad nauseam interfecti ur

Combinations established for the purpose of exaggerating abstract visual form can be very dynamic. In this combination, linearity and dotlike mass play off each other for exaggerated contrast.

Creating Visual Dialogue
between Type and Imagery

Getting type to interact with imagery poses a serious problem that must always be overcome, no matter how simple the layout. The first step in doing so is to recognize this basic fact: Just like images, type is made up of lights and darks, linear motion and volume, contours, open and closed space, mass, and texture. Consider type not only the equal of image with respect to layout—but an element that completes the image. If type can be removed from a layout and the remaining image composition still appears strong, type and image aren't talking to each other. There are as many strategies for getting type and image to meld with each other as there are ways of mixing vegetables and herbs in soup; the trick is always to establish not only some balance and similarity among the elements, but also a certain degree of contrast.

A

B

C

D

E

F

G

Type can respond to scale, directional movement, and tonal variation. Among these studies type relates to the image by virtue of: [A] similarity in general shape and structure; [B] repetition of linear movement; [C] alternation of weight; [D] restating of proportional division; [E] mimicry of depth and perspective; [F] angle alignments; [G] response to light and dark value arrangement.

DESIGN CHEF'S TIP 6

Translate Macro-Level Image and Type Treatments into Text Detailing

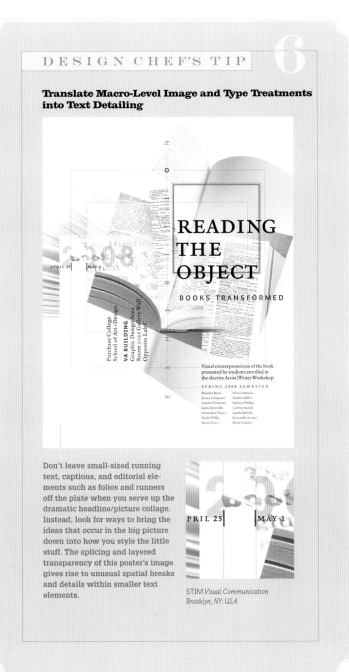

STIM *Visual Communication*
Brooklyn, NY: USA

Don't leave small-sized running text, captions, and editorial elements such as folios and runners off the plate when you serve up the dramatic headline/picture collage. Instead, look for ways to bring the ideas that occur in the big picture down into how you style the little stuff. The splicing and layered transparency of this poster's image gives rise to unusual spatial breaks and details within smaller text elements.

TASTE

TASTE

TASTE

Type appears to change spatial relationships when placed on, in, or next to an image—it either becomes part of the image or acts as a "bridge" between image and external space.

TASTE

Crafting Reader-Friendly (and Beautiful!) Text

Making a comfortable, easily read text that is pleasant to look at is much like developing reliable pastry dough. The amount of water, flour, egg, and milk and the working temperature all need to work together or the dough will be too tough, too flaky, and so on. Similarly, a good text setting is one in which a constellation of variables achieves a harmonic balance.

Text that is legible in size, encourages sequential reading, shows decisive (and consistent) rags and spacing, clearly separates paragraphs, and exhibits a minimum of hyphens, widows, and orphans—this often becomes the foundation of a strong layout.

DESIGN CHEF'S TIP

7

| ¶ | Regular | | A̅A̲ 15 pt | | Tr T₁ T̄ | A̲V̲ -5 |

0   6   12   18   24

Lorem ipsum dolor sit amet, consectetur adipiscing elit. Ut nisi lectus, adipiscing ut consequet, commodo at ante. Integer luctus blandit ipsum, sit amet pellen tesque orci aliquam eget. Phasellus a dapibus liberoma. Nulla laoreet, diam sit amet consectetur ultricies, jus totellus imperdiet libero, in consequat metus erat idni sl. Proin arcu quam, rutrum id luctus sit amet, cong ue at augue. Donec pellentesque, elit a pulvinar ullam corper, lectus urna laoreet metus, eu pulvinar mauris nulla sed diam. Aliquam erat volutpat. Aliquam portiar tor nisi vel quam feugiat eleifend. Vivamus consectet

| ¶ | Regular | | A̅A̲ 15 pt | | Tr T₁ T̄ | A̲V̲ +25 |

0   6   12   18   24

Lorem ipsum dolor sit amet, consectetur adipiscing elit. Ut nisi lectus, adipiscing ut consequat et, commodo at ante. Integer luctus blandit ipsum, sit amet pellentes que orci aliquam eget. Phasellus a dapibus libero. Nulla laoreet, diam sit amet consectetur ultricies, justo tellus imperdiet libero, in consequat metus erat id nisl. Proin arcu quam, rutrum id luctus sit amet, congue at augue. Donec pellentesque, elit a pulvinar ullamcorper, lectus urna laoreet metus, eu pulvinar mauris nulla sed diam. Aliquam erat volutpat. Aliquam porttitor nisi vel quam feugiat eleifend. Vivamus consectetur congue metus.

Tricks for Resolving Rag and Justification Problems

If the hyphenation is excessive (whether in a ragged or justified column), it may mean the type size is too big relative to the width of the column. Reduce the text size by a half-point or widen the columns by three letter-widths.

For rags that are inconsistent—soft and rippling in some places and very deep elsewhere—or if just a few lines seem hopeless, force the rag to be much deeper or active throughout; this approach provides more options for breaking difficult sequences of lines, and hides disparities in the rag from location to location.

Dramatically loosening the leading in a narrow column will diminish the irregularity of a rag.

If a sequence of lines in an otherwise consistent rag is too short or too long, select those lines and adjust their kerning independently—but not to the point that they look different. This approach may also be applied to single lines that are just too short or too long.

In a justified column where one line of text is exceptionally tight and dark, return the last word to the following line and then adjust the spacing for the newly broken line to loosen it. The opposite approach—forcing an extra word onto a very loose line—will also often work.

In justified text that seems overly loose, with a great deal of rivers, it is likely that the column measure is too wide for the type size. First try enlarging the type by a half point to see if that helps. The next step is to narrow the column by a couple of letter-widths.

1

Lorem ipsum dolor sit amet consectitur adipscing elit summa duis autem velure quod meri

Lorem ipsum dolor sit amet consectitur adipscing elit summa duis autem velure quod meri

Most often, the first step is to pick a typeface and establish a comfortable size. Because most people will read a newspaper without complaint, this can be a good barometer for choosing type size. If the type looks like 9-point Times (top) or 10-point Garamond Oldstyle (bottom) regardless of the actual face or size, chances are most readers will find it legible.

2

Lorem ipsum dolor sit amet consectitur adipscing elitas summa duis autem velure quod meri uismod. Indeo summa erat, nunc et semper, fiat equame gloriosa interfectus est

Lorem ipsum dolor sit amet consectitur adipscing elitas summa duis autem velure quod meri uismod. Indeo sum erat, nunc et semper, fiat equame gloriosa interfectus est

Strive to get fifty-five to seventy-five characters on a single line before a return. Determining text width on this average number of characters (in English) results in the most consistent overall appearance—meaning the rag will be very consistent and there will be very few hyphens. If setting justified, the result is much more consistent word spacing without rivers, and limited hyphenation.

Counting characters is fine, but grabbing the right-hand anchor point in a text box and slowly pulling it left and right to see how the text within the box reflows is a quick, on-the-fly method. At certain widths, the rag (or spacing) will suddenly snap into a state of near perfection—this state is an optimal width for that text.

3

ipsum: velut   ipsum; velut
ipsum : velut   ipsum ; velut

velure! delicit   velure? delicit
velure! delicit   velure? delicit

Colons and semicolons need additional space preceding them and less space following them. Exclamation points and question marks often benefit from being separated from their sentences by an extra bit of space. A full word space is too much, as is half a word space; but +20 to +40 tracking is usually sufficient.

4

duis autem vegure nunc et semper interfectus

The leading (measured from baseline to baseline) should be about 120 percent of the point size. This usually means that for 10-point text, the leading should be 12; for 12-point text, the leading should be 14; and so on. A rule of thumb: The leading can be tighter or looser, but it should always appear bigger than the space between

words. Leading needs to be loosened if the ascenders and descenders in the chosen typeface are exceptionally long; if the x-height is large; if the text width is greater than seventy-five characters; or if the text width is narrower than fifty characters.

5

Lorem ipsum dolor sit amet consectit adipscer elit summa duis autem velure quod meri uismor ind eosum erat, nunc et semper, quam gloriosa invectus est. Quae coelis interfectus in deo fiat eternam, duis autem velure et consequat carborundu est.

A paragraph rag should be made by hand. Aim for a consistent short/long/short rhythm from the top of the column to the bottom. The most comfortable depth for rags is between one-fifth and one-seventh the width of the text. Ideally, there are no hyphens, but if they are necessary, one every ten to fifteen lines is ideal (and never two in a row).

6

Don't allow the last line of a paragraph to begin the top of a column. This "orphan" is especially distracting if there is a space separating the paragraph that follows, and is really irritating if it occurs at the very beginning of the left-hand page. Run the text

back so that the new page starts a paragraph, or space out the preceding text so that the paragraph continues with at least three lines after the page break.

7

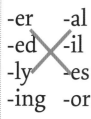

-er   -al
-ed   -il
-ly   -es
-ing   -or

Avoid breaking words across lines (hyphenating) so that short or incomplete stubs, such as those shown above, begin the line following. Make sure there are at least four letters in the word ending the line before the break.

8

Lorem ipsum dolor sit amet con sectitur adipscing elit summa duis autem.

Lorem ipsum dolor sit amet con sectitur adipscing elit summa duis autem velure fiat.

Never allow a single word, or **widow***, to end a paragraph. If* **widows** *constantly appear in the rough setting of a body of text, the column width should be adjusted. Ideally, the last line of a paragraph should be more than half the paragraph's width, but three words (no matter their length) are acceptable.*

9

When possible, avoid hard returns between paragraphs that are aligning (or nearly aligning) between adjacent columns. As the horizontal negative channels created by the returns approach each other, not only do they become distracting but also they tend to redirect the eye across the columns and break reading sequence.

10

Lorem ipsum dolor sit amet consectit adipscer elit summa duis autem velure quod meri uismor in deosum erat, nunc et semper, quam gloriosa invectus est. Quae coelis inter fectus in deo fiat eternam, duis autem velure consequat carboru-

In justified setting, the relative lightness and darkness of the lines, as well as spacing between words, should remain consistent. When lines are extremely dark (having too many characters) or light (having too few), or if there is a significant occurrence of rivers (wide gaps between words), adjust the tracking, the line breaks, and the column width as needed.

Effectively Using a Column Grid

Most any three-, four-, six-, or eight-column grids will usually work well; it's the way in which columns of text interact with negative space—and with each other—that truly determines how a grid is articulated. The spaces above and below columns play an active part in giving the columns a rhythm as they relate to each other across pages and spreads. Every approach has a dramatic impact on the overall rhythm of the pages within a publication, ranging from austere and geometric to wildly organic in feeling—all the while ordered by the underlying grid. Changing the column logic from section to section provides yet another method of differ-entiating informational areas.

Column Logic and Baseline Alignment

When columns begin to separate vertically, shifting up and down past one another—or dropping to different depths while adhering to a single hangline above—consider the relationship between lines of text across the gutter separating the columns. In a grouping of columns set justified, with no line breaks (or a hard return of the same leading) between paragraphs, the baselines between columns will align. Any other situation, and the baselines between columns will not align.

In hanging columns, text will align between columns until a paragraph change. Because the depth of the hanging columns changes, this might feel appropriate. A problem will occur in a page spread set with columns justifying top and bottom, however, if the paragraph space introduces an uneven line: The lines of text at the foot margin will be noticeably off.

UNDERSTANDING THE OPTIONS

A

B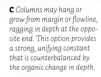

C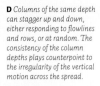

D

E

A Columns of text may justify to the head and foot margins, broken by the introduction of images into the text field and by the insertion of callouts. This approach creates a very dense page and emphasizes the image proportions over the shaping of the text, which becomes a neutral field.

B Text columns may justify to specific flowlines or module depths, creating a very rigidly geometric shift up and down across the page.

C Columns may hang or grow from margin or flowline, ragging in depth at the opposite end. This option provides a strong, unifying constant that is counterbalanced by the organic change in depth.

D Columns of the same depth can stagger up and down, either responding to flowlines and rows, or at random. The consistency of the column depths plays counterpoint to the irregularity of the vertical motion across the spread.

E The most organic approach is one in which the columns change depth as well as stagger up and down. The effect is extremely rhythmic, with text pushing and pulling fluidly against the consistency of the head and foot margins.

Positioning Images Dynamically

Given the regularity of proportions inherent in using a grid, the potential for image placement to feel a bit static or regular can be a problem designers need to overcome to produce dynamic layouts. It's very important to remember that a grid allows the designer to size and position an image any way he or she wants, as long as the image corresponds to the columns (and rows, if the grid is modular). Showing as much variation in arrangement as possible helps the reader see the grid in different ways, reinforcing its presence, while keeping him or her from getting bored. One way to ensure dynamic image placement on a grid—on a single page, across a spread, or from spread to spread—is to establish a formula for size, proportion, and position calculated to vary the composition as methodically as possible. This method, called *bounce*, usually results in dynamic layout changes from spread to spread.

Relating Full-Bleed Images to the Structure

Large images that bleed the margins offer strong counterpoint to small images and text-only pages; but even though the image fills the entire page, it doesn't mean it can ignore the grid underneath. To the contrary, such images must be scaled and positioned within the frame of the page so that some geometric element within aligns with the column or row and helps articulate it.

DESIGN CHEF'S TIP

How to Size and Position Silhouetted Images on a Column Grid

8

Regardless of where the text may fall around the image, position it so that major vertical or horizontal stresses align with column edges; alternatively, size the image so that the proportions of internal elements correspond to the proportions of columns or rows.

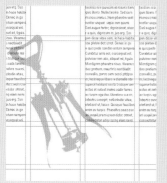

Allow the silhouetted image to move freely—even sliding it "behind" an area of solid text. Or wrap the text around the image. If the image is positioned between columns, make sure one part of it extends past the enclosing portions of the text; this will prevent it from appearing "boxed in."

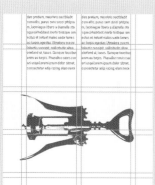

When aligning a silhouetted image to a text column, enlarge the image so that its contours expand beyond the guides that establish the column, especially if it's a circular or organic form; otherwise, the image will appear too small to visually correspond to the width of the column.

Step-by-Step

Creating Rhythmic Image Arrangements, or "Bounce," on a Grid Structure

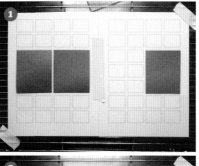

Begin with three images of the same size. Working with odd numbers of elements tends to throw regularity off a bit. Place the images in the layout, aligned by their heights and distributed across the spread according to the columns.

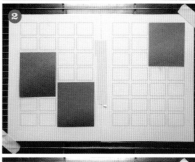

Move the first image up and the second image down, creating triangular movement—the most basic kind of bounce. The top and bottom edges of the image boxes may align or not.

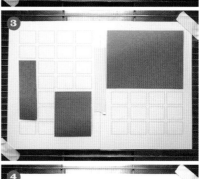

Change the proportions of two images: Substitute a narrow vertical for one, and a relatively deep horizontal for the other. Adjusting the images' relative sizes and proximity increases their three-dimensional play.

Once a basic bounce layout is set for a spread, use the same image elements on the next spread—but swap their positions high/low and left/right. The viewer will recognize the proportions and sizes, and appreciate the new experience. Another simple change is to group all the images in one area, perhaps low on the first spread... and on the subsequent spread, move them all high.

intuition

metaphor

a b c d e f g
h i j k l m n
o p q r s t u
v w x y z

BINDER & BAYER
NEW AMSTERDAM
Geometric Forms
NET WT.

Premium Quality   Naturalistic
SIMPLE ICONS
REFINED DRAWING
BUMBLEBEE

CLARO
dal 1897

Negative Space

Enriched Openn
For Asymmetry

No.35 Vertical

INGREDIENTS:
AIR, EXPANSIVENE
MOVEMENT, QUIE
VISUAL REST, CONTRA

DESIGNER'S

Compositio

CONTR

GREAT FOR VISUAL DY

PREMIUM
**RUBBER
CEMENT**
ACID FREE

DANGER: EXTREMELY FLAMMABLE.
READ CAUTIONS ON LABEL
CAREFULLY BEFORE USING

Beautiful deep black Indian
Ink that is indelible and
lightfast. When diluted with
water it becomes less indelible.
Excellent for calligraphy with
pen, brushes and airbrush. Not
recommended for fountain pens.

POUR IT ON, DON'T PA

3 LB NET WT (1.

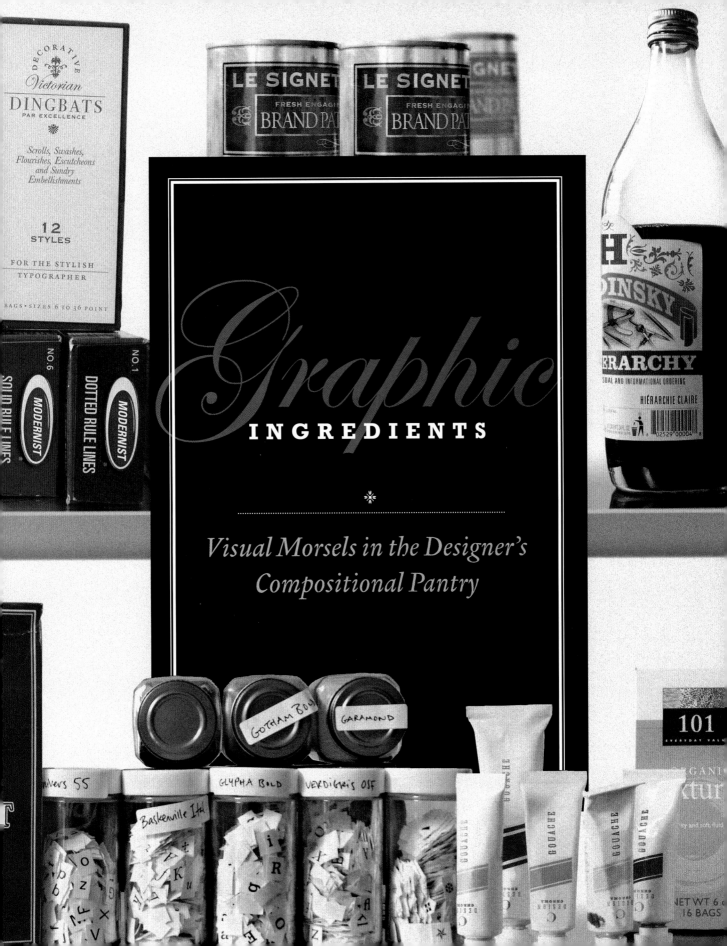

Pictorial
Staples

IMAGERY IS, PERHAPS, the heart of visual communication. Although text usually supports designed messages, symbols, icons, photographs, and illustrations speak to audiences with the greatest impact. In the visual cupboard, the designer will find a tremendous range of options for preparing visually satisfying communications. Photography offers depth and credibility that an audience can sink their teeth into, while illustration customizes communication and adds a human element. For quick bites of information, or where a harder-edged, contemporary feel is needed, try icons and abstract graphic languages. Texture and pattern add detail and depth to the blandest of layouts. Many of the individual ingredients in this section may be easily altered (e.g., enlarging the scale of a pattern to create larger graphic elements, or housing an icon within a shape) or combined for greater visual richness. The designer who is well versed in the distinct qualities of the pictorial ingredients at his or her fingertips can experiment with their use to create dynamic and inventive visual treats.

FUNDAMENTAL FORMS *Basic Shapes and Behaviors* **01**

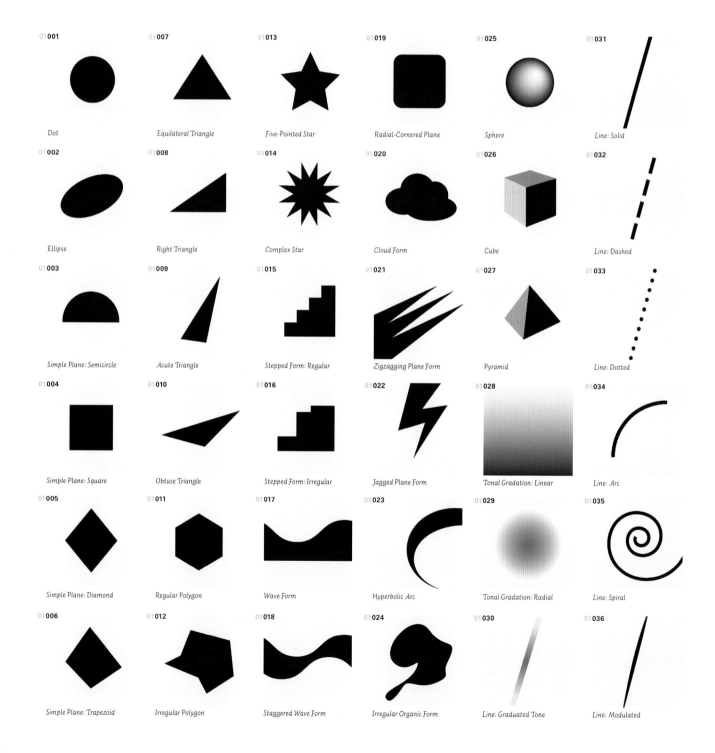

01**001**
Dot

01**007**
Equilateral Triangle

01**013**
Five-Pointed Star

01**019**
Radial-Cornered Plane

01**025**
Sphere

01**031**
Line: Solid

01**002**
Ellipse

01**008**
Right Triangle

01**014**
Complex Star

01**020**
Cloud Form

01**026**
Cube

01**032**
Line: Dashed

01**003**
Simple Plane: Semicircle

01**009**
Acute Triangle

01**015**
Stepped Form: Regular

01**021**
Zigzagging Plane Form

01**027**
Pyramid

01**033**
Line: Dotted

01**004**
Simple Plane: Square

01**010**
Obtuse Triangle

01**016**
Stepped Form: Irregular

01**022**
Jagged Plane Form

01**028**
Tonal Gradation: Linear

01**034**
Line: Arc

01**005**
Simple Plane: Diamond

01**011**
Regular Polygon

01**017**
Wave Form

01**023**
Hyperbolic Arc

01**029**
Tonal Gradation: Radial

01**035**
Line: Spiral

01**006**
Simple Plane: Trapezoid

01**012**
Irregular Polygon

01**018**
Staggered Wave Form

01**024**
Irregular Organic Form

01**030**
Line: Graduated Tone

01**036**
Line: Modulated

The simplest visual elements—circular, planar, linear, solid, and graded—that make up the basis of all other compositional forms are outlined here. Their seeming simplicity belies their tremendous graphic power, whether used alone or in combination, as building blocks for patterns, or as backdrops for type and image. Identifying and understanding the most basic forms is the design chef's first step toward mastering all others.

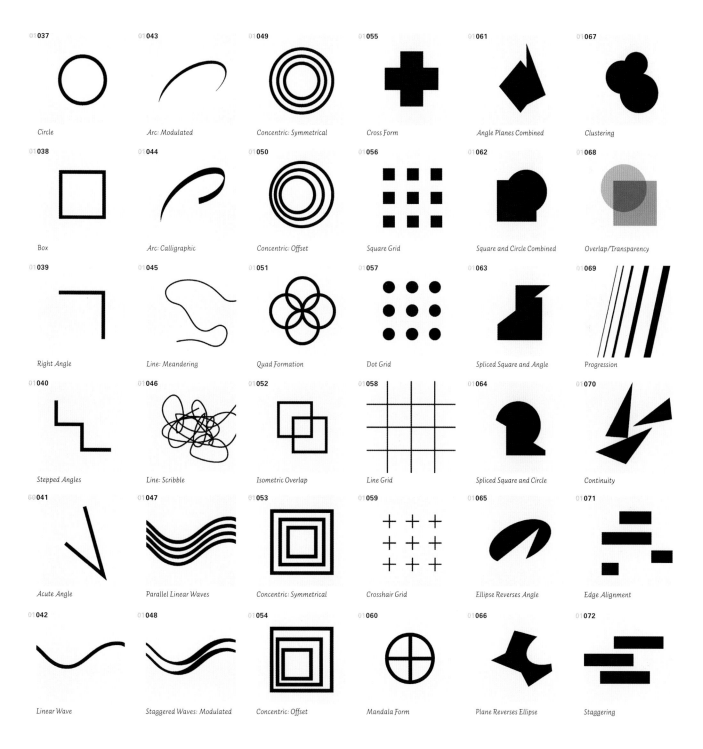

01**037**	01**043**	01**049**	01**055**	01**061**	01**067**
Circle	Arc: Modulated	Concentric: Symmetrical	Cross Form	Angle Planes Combined	Clustering
01**038**	01**044**	01**050**	01**056**	01**062**	01**068**
Box	Arc: Calligraphic	Concentric: Offset	Square Grid	Square and Circle Combined	Overlap/Transparency
01**039**	01**045**	01**051**	01**057**	01**063**	01**069**
Right Angle	Line: Meandering	Quad Formation	Dot Grid	Spliced Square and Angle	Progression
01**040**	01**046**	01**052**	01**058**	01**064**	01**070**
Stepped Angles	Line: Scribble	Isometric Overlap	Line Grid	Spliced Square and Circle	Continuity
60**041**	01**047**	01**053**	01**059**	01**065**	01**071**
Acute Angle	Parallel Linear Waves	Concentric: Symmetrical	Crosshair Grid	Ellipse Reverses Angle	Edge Alignment
01**042**	01**048**	01**054**	01**060**	01**066**	01**072**
Linear Wave	Staggered Waves: Modulated	Concentric: Offset	Mandala Form	Plane Reverses Ellipse	Staggering

ICONIC IMAGES *Naturalistic*

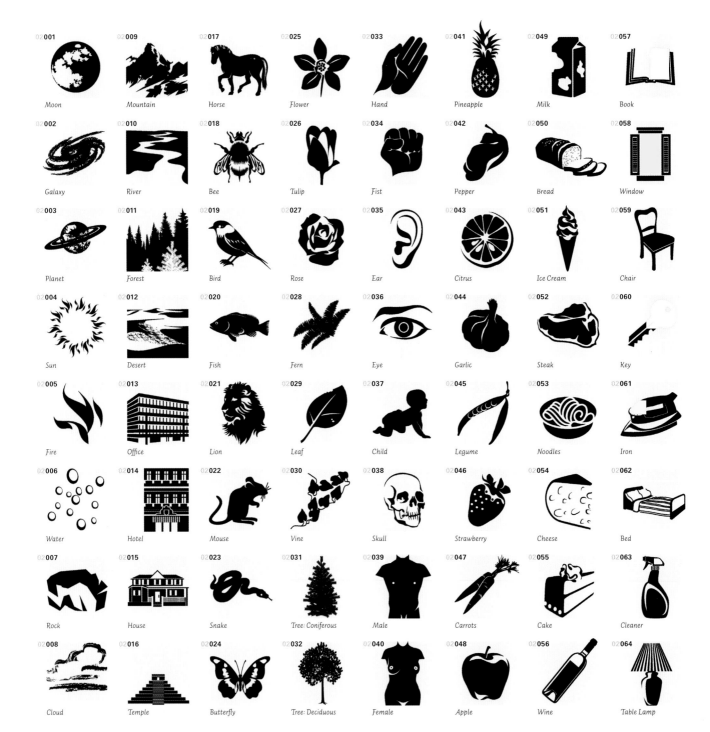

02**001** Moon	02**009** Mountain	02**017** Horse	02**025** Flower	02**033** Hand	02**041** Pineapple	02**049** Milk	02**057** Book
02**002** Galaxy	02**010** River	02**018** Bee	02**026** Tulip	02**034** Fist	02**042** Pepper	02**050** Bread	02**058** Window
02**003** Planet	02**011** Forest	02**019** Bird	02**027** Rose	02**035** Ear	02**043** Citrus	02**051** Ice Cream	02**059** Chair
02**004** Sun	02**012** Desert	02**020** Fish	02**028** Fern	02**036** Eye	02**044** Garlic	02**052** Steak	02**060** Key
02**005** Fire	02**013** Office	02**021** Lion	02**029** Leaf	02**037** Child	02**045** Legume	02**053** Noodles	02**061** Iron
02**006** Water	02**014** Hotel	02**022** Mouse	02**030** Vine	02**038** Skull	02**046** Strawberry	02**054** Cheese	02**062** Bed
02**007** Rock	02**015** House	02**023** Snake	02**031** Tree: Coniferous	02**039** Male	02**047** Carrots	02**055** Cake	02**063** Cleaner
02**008** Cloud	02**016** Temple	02**024** Butterfly	02**032** Tree: Deciduous	02**040** Female	02**048** Apple	02**056** Wine	02**064** Table Lamp

Simple and clean, icons offer immediate recognizability and concrete messages in a distilled, illustrative form. Use them alone or housed in graphic shapes, as small notational elements, or as large-scale primary illustrations.

The simplicity of their form allows them to accept texture and participate actively in a collage with other imagery.

02 065 Blender	02 073 Comb	02 081 Wrench	02 089 Clock	02 097 Computer	02 105 Microscope	02 113 Pill	02 121 Bicycle
02 066 Kettle	02 074 Umbrella	02 082 Hammer	02 090 Compass: Directional	02 098 Telephone	02 106 Cell	02 114 Syringe	02 122 Auto
02 067 Whisk	02 075 Needle+Thread	02 083 Saw	02 091 Compass	02 099 Stapler	02 107 Satellite	02 115 Crutch	02 123 Airplane
02 068 Pot	02 076 Wallet	02 084 Gear	02 092 Tweezers	02 100 Scissors	02 108 Test Tube	02 116 Monitor	02 124 Rocket
02 069 Oven MItt	02 077 Hair Dryer	02 085 Screwdriver	02 093 Camera	02 101 Pen	02 109 Brain	02 117 Thermometer	02 125 Boat
02 070 Spatula	02 078 Perfume	02 086 Axe	02 094 Army Knife	02 102 Filing Cabinet	02 110 Atom	02 118 Scalpel	02 126 Train
02 071 Toaster	02 079 Wristwatch	02 087 Nut and Bolt	02 095 Weight Scale	02 103 Desk	02 111 Beaker	02 119 Stethoscope	02 127 Bus
02 072 Measures	02 080 Toothbrush	02 088 Drill	02 096 Magnifying Glass	02 104 Calculator	02 112 Telescope	02 120 Bandage	02 128 Truck

ICONIC IMAGES *Stylized Languages*

03

03001

Curve and Plane

03005

Simplified Naturalistic

03009

Reduced Modulated Lines

03013

Organic Planar Translation

03002

Plane/Line Division

03006

Outline and Pattern

03010

Planar Reduction/Literal Texture

03014

Angle/Curve Reduction

03003

Planar Reduction and Line Pattern

03007

Bold Line/Dot Translation

03011

Planar Reduction and Pattern

03015

Planar Reduction

03004

Modulated Lines

03008

Gestural Outline

03012

Simple Planar Reduction

03016

Seminaturalistic Reduction: Linear

Working from a naturalistic form as a base, designers may opt for more stylized icons for a bolder, more abstract, or metaphorical quality, supported by the clarity offered by the underlying concrete depiction. Shown here are a number of varied approaches to stylizing an icon, based on the fish form in the previous category.

03**017**

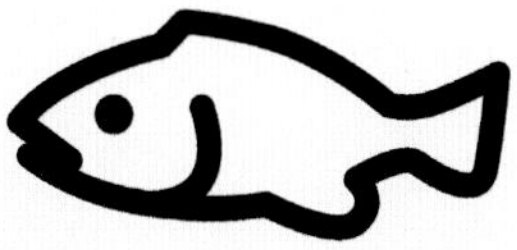

Simplified Naturalistic: Linear

03**021**

Ripped or Treated Edges

03**025**

Modulated Line Translation

03**029**

All-Angular Plane Reduction

03**018**

Naturalistic Silhouette: Dot Pattern

03**022**

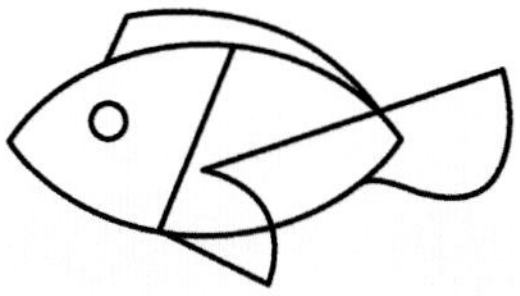

Linear Construction

03**026**

Form As Dot Grid

03**030**

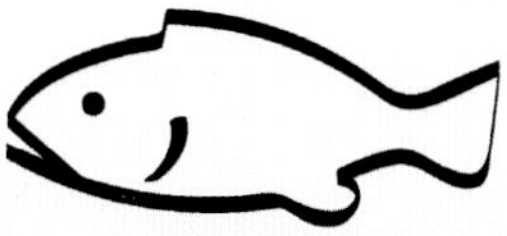

Calligraphic Line Translation

03**019**

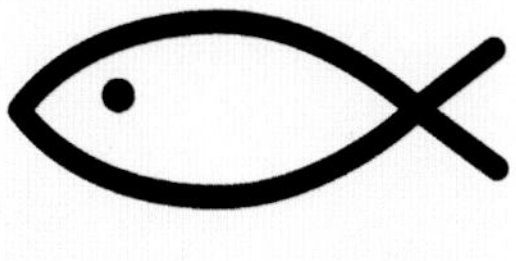

Elemental Reduction: Linear

03**023**

Planar Reduction and Pattern Detailing

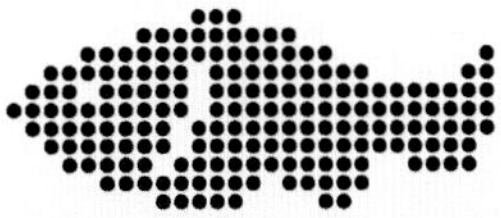

03**027**

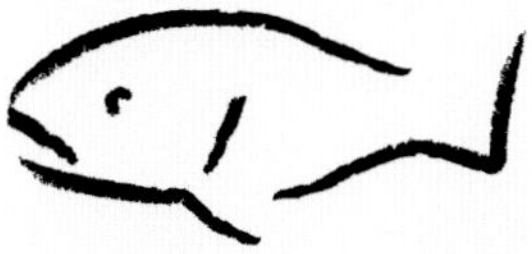

Softened Line Translation

03**031**

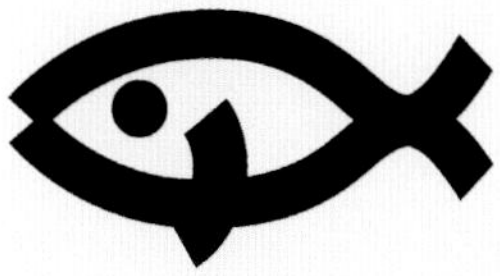

Exaggerated Line/Dot Translation

03**020**

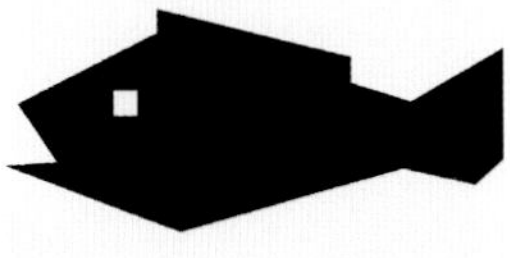

All-Angle Silhouette

03**024**

Silhouette and Overlayed Pattern

03**028**

Silhouette and Relevant Texture

03**032**

Deconstructed Edges

PHOTOGRAPHY *Color and Toning Treatments*

04

04 **001**

CMYK: Full Color

04 **002**

CMYK: Even Ghosting

04 **003**

CMYK: Ghosting: Supersaturated

04 **004**

CMYK: Full Density: Desaturated

04 **005**

CMYK: Color Balance Shift: Cyan

04 **006**

CMYK: Overall Hue Shift: Warm

04 **007**

CMYK: Low Contrast: Supersaturated

04 **008**

CMYK: Solid Color Overprint

04 **009**

BW Halftone

04 **010**

BW Halftone: Even Ghosting: Unchanged
Contrast

04 **011**

BW Halftone: Ghosting: High Contrast

04 **012**

BW Halftone: Ghosting: Low Contrast

04 **013**

BW Halftone: High Contrast

04 **014**

BW Halftone: Low Contrast: Midtone

04 **015**

BW Halftone: High Contrast: Midtone

04 **016**

BW Halftone: Solid Color Overprint

The simplicity of altering the color or tonality of photographs belies its potential to achieve visual interest. Varying contrast levels and ink mixture can offer a variety of distinctive results, especially for budget-conscious one- or two-color projects. Tonal treatments can also help enhance communication by changing the perceived feeling of images.

04**017**

Color Halftone

04**021**

Duotone: Black plus Warm Gray

04**025**

Duotone: Black plus Color: Black Dominant

04**029**

Duotone: Two Colors

04**018**

Color Halftone: Reversed from Background:
Light

04**022**

Duotone: Black plus Warm Gray: Even Ghosting

04**026**

Duotone: Black plus Color: Color Dominant

04**030**

Duotone: Two Colors: Color 1 Dominant

04**019**

Color Halftone: Reversed from Background:
Vibrant

04**023**

Duotone: Black plus Color

04**027**

Duotone: Black plus Color: Color Midtone
Range Exaggerated

04**031**

Duotone: Two Colors: Color 2 Dominant

04**020**

Color Halftone: Overprint Solid Color

04**024**

Duotone: Black plus Color: Even Ghosting

04**028**

Duotone: Black plus Color: Black Dominant in
Shadows/Color Ghosted

04**032**

Duotone: Two Colors: Selective Highlight and
Midtone Application

PHOTOGRAPHY *Texture and Filter Treatments*

05

CMYK: Coarse Dot Screen

BW: Pixel Dither

Color Painting over CMYK Image

Posterization: BW: One Level

BW: Coarse Dot Screen

CMYK: Linear Mezzotint

Color Painting over BW Image

Posterization: BW: Four Levels

CMYK: Coarse Line Screen

BW: Reticulation Pattern

Color Painting over Mezzotint Image

Posterization: CMYK: Eight Levels

BW: Coarse Line Screen

CMYK: Noise Texture

Color Painting over Coarse Dot Screen

BW: Xerography

More dramatic, even, than tonal change, is the possibility of introducing texture within a photographic image—whether digitally or through conventional means. Textural alterations lend tactility, may evoke symbolism and metaphor, or help relate photographs to illustrative elements through similar visual vocabulary.

Linear Pattern Overlay: Opaque

Typographic Overlay: Opaque

Digital Pointillization

Digital Diffusion

Linear Pattern Overlay: Transparent

Typographic Overlay: Transparent: Color Blended

Digital Solarization

Digital Blurring

Ornamental Pattern Overlay: Transparent

Photographic Texture Overlay: Ghosted

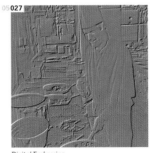
Digital Embossing

Digital Mosaic Pixellation

Ornamental Pattern Overlay: Transparent: Color Blended

Photographic Texture Overlay: Color Blended

Digital Edge Enhancement

Digital Fragmenting

PHOTOGRAPHY *Form Manipulations*

06

06001

Selective Toning

06002

Selective Blurring

06003

Selective Filtering Treatment

06004

Selective Resizing

06005

Silhouetted: Tight Contour

06006

Silhouetted: Simplified Contour: Angular

06007

Silhouetted: Simplified Contour: Curvilinear

06008

Silhouetted: Ripped Contour

06009

Masking: Secondary Image

06010

Masking: Large-Scale Pattern: Angular

06011

Masking: Large-Scale Pattern: Grid

06012

Masking: Large-Scale Texture

06013

Cutting and Separation: Part-Relative

06014

Cutting and Separation: Arbitrary

06015

Recomposition: Integral

06016

Recomposition: Additive

Presented here are a variety of options for affecting the physical form of photographic content: selective alterations of internal components; silhouetting; deconstructing and reordering parts; and splicing and combining multiple images. Together with other toning or texturing techniques, these approaches provide further possibilities for evolving photography into unique visual languages.

06**017**
Component Distortion

06**021**
Vignetted or Feathered Edge

06**025**
Splicing: Staggered

06**029**
Image Repeated: Offset: Overlaid

06**018**
Overall Distortion

06**022**
Alternate Frame Shape: Angular

06**026**
Splicing: Alternation with Secondary Image

06**030**
Image Repeated: Offset: Rotated: Overlaid

06**019**
Perspective

06**023**
Alternate Frame Shape: Curvilinear

06**027**
Splicing: Alternation with Image Inverse

06**031**
Overlay: Secondary Image

06**020**
Spherizing

06**024**
Alternate Frame Shape: Organic

06**028**
Splicing: Alternation with Rotated Splices

06**032**
Overlay: Secondary Image: Spliced

ILLUSTRATION *Styles and Media*

07

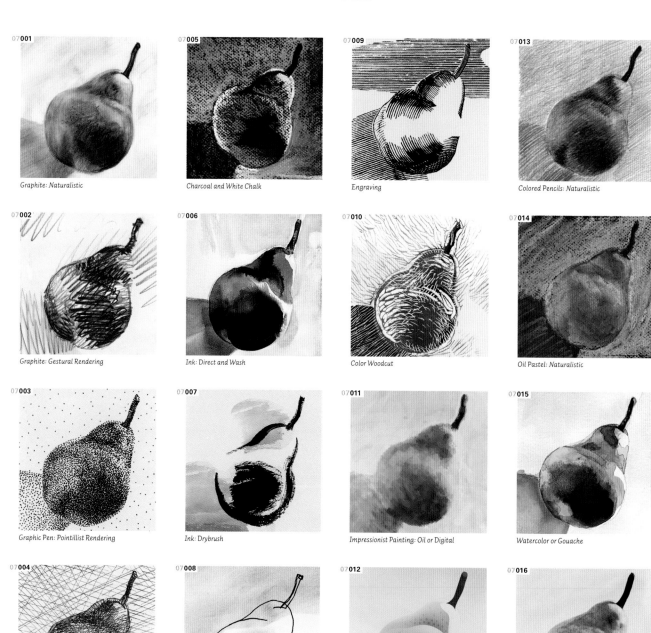

07**001** Graphite: Naturalistic

07**005** Charcoal and White Chalk

07**009** Engraving

07**013** Colored Pencils: Naturalistic

07**002** Graphite: Gestural Rendering

07**006** Ink: Direct and Wash

07**010** Color Woodcut

07**014** Oil Pastel: Naturalistic

07**003** Graphic Pen: Pointillist Rendering

07**007** Ink: Drybrush

07**011** Impressionist Painting: Oil or Digital

07**015** Watercolor or Gouache

07**004** Ballpoint Pen: Crosshatch

07**008** Etching with Aquatint

07**012** Idealized Vector Drawing

07**016** Aribrushed Photorealism

Illustration frees designers from real-world constraints of depiction inherent in photography. In this sampling: conventional styles created with paint, collage, and printmaking, as well as graphic vector-based approaches and digital montage. The left-hand page presents naturalistic approaches; on the right-hand page, interpretive styles are shown. Whether handmade or digital, drawing and painting techniques impart a human touch and a sense of invention.

07**017**

Icon Clustering

07**021**

Interpretive Doodling

07**025**
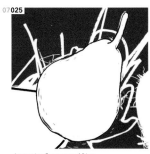
Aggressive Contour and Line

07**029**

Pop Art

07**018**
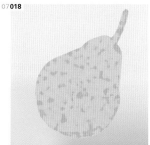
Texture and Gradation Fill

07**022**

Vector Symbol Kitsch

07**026**

Silhouette and Pattern

07**030**

Dot or Pixel Matrix

07**019**

Decorative Cuteness

07**023**

Playful Painted-Pattern Cutouts

07**027**
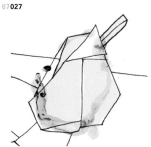
Linear Hand-Drawn Cubism with Paint

07**031**

Vector Cartoon Environment

07**020**
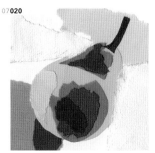
Collage: Ripped and Cut Paper

07**024**
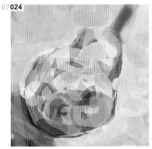
Lumnious Digital Painting

07**028**

Color-Field Brutalism

07**032**
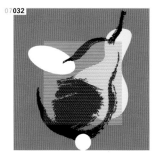
Retro Mixed-Media Collage

ABSTRACT LANGUAGES *Geometric*

08

08**001**

Urban

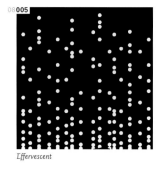

08**005**

Effervescent

08**009**

Monumental

08**013**

Mapping

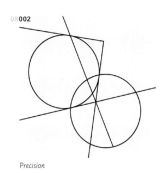

08**002**

Precision

08**006**

Traffic or Momentum

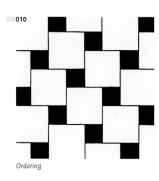

08**010**

Ordering

08**014**

Intimidation

08**003**

Conflict

08**007**

Rage

08**011**

Unity

08**015**

Internal Mechanisms

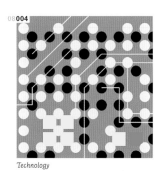

08**004**

Technology

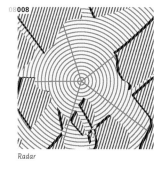

08**008**

Radar

08**012**

Fractal

08**016**

Interfacing

The power of abstraction to communicate, as well as to create unique, custom design statements, is demonstrated in this collection of geometric shapes and environments. Use these languages—evoking architecture, industry, science, and other concepts suggested by pure geometry—as backgrounds, components for collage, or stand-alone images. Cropping, scale changes, positive/negative reversal, and repetition may introduce variation for branding systems or to build more complex forms.

Primitive/Figural

Energetic

Digital Transmission

Planar Perspective

Faceted

Architectural

Atomic or Microbial

Destabilized

Fractured

Cellular

Crystalline

Navigating

Network

Messaging

Interpolating

Landscape/Sunrise

ABSTRACT LANGUAGES *Organic*

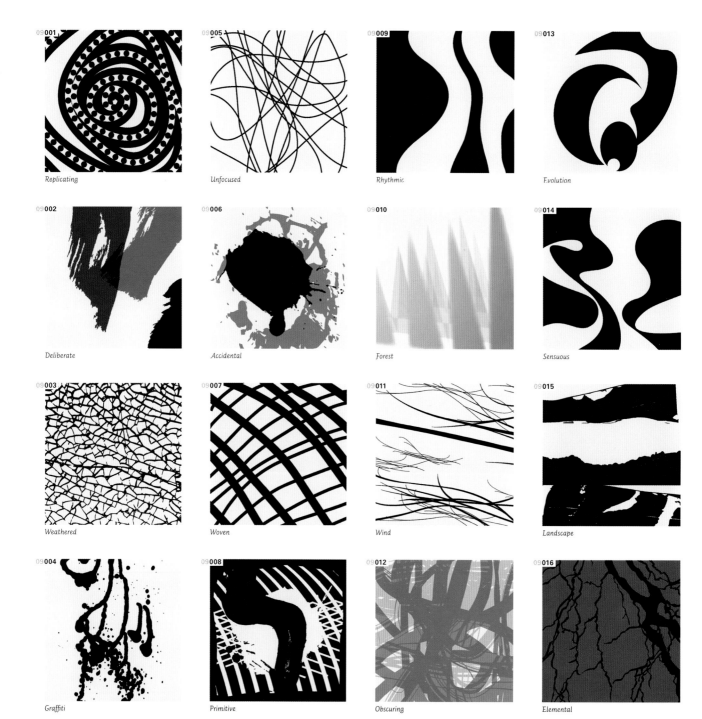

09001 Replicating

09005 Unfocused

09009 Rhythmic

09013 Evolution

09002 Deliberate

09006 Accidental

09010 Forest

09014 Sensuous

09003 Weathered

09007 Woven

09011 Wind

09015 Landscape

09004 Graffiti

09008 Primitive

09012 Obscuring

09016 Elemental

These abstract languages, in their softness, irregularity, and curvilinear qualities, reference the endless diversity of natural form. Use them as backgrounds or housing for photography, in combination with geometric abstraction or icons, as inspiration for logos, or as support for typographic configurations—for messages as far-ranging as the environment, emotions, life sciences, and poetic metaphor.

09**017**
Nebulous

09**021**
Reproduction

09**025**
Formulating

09**029**
Layered

09**018**
Intuitive

09**022**
Robust

09**026**
Activity

09**030**
Roiling

09**019**
Dissolution

09**023**
Biological

09**027**
Topographical

09**031**
Contemplative

09**020**
Stormy

09**024**
Oppositional

09**028**
Rugged

09**032**
Building

TEXTURES *Representational*

10

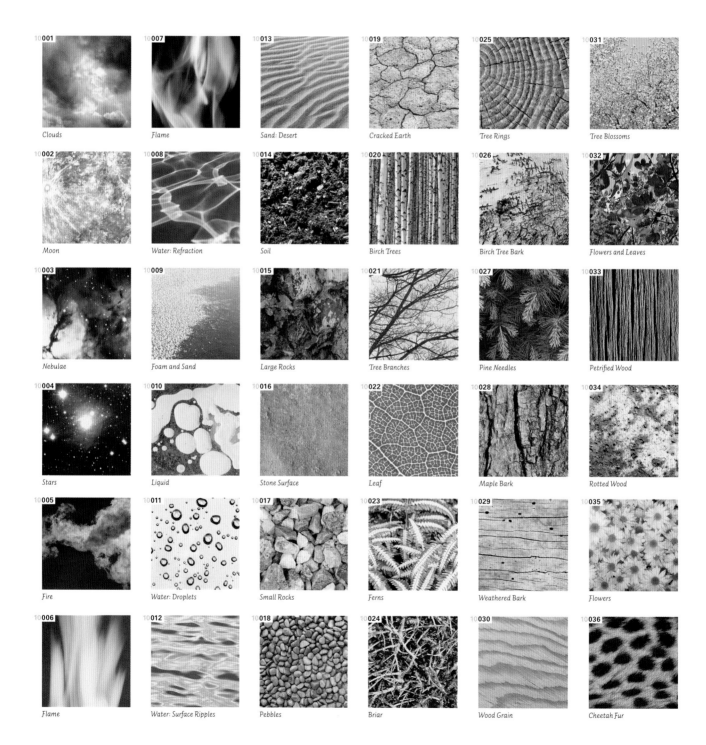

10 001 Clouds	10 007 Flame	10 013 Sand: Desert	10 019 Cracked Earth	10 025 Tree Rings	10 031 Tree Blossoms
10 002 Moon	10 008 Water: Refraction	10 014 Soil	10 020 Birch Trees	10 026 Birch Tree Bark	10 032 Flowers and Leaves
10 003 Nebulae	10 009 Foam and Sand	10 015 Large Rocks	10 021 Tree Branches	10 027 Pine Needles	10 033 Petrified Wood
10 004 Stars	10 010 Liquid	10 016 Stone Surface	10 022 Leaf	10 028 Maple Bark	10 034 Rotted Wood
10 005 Fire	10 011 Water: Droplets	10 017 Small Rocks	10 023 Ferns	10 029 Weathered Bark	10 035 Flowers
10 006 Flame	10 012 Water: Surface Ripples	10 018 Pebbles	10 024 Briar	10 030 Wood Grain	10 036 Cheetah Fur

As page backgrounds, fills for graphical forms, or overlays for image or type, textures whose sources a viewer is able to recognize present a concrete, grounded reference that can speed communication. These textures are drawn from archetypal sources, such as the elements, materials in the environment, animals, and manmade objects.

10 037 Tiger Stripes	10 043 Leopard Fur	10 049 Snakeskin	10 055 Bed Linens	10 061 Loomed Textile	10 067 Watercolor Paper
10 038 Bear Fur	10 044 Alligator Skin	10 050 Leather	10 056 Brush Painting	10 062 Brick	10 068 Sequins
10 039 Cowhide	10 045 Elephant Hide	10 051 Folded Paper	10 057 Scribble	10 063 Curled Paper	10 069 Circuit Board
10 040 Zebra Hide	10 046 Human Skin	10 052 Gauze Fabric	10 058 Ink Wash	10 064 Coins	10 070 Wires
10 041 Butterfly Wing	10 047 Basal Cells	10 053 Linen Paper	10 059 Burlap	10 065 Hardware	10 071 Glass
10 042 Feathers	10 048 Striated Muscle Cells	10 054 Rag Paper	10 060 Furled Silk	10 066 Paper Clips	10 072 Rusted Steel

TEXTURES *Abstract*

11

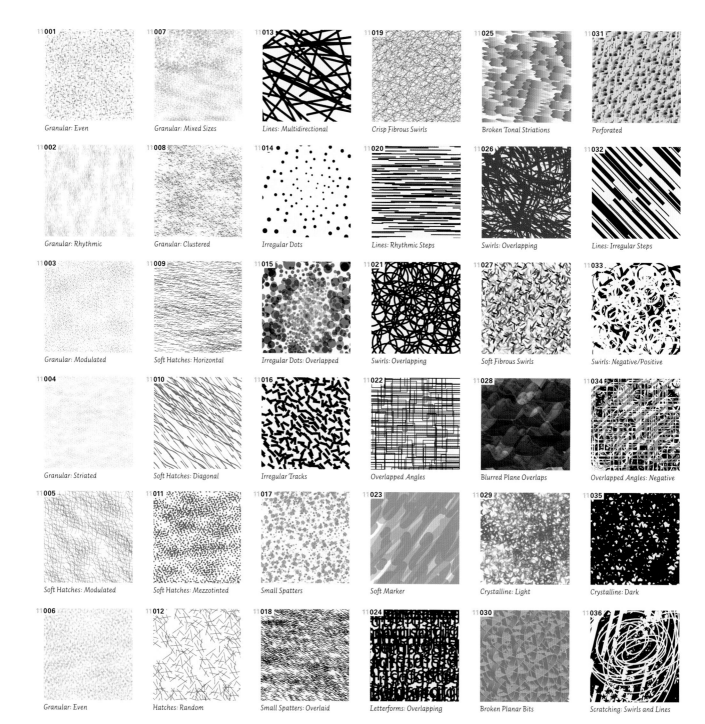

11001 Granular: Even

11002 Granular: Rhythmic

11003 Granular: Modulated

11004 Granular: Striated

11005 Soft Hatches: Modulated

11006 Granular: Even

11007 Granular: Mixed Sizes

11008 Granular: Clustered

11009 Soft Hatches: Horizontal

11010 Soft Hatches: Diagonal

11011 Soft Hatches: Mezzotinted

11012 Hatches: Random

11013 Lines: Multidirectional

11014 Irregular Dots

11015 Irregular Dots: Overlapped

11016 Irregular Tracks

11017 Small Spatters

11018 Small Spatters: Overlaid

11019 Crisp Fibrous Swirls

11020 Lines: Rhythmic Steps

11021 Swirls: Overlapping

11022 Overlapped Angles

11023 Soft Marker

11024 Letterforms: Overlapping

11025 Broken Tonal Striations

11026 Swirls: Overlapping

11027 Soft Fibrous Swirls

11028 Blurred Plane Overlaps

11029 Crystalline: Light

11030 Broken Planar Bits

11031 Perforated

11032 Lines: Irregular Steps

11033 Swirls: Negative/Positive

11034 Overlapped Angles: Negative

11035 Crystalline: Dark

11036 Scratching: Swirls and Lines

The textures in this category are simply that—randomized, abstract surface activity without the limitations imposed by recognizability. As such, their use as overlays, fills, or backgrounds offers room for interpretation or suggests real-world associations on a more conceptual level. Use them on their own, combine them with representational textures, or use them to enrich photographs, icons, and illustrations.

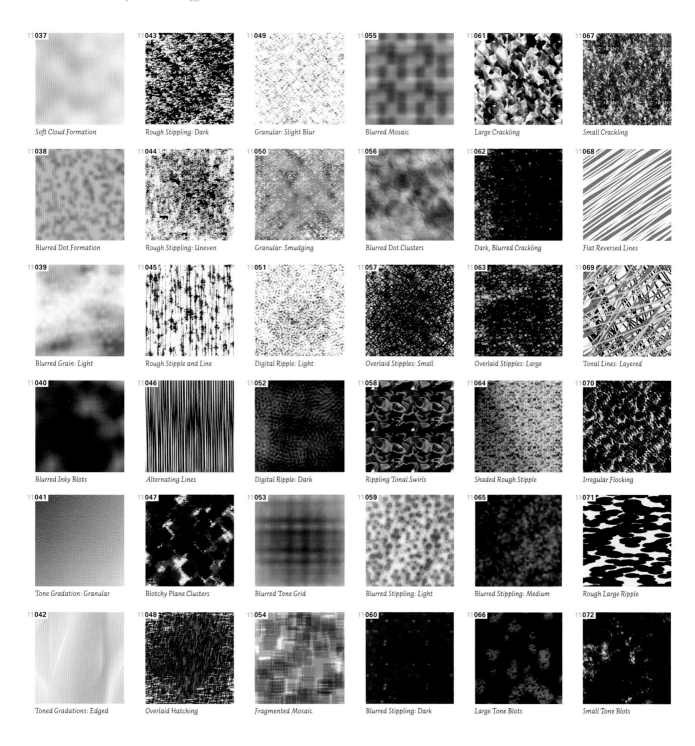

11037 Soft Cloud Formation

11043 Rough Stippling: Dark

11049 Granular: Slight Blur

11055 Blurred Mosaic

11061 Large Crackling

11067 Small Crackling

11038 Blurred Dot Formation

11044 Rough Stippling: Uneven

11050 Granular: Smudging

11056 Blurred Dot Clusters

11062 Dark, Blurred Crackling

11068 Flat Reversed Lines

11039 Blurred Grain: Light

11045 Rough Stipple and Line

11051 Digital Ripple: Light

11057 Overlaid Stipples: Small

11063 Overlaid Stipples: Large

11069 Tonal Lines: Layered

11040 Blurred Inky Blots

11046 Alternating Lines

11052 Digital Ripple: Dark

11058 Rippling Tonal Swirls

11064 Shaded Rough Stipple

11070 Irregular Flocking

11041 Tone Gradation: Granular

11047 Blotchy Plane Clusters

11053 Blurred Tone Grid

11059 Blurred Stippling: Light

11065 Blurred Stippling: Medium

11071 Rough Large Ripple

11042 Toned Gradations: Edged

11048 Overlaid Hatching

11054 Fragmented Mosaic

11060 Blurred Stippling: Dark

11066 Large Tone Blots

11072 Small Tone Blots

PATTERNS *Concrete: Photographic*

12

12**001** Mesh	12**007** Rolled Towels	12**013** Crates	12**019** Struts and Wires	12**025** Tire Tread	12**031** Glass and Steel Facade
12**002** Mixing Board	12**008** Circuit Board	12**014** Lace	12**020** Metal Cables	12**026** Ornamental Ironwork	12**032** Plaid Fabric
12**003** Palladian Windows	12**009** Corrugated Cardboard	12**015** Baling Wire	12**021** Steel Plating	12**027** Mailbox Doors	12**033** Ribbed Stone
12**004** Dot Screen	12**010** Stacked Pots	12**016** Noodles	12**022** Metal Grate	12**028** Cheese Grater	12**034** Woven Rope
12**005** Office Windows	12**011** Bamboo	12**017** Bricks	12**023** Basket Weave	12**029** Doily	12**035** Plant Stem
12**006** Cedar Shakes	12**012** Glazed Tiles	12**018** Wood	12**024** Cement Blocks	12**030** Strawberry Seeds	12**036** Computer Keyboard

Repeating structures of representational and semiconcrete forms can provide backdrops for layouts or packaging, fills for abstract shapes, or foundations for complex collages where the element of recognition helps add depth to simpler, more concise images. Explore combinations of these pattern elements to create rich, illustrative tapestries.

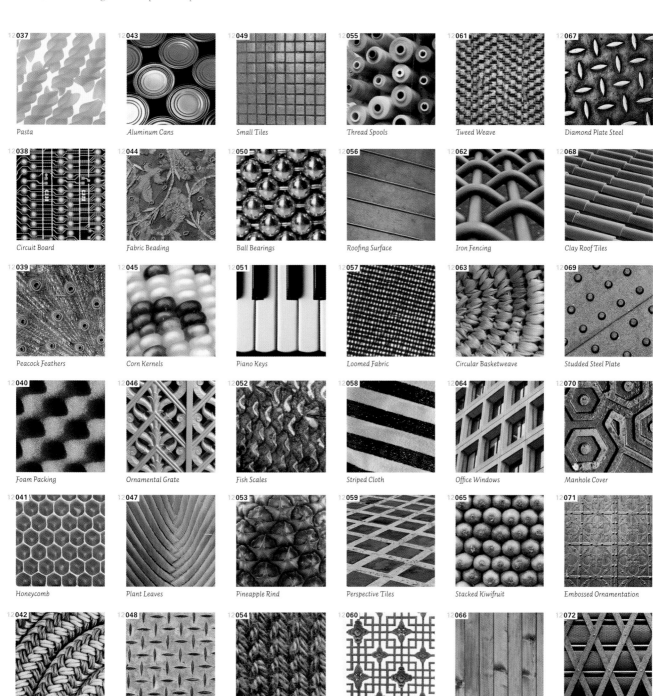

037 Pasta

043 Aluminum Cans

049 Small Tiles

055 Thread Spools

061 Tweed Weave

067 Diamond Plate Steel

038 Circuit Board

044 Fabric Beading

050 Ball Bearings

056 Roofing Surface

062 Iron Fencing

068 Clay Roof Tiles

039 Peacock Feathers

045 Corn Kernels

051 Piano Keys

057 Loomed Fabric

063 Circular Basketweave

069 Studded Steel Plate

040 Foam Packing

046 Ornamental Grate

052 Fish Scales

058 Striped Cloth

064 Office Windows

070 Manhole Cover

041 Honeycomb

047 Plant Leaves

053 Pineapple Rind

059 Perspective Tiles

065 Stacked Kiwifruit

071 Embossed Ornamentation

042 Woven Wire Sheathing

048 Diamond Plate Steel

054 Crochet

060 Ornamental Screen

066 Wood Flooring

072 Duct Grate

PATTERNS *Ornamental*

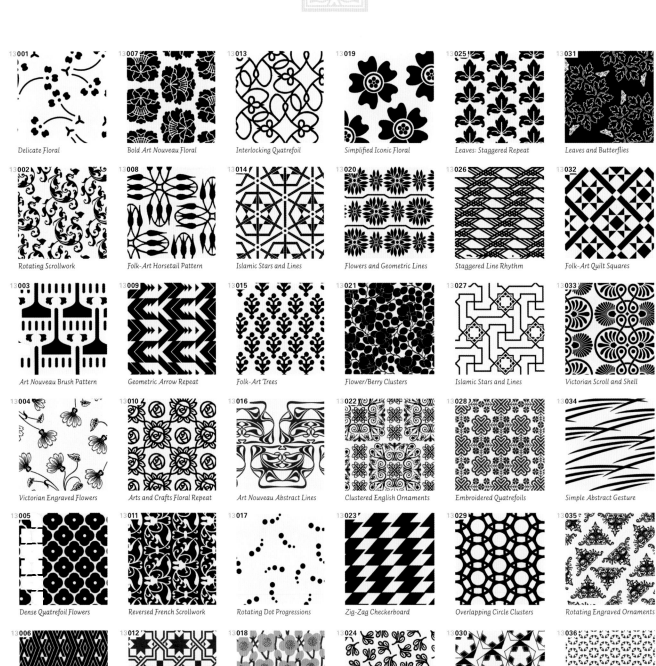

13001 Delicate Floral	**13007** Bold Art Nouveau Floral	**13013** Interlocking Quatrefoil
13002 Rotating Scrollwork	**13008** Folk-Art Horsetail Pattern	**13014** Islamic Stars and Lines
13003 Art Nouveau Brush Pattern	**13009** Geometric Arrow Repeat	**13015** Folk-Art Trees
13004 Victorian Engraved Flowers	**13010** Arts and Crafts Floral Repeat	**13016** Art Nouveau Abstract Lines
13005 Dense Quatrefoil Flowers	**13011** Reversed French Scrollwork	**13017** Rotating Dot Progressions
13006 Native American Weave	**13012** Islamic Stars and Lines	**13018** Two-Tone Flowers/Branches

13019 Simplified Iconic Floral	**13025** Leaves: Staggered Repeat	**13031** Leaves and Butterflies
13020 Flowers and Geometric Lines	**13026** Staggered Line Rhythm	**13032** Folk-Art Quilt Squares
13021 Flower/Berry Clusters	**13027** Islamic Stars and Lines	**13033** Victorian Scroll and Shell
13022 Clustered English Ornaments	**13028** Embroidered Quatrefoils	**13034** Simple Abstract Gesture
13023 Zig-Zag Checkerboard	**13029** Overlapping Circle Clusters	**13035** Rotating Engraved Ornaments
13024 Rotating Bud Clusters	**13030** Art Deco Pentagram	**13036** Dense Circle/Triangle Repeat

These decorative patterns run the gamut from Old-World inspirations in architectural engravings and textiles to stripped-down, modern, yet still intricate, interwoven rhythms of geometry. Overlaying related patterns, enlarging and reducing their scales, rotating them in different locations—as well as using them to interact with photography and illustration—provides limitless possibilities.

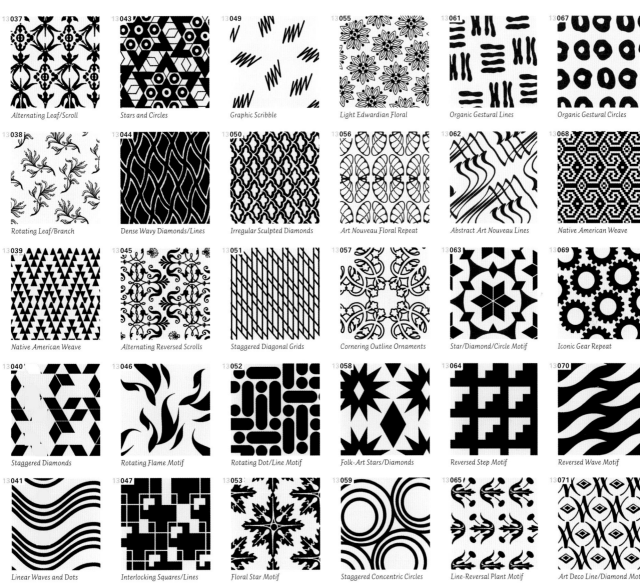

13037 Alternating Leaf/Scroll	13043 Stars and Circles	13049 Graphic Scribble	13055 Light Edwardian Floral	13061 Organic Gestural Lines	13067 Organic Gestural Circles
13038 Rotating Leaf/Branch	13044 Dense Wavy Diamonds/Lines	13050 Irregular Sculpted Diamonds	13056 Art Nouveau Floral Repeat	13062 Abstract Art Nouveau Lines	13068 Native American Weave
13039 Native American Weave	13045 Alternating Reversed Scrolls	13051 Staggered Diagonal Grids	13057 Cornering Outline Ornaments	13063 Star/Diamond/Circle Motif	13069 Iconic Gear Repeat
13040 Staggered Diamonds	13046 Rotating Flame Motif	13052 Rotating Dot/Line Motif	13058 Folk-Art Stars/Diamonds	13064 Reversed Step Motif	13070 Reversed Wave Motif
13041 Linear Waves and Dots	13047 Interlocking Squares/Lines	13053 Floral Star Motif	13059 Staggered Concentric Circles	13065 Line-Reversal Plant Motif	13071 Art Deco Line/Diamond Motif
13042 Folk-Art Star Flowers	13048 Neoclassical Ornament Repeat	13054 Art Deco Wave Chevrons	13060 Alternating Flowers/Stars	13066 Fish Scale Motif	13072 Art Deco Cube/Arrow Motif

PATTERNS *Geometric: Lines*

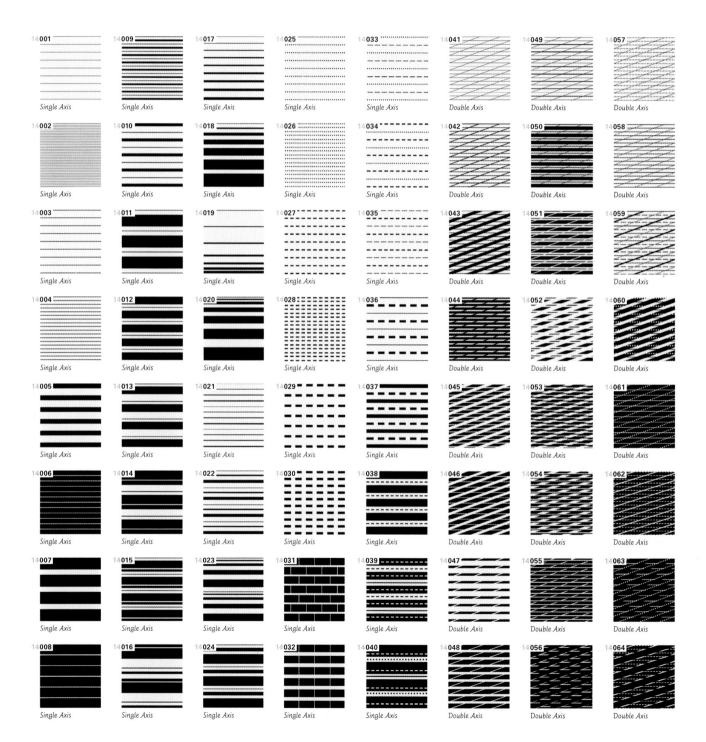

14001 Single Axis	14009 Single Axis	14017 Single Axis	14025 Single Axis	14033 Single Axis	14041 Double Axis	14049 Double Axis	14057 Double Axis
14002 Single Axis	14010 Single Axis	14018 Single Axis	14026 Single Axis	14034 Single Axis	14042 Double Axis	14050 Double Axis	14058 Double Axis
14003 Single Axis	14011 Single Axis	14019 Single Axis	14027 Single Axis	14035 Single Axis	14043 Double Axis	14051 Double Axis	14059 Double Axis
14004 Single Axis	14012 Single Axis	14020 Single Axis	14028 Single Axis	14036 Single Axis	14044 Double Axis	14052 Double Axis	14060 Double Axis
14005 Single Axis	14013 Single Axis	14021 Single Axis	14029 Single Axis	14037 Single Axis	14045 Double Axis	14053 Double Axis	14061 Double Axis
14006 Single Axis	14014 Single Axis	14022 Single Axis	14030 Single Axis	14038 Single Axis	14046 Double Axis	14054 Double Axis	14062 Double Axis
14007 Single Axis	14015 Single Axis	14023 Single Axis	14031 Single Axis	14039 Single Axis	14047 Double Axis	14055 Double Axis	14063 Double Axis
14008 Single Axis	14016 Single Axis	14024 Single Axis	14032 Single Axis	14040 Single Axis	14048 Double Axis	14056 Double Axis	14064 Double Axis

Patterns such as those shown here create directional movement and optical rhythm. Enlarging the scale of a pattern, relative to the format in which it is used, increases the number of options—as do rotating it, changing the tonality or color of its line elements, and so on.

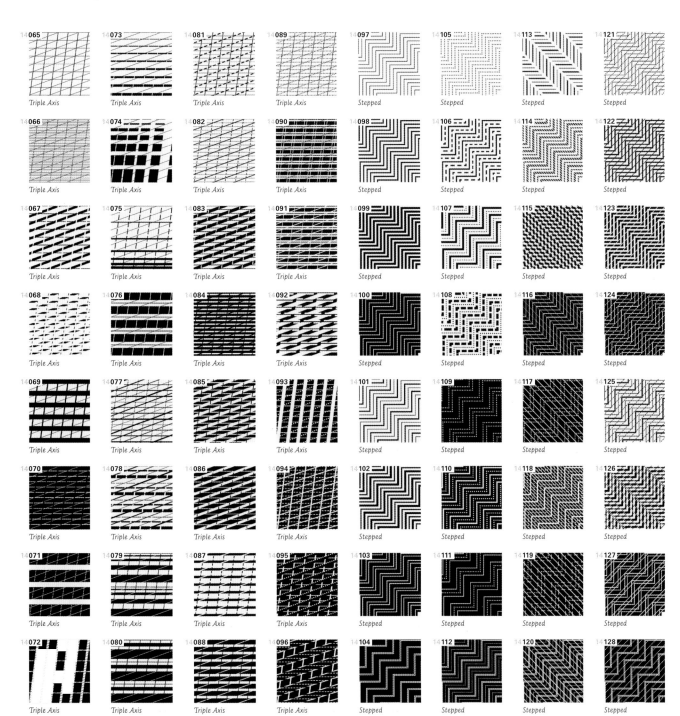

14 065	14 073	14 081	14 089	14 097	14 105	14 113	14 121
Triple Axis	Triple Axis	Triple Axis	Triple Axis	Stepped	Stepped	Stepped	Stepped
14 066	14 074	14 082	14 090	14 098	14 106	14 114	14 122
Triple Axis	Triple Axis	Triple Axis	Triple Axis	Stepped	Stepped	Stepped	Stepped
14 067	14 075	14 083	14 091	14 099	14 107	14 115	14 123
Triple Axis	Triple Axis	Triple Axis	Triple Axis	Stepped	Stepped	Stepped	Stepped
14 068	14 076	14 084	14 092	14 100	14 108	14 116	14 124
Triple Axis	Triple Axis	Triple Axis	Triple Axis	Stepped	Stepped	Stepped	Stepped
14 069	14 077	14 085	14 093	14 101	14 109	14 117	14 125
Triple Axis	Triple Axis	Triple Axis	Triple Axis	Stepped	Stepped	Stepped	Stepped
14 070	14 078	14 086	14 094	14 102	14 110	14 118	14 126
Triple Axis	Triple Axis	Triple Axis	Triple Axis	Stepped	Stepped	Stepped	Stepped
14 071	14 079	14 087	14 095	14 103	14 111	14 119	14 127
Triple Axis	Triple Axis	Triple Axis	Triple Axis	Stepped	Stepped	Stepped	Stepped
14 072	14 080	14 088	14 096	14 104	14 112	14 120	14 128
Triple Axis	Triple Axis	Triple Axis	Triple Axis	Stepped	Stepped	Stepped	Stepped

PATTERNS *Geometric: Curves*

15001	15009	15017	15025	15033	15041	15049	15057
Concentric	Concentric	Concentric	Concentric	Concentric	Doubled	Tripled	Offset
15002	15010	15018	15026	15034	15042	15050	15058
Concentric	Concentric	Concentric	Concentric	Concentric	Doubled	Tripled	Offset
15003	15011	15019	15027	15035	15043	15051	15059
Concentric	Concentric	Concentric	Concentric	Concentric	Doubled	Tripled	Offset
15004	15012	15020	15028	15036	15044	15052	15060
Concentric	Concentric	Concentric	Concentric	Concentric	Doubled	Tripled	Offset
15005	15013	15021	15029	15037	15045	15053	15061
Concentric	Concentric	Concentric	Concentric	Concentric	Doubled	Tripled	Offset
15006	15014	15022	15030	15038	15046	15054	15062
Concentric	Concentric	Concentric	Concentric	Concentric	Doubled	Tripled	Offset
15007	15015	15023	15031	15039	15047	15055	15063
Concentric	Concentric	Concentric	Concentric	Concentric	Doubled	Tripled	Offset
15008	15016	15024	15032	15040	15048	15056	15064
Concentric	Concentric	Concentric	Concentric	Concentric	Doubled	Tripled	Offset

The pure directionality and vibration of linear patterns is made more complex when the line elements are curved or waved, as in the selection provided here. At extremely large scales, these structures can be used not only to activate surface area but also to create exceptionally three-dimensional environments or direct the eye from one element to another. At very small scales, they make very active fills within shapes or within other enlarged pattern elements.

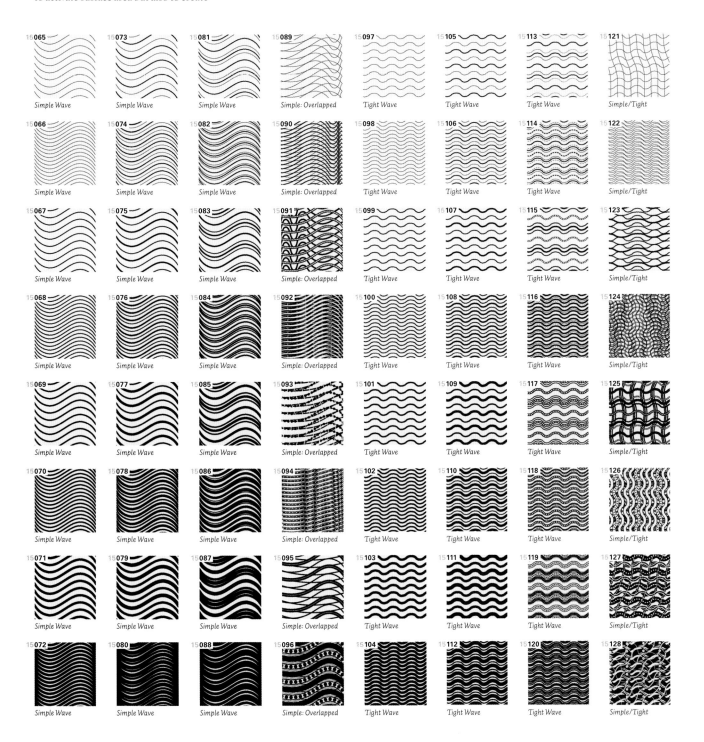

PATTERNS *Geometric: Grids*

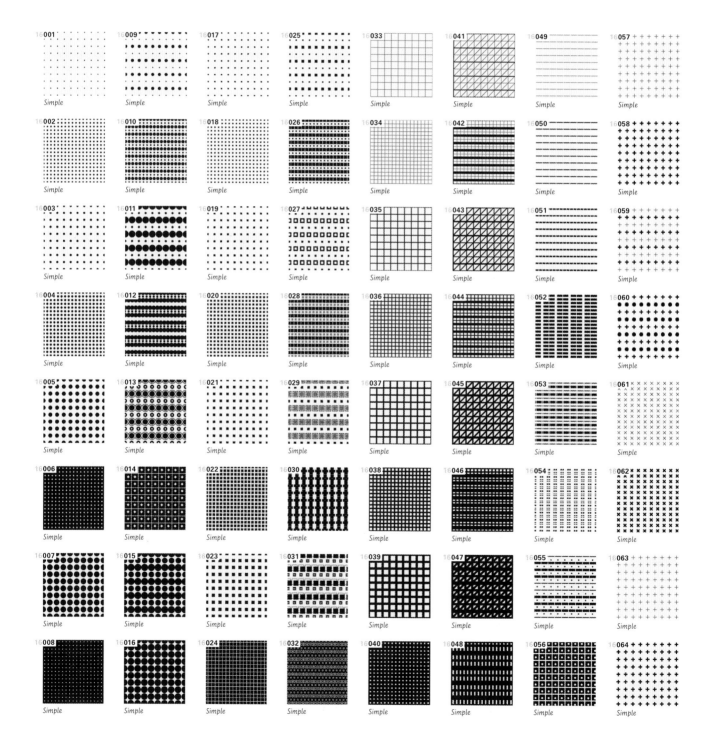

The patterns shown here are all based on modular, square-based repeating structures—whether the pattern components are square themselves, linear, or dotlike in shape. From simple checker patterns to intricate configurations of several base components, these patterns are systematic, architectonic, and three-dimensional.

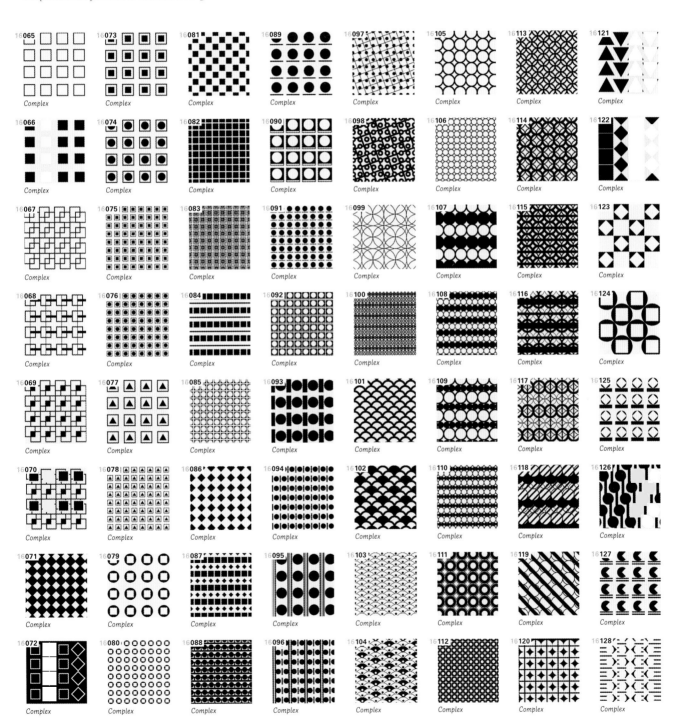

16 065 *Complex*	16 073 *Complex*	16 081 *Complex*	16 089 *Complex*	16 097 *Complex*	16 105 *Complex*	16 113 *Complex*	16 121 *Complex*
16 066 *Complex*	16 074 *Complex*	16 082 *Complex*	16 090 *Complex*	16 098 *Complex*	16 106 *Complex*	16 114 *Complex*	16 122 *Complex*
16 067 *Complex*	16 075 *Complex*	16 083 *Complex*	16 091 *Complex*	16 099 *Complex*	16 107 *Complex*	16 115 *Complex*	16 123 *Complex*
16 068 *Complex*	16 076 *Complex*	16 084 *Complex*	16 092 *Complex*	16 100 *Complex*	16 108 *Complex*	16 116 *Complex*	16 124 *Complex*
16 069 *Complex*	16 077 *Complex*	16 085 *Complex*	16 093 *Complex*	16 101 *Complex*	16 109 *Complex*	16 117 *Complex*	16 125 *Complex*
16 070 *Complex*	16 078 *Complex*	16 086 *Complex*	16 094 *Complex*	16 102 *Complex*	16 110 *Complex*	16 118 *Complex*	16 126 *Complex*
16 071 *Complex*	16 079 *Complex*	16 087 *Complex*	16 095 *Complex*	16 103 *Complex*	16 111 *Complex*	16 119 *Complex*	16 127 *Complex*
16 072 *Complex*	16 080 *Complex*	16 088 *Complex*	16 096 *Complex*	16 104 *Complex*	16 112 *Complex*	16 120 *Complex*	16 128 *Complex*

BORDERS *Page and Object Edge Forms*

17

17**001**

Linear Pattern

17**002**

Linear Pattern

17**003**

Linear Pattern

17**004**

Linear Pattern

17**005**

Linear Pattern

17**006**

Linear Pattern

17**007**

Linear Pattern

17**008**

Linear Pattern

17**009**

Linear Pattern

17**010**

Linear Pattern

17**011**

Linear Pattern

17**012**

Linear Pattern

17**013**

Gridded Pattern

17**014**

Gridded Pattern

17**015**

Gridded Pattern

17**016**

Gridded Pattern

17**017**

Gridded Pattern

17**018**

Gridded Pattern

17**019**

Gridded Pattern

17**020**

Waved Line Screen

17**021**

Gridded Pattern

17**022**

Gridded Pattern

17**023**

Gridded Pattern

17**024**

Gridded Pattern

17**025**

Rough Rip: Shallow or Deep

17**026**

Brush Stroke

17**027**

Charcoal Stroke

17**028**

Torn Spiral Paper

17**029**

Torn Ring-Bound Paper

17**030**

Engraved Page Curl

17**031**

Stitching

17**032**

Fibrous Edge

17**033**

Photographic Paper Edge: Deckled or Crumpled

17**034**

Watercolor Edge: Wet Bleed

17**035**

Wire Binding: Spine/Interior

17**036**

Wire Binding: Spine/Edge View

Use these edging devices—striped bands, rips, brush strokes, double lines, and so on—to enclose images, surround typographic elements, alter the edges of abstract graphic forms, or border page edges. Carefully cropped, they are also useful as shapes unto themselves, or as containers for icons, patterns, page numbers, or titling elements.

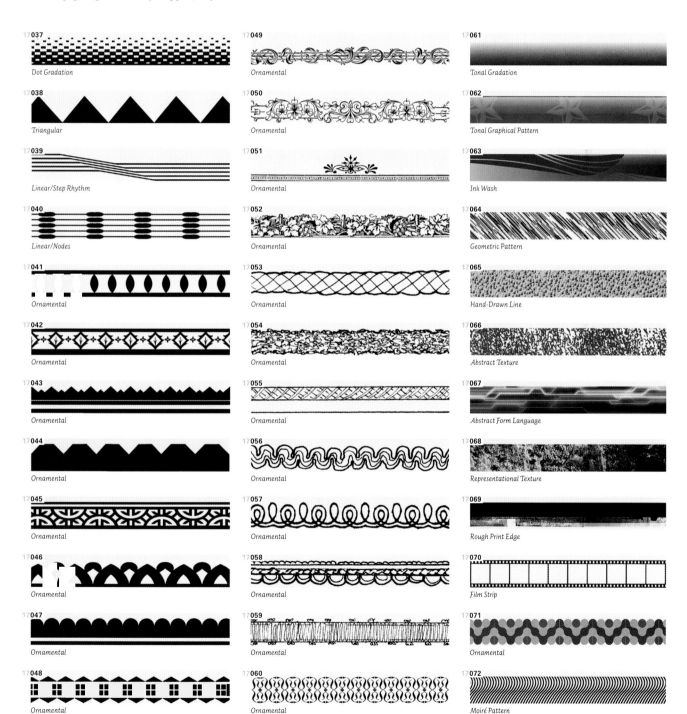

17**037**
Dot Gradation

17**038**
Triangular

17**039**
Linear/Step Rhythm

17**040**
Linear/Nodes

17**041**
Ornamental

17**042**
Ornamental

17**043**
Ornamental

17**044**
Ornamental

17**045**
Ornamental

17**046**
Ornamental

17**047**
Ornamental

17**048**
Ornamental

17**049**
Ornamental

17**050**
Ornamental

17**051**
Ornamental

17**052**
Ornamental

17**053**
Ornamental

17**054**
Ornamental

17**055**
Ornamental

17**056**
Ornamental

17**057**
Ornamental

17**058**
Ornamental

17**059**
Ornamental

17**060**
Ornamental

17**061**
Tonal Gradation

17**062**
Tonal Graphical Pattern

17**063**
Ink Wash

17**064**
Geometric Pattern

17**065**
Hand-Drawn Line

17**066**
Abstract Texture

17**067**
Abstract Form Language

17**068**
Representational Texture

17**069**
Rough Print Edge

17**070**
Film Strip

17**071**
Ornamental

17**072**
Moiré Pattern

SYMBOLS AND SIGNS *Visual Metaphors*

18

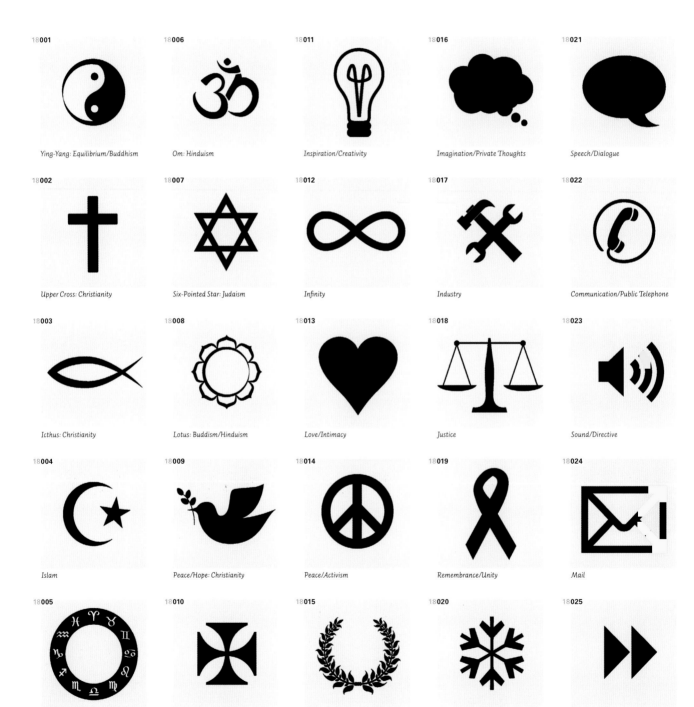

18**001**

Ying-Yang: Equilibrium/Buddhism

18**002**

Upper Cross: Christianity

18**003**

Icthus: Christianity

18**004**

Islam

18**005**

Zodiac

18**006**

Om: Hinduism

18**007**

Six-Pointed Star: Judaism

18**008**

Lotus: Buddism/Hinduism

18**009**

Peace/Hope: Christianity

18**010**

Maltese Cross: Treasure/Piracy

18**011**

Inspiration/Creativity

18**012**

Infinity

18**013**

Love/Intimacy

18**014**

Peace/Activism

18**015**

Laurel Wreath: Victory/Imperialism

18**016**

Imagination/Private Thoughts

18**017**

Industry

18**018**

Justice

18**019**

Remembrance/Unity

18**020**

Snowflake: Winter/General Seasons

18**021**

Speech/Dialogue

18**022**

Communication/Public Telephone

18**023**

Sound/Directive

18**024**

Mail

18**025**

Fast-Forward

In addition to using literal images for direct representation, a designer may opt for symbolic forms, or for representational images that have acquired metaphorical meaning.

Shown here is but a small sampling of commonly understood symbols that can add humor or unexpected conceptual overlay.

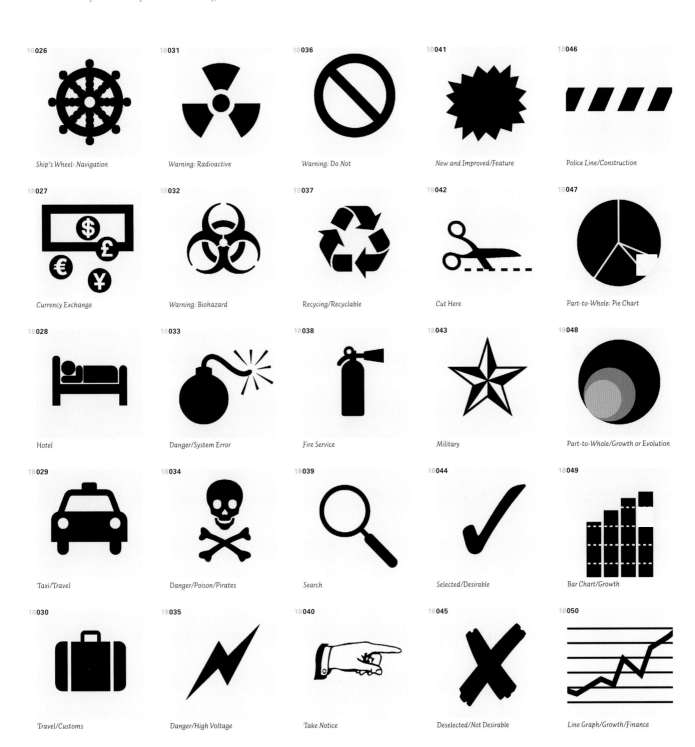

18**026**

Ship's Wheel: Navigation

18**031**

Warning: Radioactive

18**036**

Warning: Do Not

18**041**

New and Improved/Feature

18**046**

Police Line/Construction

18**027**

Currency Exchange

18**032**

Warning: Biohazard

18**037**

Recycling/Recyclable

18**042**

Cut Here

18**047**

Part-to-Whole: Pie Chart

18**028**

Hotel

18**033**

Danger/System Error

18**038**

Fire Service

18**043**

Military

18**048**

Part-to-Whole/Growth or Evolution

18**029**

Taxi/Travel

18**034**

Danger/Poison/Pirates

18**039**

Search

18**044**

Selected/Desirable

18**049**

Bar Chart/Growth

18**030**

Travel/Customs

18**035**

Danger/High Voltage

18**040**

Take Notice

18**045**

Deselected/Not Desirable

18**050**

Line Graph/Growth/Finance

Chromatic
Flavors

WHILE THE PERCEPTION OF COLOR may be highly subjective, there is no denying its power to stimulate and influence us. Even the most seasoned designers, however, are often at a loss when selecting colors, especially when the budget is tight and printing is at a premium. The first few ingredient categories here offer purely formal options for two- and three-color palettes—sets of colors chosen as partners because their optical interactions are especially dynamic. Two-color palettes are excellent starting points for branding or identity programs—if a given project already comes with a corporate color or two, one of the simple palettes here may be used for support. Even when full-color printing is an option, limiting one's color palette to two or three colors will create a stronger impression. Audiences' emotional and cultural expectations play important roles in developing color for products and services, as well as for projects of a metaphorical nature. Colors based on time periods, moods, age groups, and concepts as diverse as health care and telecommunications, men's grooming, and forestry are distilled here into palettes that will ensure a reliable chromatic flavor that you can build on to create complex color systems in any project.

TWO-COLOR PALETTES *Formal*

19

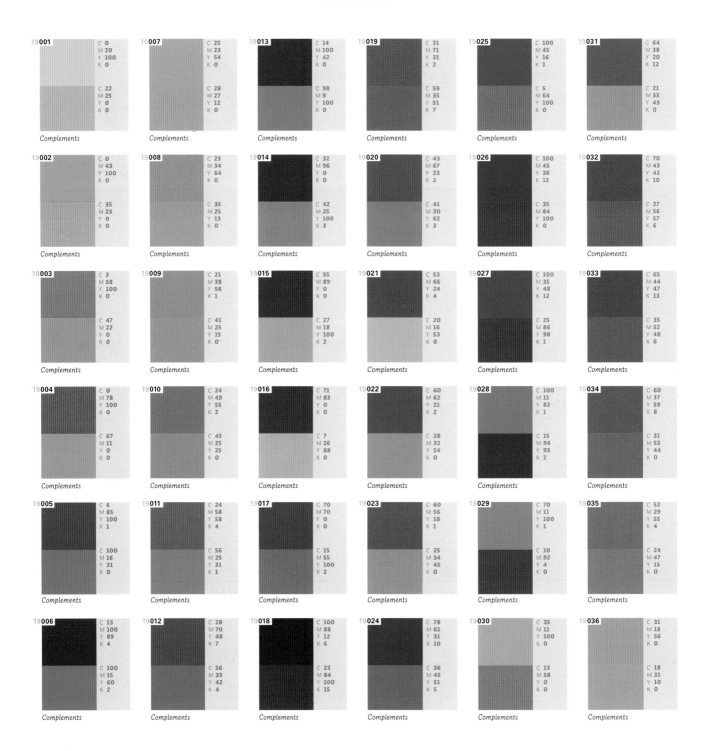

| 19**001** | C 0 M 20 Y 100 K 0 / C 22 M 25 Y 0 K 0 | 19**007** | C 25 M 23 Y 54 K 0 / C 28 M 27 Y 12 K 0 | 19**013** | C 14 M 100 Y 42 K 0 / C 98 M 9 Y 0 K 0 | 19**019** | C 31 M 71 Y 31 K 2 / C 59 M 35 Y 51 K 7 | 19**025** | C 100 M 45 Y 16 K 1 / C 5 M 64 Y 100 K 0 | 19**031** | C 64 M 38 Y 20 K 12 / C 21 M 33 Y 43 K 0 |

Complements (×6)

| 19**002** | C 0 M 43 Y 100 K 0 / C 35 M 23 Y 0 K 0 | 19**008** | C 23 M 34 Y 64 K 0 / C 35 M 25 Y 13 K 0 | 19**014** | C 32 M 96 Y 0 K 0 / C 42 M 25 Y 100 K 3 | 19**020** | C 43 M 67 Y 23 K 2 / C 41 M 30 Y 62 K 3 | 19**026** | C 100 M 45 Y 36 K 12 / C 35 M 84 Y 100 K 0 | 19**032** | C 70 M 43 Y 42 K 10 / C 27 M 56 Y 57 K 6 |

Complements (×6)

| 19**003** | C 3 M 58 Y 100 K 0 / C 47 M 22 Y 0 K 0 | 19**009** | C 21 M 38 Y 58 K 1 / C 41 M 25 Y 15 K 0 | 19**015** | C 55 M 89 Y 0 K 0 / C 27 M 18 Y 100 K 2 | 19**021** | C 53 M 66 Y 24 K 4 / C 20 M 16 Y 53 K 0 | 19**027** | C 100 M 35 Y 48 K 12 / C 25 M 86 Y 98 K 1 | 19**033** | C 65 M 44 Y 47 K 13 / C 35 M 52 Y 48 K 6 |

Complements (×6)

| 19**004** | C 0 M 78 Y 100 K 0 / C 67 M 11 Y 0 K 0 | 19**010** | C 24 M 49 Y 55 K 2 / C 45 M 25 Y 25 K 0 | 19**016** | C 71 M 83 Y 0 K 0 / C 7 M 26 Y 88 K 0 | 19**022** | C 60 M 62 Y 21 K 2 / C 28 M 32 Y 54 K 0 | 19**028** | C 100 M 11 Y 82 K 1 / C 15 M 94 Y 93 K 2 | 19**034** | C 60 M 37 Y 59 K 8 / C 31 M 53 Y 44 K 0 |

Complements (×6)

| 19**005** | C 6 M 85 Y 100 K 1 / C 100 M 16 Y 31 K 0 | 19**011** | C 24 M 58 Y 58 K 4 / C 56 M 25 Y 31 K 1 | 19**017** | C 70 M 70 Y 0 K 0 / C 15 M 55 Y 100 K 2 | 19**023** | C 60 M 56 Y 18 K 1 / C 25 M 34 Y 45 K 0 | 19**029** | C 70 M 11 Y 100 K 1 / C 10 M 92 Y 4 K 0 | 19**035** | C 52 M 29 Y 55 K 4 / C 24 M 47 Y 15 K 0 |

Complements (×6)

| 19**006** | C 13 M 100 Y 89 K 4 / C 100 M 15 Y 60 K 2 | 19**012** | C 28 M 70 Y 48 K 7 / C 56 M 33 Y 42 K 4 | 19**018** | C 100 M 88 Y 12 K 6 / C 23 M 84 Y 100 K 15 | 19**024** | C 78 M 61 Y 31 K 10 / C 36 M 45 Y 51 K 5 | 19**030** | C 35 M 11 Y 100 K 0 / C 13 M 58 Y 0 K 0 | 19**036** | C 31 M 18 Y 56 K 0 / C 18 M 31 Y 10 K 0 |

Complements (×6)

A simple, yet rich, chromatic relationship between two colors can be the foundation for a strong color language, whether used literally by printing in two spot-ink colors or limiting oneself in a process-color project. The colors in each pair may be tinted or overprinted to produce color families. The values of all the swatches are dark enough to be used for type, as well as imagery.

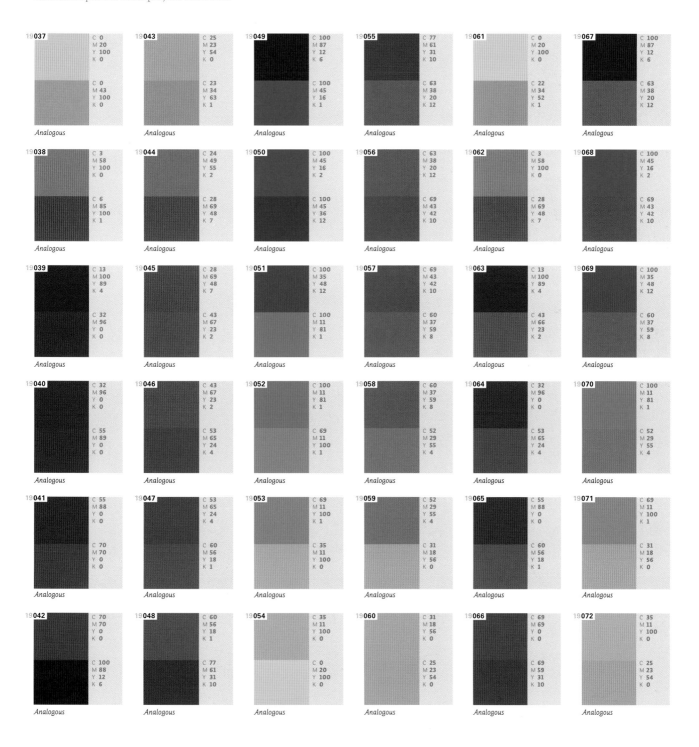

19037	C 0 M 20 Y 100 K 0 / C 0 M 43 Y 100 K 0	19043	C 25 M 23 Y 54 K 0 / C 23 M 34 Y 63 K 1	19049	C 100 M 87 Y 12 K 6 / C 100 M 45 Y 16 K 1	19055	C 77 M 61 Y 31 K 10 / C 63 M 38 Y 20 K 12	19061	C 0 M 20 Y 100 K 0 / C 22 M 34 Y 52 K 1	19067	C 100 M 87 Y 12 K 6 / C 63 M 38 Y 20 K 12
Analogous		*Analogous*		*Analogous*		*Analogous*		*Analogous*		*Analogous*	

19038 — C 3 M 58 Y 100 K 0 / C 6 M 85 Y 100 K 1 — *Analogous*
19044 — C 24 M 49 Y 55 K 2 / C 28 M 69 Y 48 K 7 — *Analogous*
19050 — C 100 M 45 Y 16 K 2 / C 100 M 45 Y 36 K 12 — *Analogous*
19056 — C 63 M 38 Y 20 K 12 / C 69 M 43 Y 42 K 10 — *Analogous*
19062 — C 3 M 58 Y 100 K 0 / C 28 M 69 Y 48 K 7 — *Analogous*
19068 — C 100 M 45 Y 16 K 2 / C 69 M 43 Y 42 K 10 — *Analogous*

19039 — C 13 M 100 Y 89 K 4 / C 32 M 96 Y 0 K 0 — *Analogous*
19045 — C 28 M 69 Y 48 K 7 / C 43 M 67 Y 23 K 2 — *Analogous*
19051 — C 100 M 35 Y 48 K 12 / C 100 M 11 Y 81 K 1 — *Analogous*
19057 — C 69 M 43 Y 42 K 10 / C 60 M 37 Y 59 K 8 — *Analogous*
19063 — C 13 M 100 Y 89 K 4 / C 43 M 66 Y 23 K 2 — *Analogous*
19069 — C 100 M 35 Y 48 K 12 / C 60 M 37 Y 59 K 8 — *Analogous*

19040 — C 32 M 96 Y 0 K 0 / C 55 M 89 Y 0 K 0 — *Analogous*
19046 — C 43 M 67 Y 23 K 2 / C 53 M 65 Y 24 K 4 — *Analogous*
19052 — C 100 M 11 Y 81 K 1 / C 69 M 11 Y 100 K 1 — *Analogous*
19058 — C 60 M 37 Y 59 K 8 / C 52 M 29 Y 55 K 4 — *Analogous*
19064 — C 32 M 96 Y 0 K 0 / C 53 M 65 Y 24 K 4 — *Analogous*
19070 — C 100 M 11 Y 81 K 1 / C 52 M 29 Y 55 K 4 — *Analogous*

19041 — C 55 M 88 Y 0 K 0 / C 70 M 70 Y 0 K 0 — *Analogous*
19047 — C 53 M 65 Y 24 K 4 / C 60 M 56 Y 18 K 1 — *Analogous*
19053 — C 69 M 11 Y 100 K 1 / C 35 M 11 Y 100 K 0 — *Analogous*
19059 — C 52 M 29 Y 55 K 4 / C 31 M 18 Y 56 K 0 — *Analogous*
19065 — C 55 M 88 Y 0 K 0 / C 60 M 56 Y 18 K 1 — *Analogous*
19071 — C 69 M 11 Y 100 K 1 / C 31 M 18 Y 56 K 0 — *Analogous*

19042 — C 70 M 70 Y 0 K 0 / C 100 M 88 Y 12 K 6 — *Analogous*
19048 — C 60 M 56 Y 18 K 1 / C 77 M 61 Y 31 K 10 — *Analogous*
19054 — C 35 M 11 Y 100 K 0 / C 0 M 20 Y 100 K 0 — *Analogous*
19060 — C 31 M 18 Y 56 K 0 / C 25 M 23 Y 54 K 0 — *Analogous*
19066 — C 69 M 69 Y 0 K 0 / C 69 M 59 Y 31 K 10 — *Analogous*
19072 — C 35 M 11 Y 100 K 0 / C 25 M 23 Y 54 K 0 — *Analogous*

TWO-COLOR PALETTES *One Color + Neutral*

20

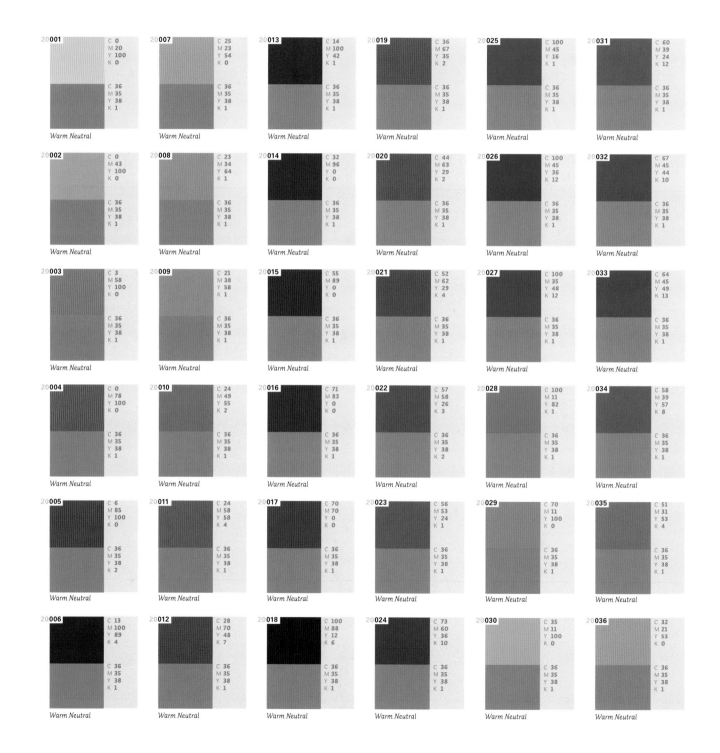

20**001** C 0 / M 20 / Y 100 / K 0 — C 36 / M 35 / Y 38 / K 1 *Warm Neutral*	20**007** C 25 / M 23 / Y 54 / K 0 — C 36 / M 35 / Y 38 / K 1 *Warm Neutral*	20**013** C 14 / M 100 / Y 42 / K 1 — C 36 / M 35 / Y 38 / K 1 *Warm Neutral*

20**001**
C 0
M 20
Y 100
K 0

C 36
M 35
Y 38
K 1
Warm Neutral

20**007**
C 25
M 23
Y 54
K 0

C 36
M 35
Y 38
K 1
Warm Neutral

20**013**
C 14
M 100
Y 42
K 1

C 36
M 35
Y 38
K 1
Warm Neutral

20**019**
C 36
M 67
Y 35
K 2

C 36
M 35
Y 38
K 1
Warm Neutral

20**025**
C 100
M 45
Y 16
K 1

C 36
M 35
Y 38
K 1
Warm Neutral

20**031**
C 60
M 39
Y 24
K 12

C 36
M 35
Y 38
K 1
Warm Neutral

20**002**
C 0
M 43
Y 100
K 0

C 36
M 35
Y 38
K 1
Warm Neutral

20**008**
C 23
M 34
Y 64
K 1

C 36
M 35
Y 38
K 1
Warm Neutral

20**014**
C 32
M 96
Y 0
K 0

C 36
M 35
Y 38
K 1
Warm Neutral

20**020**
C 44
M 63
Y 29
K 2

C 36
M 35
Y 38
K 1
Warm Neutral

20**026**
C 100
M 45
Y 36
K 12

C 36
M 35
Y 38
K 1
Warm Neutral

20**032**
C 67
M 45
Y 44
K 10

C 36
M 35
Y 38
K 1
Warm Neutral

20**003**
C 3
M 58
Y 100
K 0

C 36
M 35
Y 38
K 1
Warm Neutral

20**009**
C 21
M 38
Y 58
K 1

C 36
M 35
Y 38
K 1
Warm Neutral

20**015**
C 55
M 89
Y 0
K 0

C 36
M 35
Y 38
K 1
Warm Neutral

20**021**
C 52
M 62
Y 29
K 4

C 36
M 35
Y 38
K 1
Warm Neutral

20**027**
C 100
M 35
Y 48
K 12

C 36
M 35
Y 38
K 1
Warm Neutral

20**033**
C 64
M 45
Y 49
K 13

C 36
M 35
Y 38
K 1
Warm Neutral

20**004**
C 0
M 78
Y 100
K 0

C 36
M 35
Y 38
K 1
Warm Neutral

20**010**
C 24
M 49
Y 55
K 2

C 36
M 35
Y 38
K 1
Warm Neutral

20**016**
C 71
M 83
Y 0
K 0

C 36
M 35
Y 38
K 1
Warm Neutral

20**022**
C 57
M 58
Y 26
K 3

C 36
M 35
Y 38
K 2
Warm Neutral

20**028**
C 100
M 11
Y 82
K 1

C 36
M 35
Y 38
K 1
Warm Neutral

20**034**
C 58
M 39
Y 57
K 8

C 36
M 35
Y 38
K 1
Warm Neutral

20**005**
C 6
M 85
Y 100
K 0

C 36
M 35
Y 38
K 2
Warm Neutral

20**011**
C 24
M 58
Y 58
K 4

C 36
M 35
Y 38
K 1
Warm Neutral

20**017**
C 70
M 70
Y 0
K 0

C 36
M 35
Y 38
K 1
Warm Neutral

20**023**
C 56
M 53
Y 24
K 1

C 36
M 35
Y 38
K 1
Warm Neutral

20**029**
C 70
M 11
Y 100
K 0

C 36
M 35
Y 38
K 1
Warm Neutral

20**035**
C 51
M 31
Y 53
K 4

C 36
M 35
Y 38
K 1
Warm Neutral

20**006**
C 13
M 100
Y 89
K 4

C 36
M 35
Y 38
K 1
Warm Neutral

20**012**
C 28
M 70
Y 48
K 7

C 36
M 35
Y 38
K 1
Warm Neutral

20**018**
C 100
M 88
Y 12
K 6

C 36
M 35
Y 38
K 1
Warm Neutral

20**024**
C 73
M 60
Y 36
K 10

C 36
M 35
Y 38
K 1
Warm Neutral

20**030**
C 35
M 11
Y 100
K 0

C 36
M 35
Y 38
K 1
Warm Neutral

20**036**
C 32
M 21
Y 53
K 0

C 36
M 35
Y 38
K 1
Warm Neutral

For a bold and very specific color impression, combine a saturated color with a neutral color—instead of with black, which can deaden the chromatic intensity of other colors with which it is juxtaposed. Each of the vibrant colors is shown twice: on the left page paired with a warm neutral gray, and on the right page paired with a cool neutral gray, to show the effect of temperature difference.

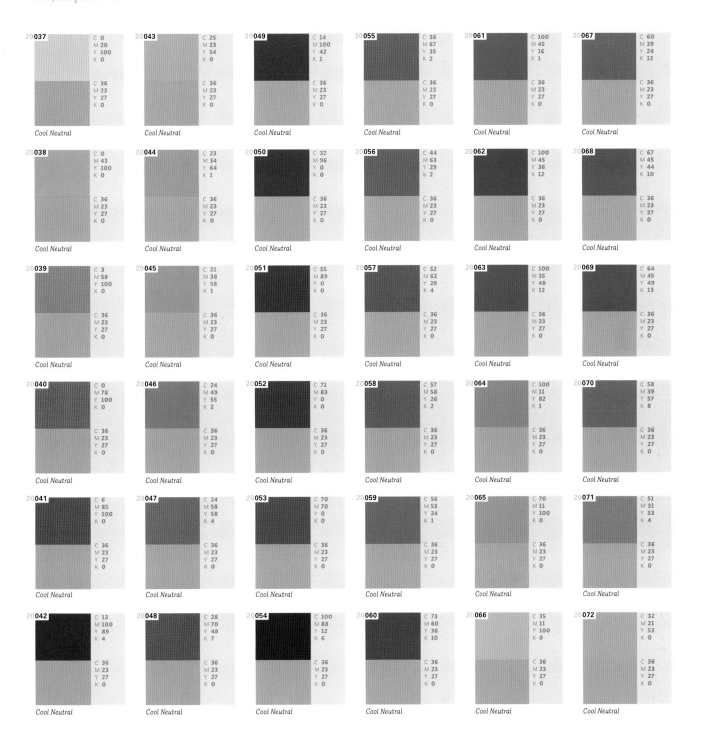

20 **037** C 0 / M 20 / Y 100 / K 0 — C 36 / M 23 / Y 27 / K 0 — *Cool Neutral*

20 **043** C 25 / M 23 / Y 54 / K 0 — C 36 / M 23 / Y 27 / K 0 — *Cool Neutral*

20 **049** C 14 / M 100 / Y 42 / K 1 — C 36 / M 23 / Y 27 / K 0 — *Cool Neutral*

20 **055** C 36 / M 67 / Y 35 / K 2 — C 36 / M 23 / Y 27 / K 0 — *Cool Neutral*

20 **061** C 100 / M 45 / Y 16 / K 1 — C 36 / M 23 / Y 27 / K 0 — *Cool Neutral*

20 **067** C 60 / M 39 / Y 24 / K 12 — C 36 / M 23 / Y 27 / K 0 — *Cool Neutral*

20 **038** C 0 / M 43 / Y 100 / K 0 — C 36 / M 23 / Y 27 / K 0 — *Cool Neutral*

20 **044** C 23 / M 34 / Y 64 / K 1 — C 36 / M 23 / Y 27 / K 0 — *Cool Neutral*

20 **050** C 32 / M 96 / Y 0 / K 0 — C 36 / M 23 / Y 27 / K 0 — *Cool Neutral*

20 **056** C 44 / M 63 / Y 29 / K 2 — C 36 / M 23 / Y 27 / K 0 — *Cool Neutral*

20 **062** C 100 / M 45 / Y 36 / K 12 — C 36 / M 23 / Y 27 / K 0 — *Cool Neutral*

20 **068** C 67 / M 45 / Y 44 / K 10 — C 36 / M 23 / Y 27 / K 0 — *Cool Neutral*

20 **039** C 3 / M 58 / Y 100 / K 0 — C 36 / M 23 / Y 27 / K 0 — *Cool Neutral*

20 **045** C 21 / M 38 / Y 58 / K 1 — C 36 / M 23 / Y 27 / K 0 — *Cool Neutral*

20 **051** C 55 / M 89 / Y 0 / K 0 — C 36 / M 23 / Y 27 / K 0 — *Cool Neutral*

20 **057** C 52 / M 62 / Y 29 / K 4 — C 36 / M 23 / Y 27 / K 0 — *Cool Neutral*

20 **063** C 100 / M 35 / Y 48 / K 12 — C 36 / M 23 / Y 27 / K 0 — *Cool Neutral*

20 **069** C 64 / M 45 / Y 49 / K 13 — C 36 / M 23 / Y 27 / K 0 — *Cool Neutral*

20 **040** C 0 / M 78 / Y 100 / K 0 — C 36 / M 23 / Y 27 / K 0 — *Cool Neutral*

20 **046** C 24 / M 49 / Y 55 / K 2 — C 36 / M 23 / Y 27 / K 0 — *Cool Neutral*

20 **052** C 71 / M 83 / Y 0 / K 0 — C 36 / M 23 / Y 27 / K 0 — *Cool Neutral*

20 **058** C 57 / M 58 / Y 26 / K 2 — C 36 / M 23 / Y 27 / K 0 — *Cool Neutral*

20 **064** C 100 / M 11 / Y 82 / K 1 — C 36 / M 23 / Y 27 / K 0 — *Cool Neutral*

20 **070** C 58 / M 39 / Y 57 / K 8 — C 36 / M 23 / Y 27 / K 0 — *Cool Neutral*

20 **041** C 6 / M 85 / Y 100 / K 0 — C 36 / M 23 / Y 27 / K 0 — *Cool Neutral*

20 **047** C 24 / M 58 / Y 58 / K 4 — C 36 / M 23 / Y 27 / K 0 — *Cool Neutral*

20 **053** C 70 / M 70 / Y 0 / K 0 — C 36 / M 23 / Y 27 / K 0 — *Cool Neutral*

20 **059** C 56 / M 53 / Y 24 / K 1 — C 36 / M 23 / Y 27 / K 0 — *Cool Neutral*

20 **065** C 70 / M 11 / Y 100 / K 0 — C 36 / M 23 / Y 27 / K 0 — *Cool Neutral*

20 **071** C 51 / M 31 / Y 53 / K 4 — C 36 / M 23 / Y 27 / K 0 — *Cool Neutral*

20 **042** C 13 / M 100 / Y 89 / K 4 — C 36 / M 23 / Y 27 / K 0 — *Cool Neutral*

20 **048** C 28 / M 70 / Y 48 / K 7 — C 36 / M 23 / Y 27 / K 0 — *Cool Neutral*

20 **054** C 100 / M 88 / Y 12 / K 6 — C 36 / M 23 / Y 27 / K 0 — *Cool Neutral*

20 **060** C 73 / M 60 / Y 36 / K 10 — C 36 / M 23 / Y 27 / K 0 — *Cool Neutral*

20 **066** C 35 / M 11 / Y 100 / K 0 — C 36 / M 23 / Y 27 / K 0 — *Cool Neutral*

20 **072** C 32 / M 21 / Y 53 / K 0 — C 36 / M 23 / Y 27 / K 0 — *Cool Neutral*

THREE-COLOR PALETTES *Formal*

21

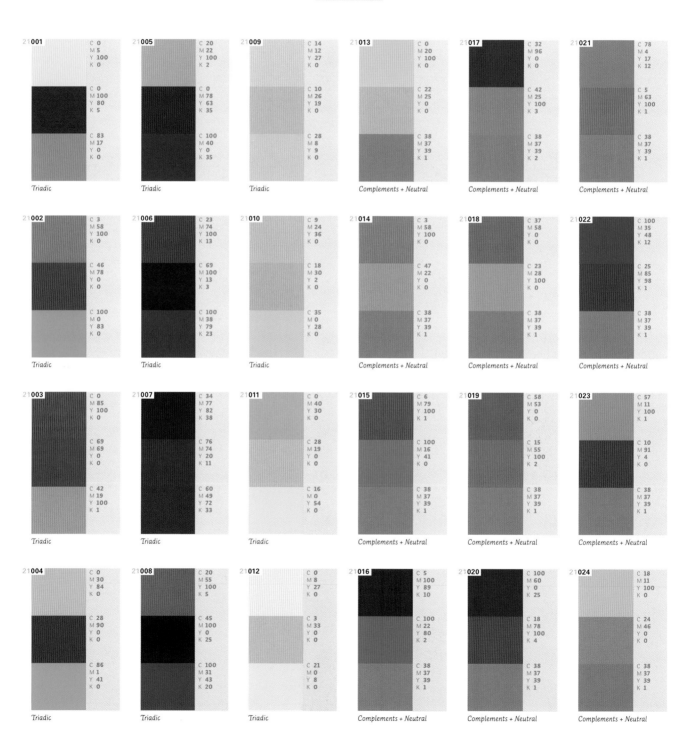

21001
C 0
M 5
Y 100
K 0

C 0
M 100
Y 80
K 5

C 83
M 17
Y 0
K 0

Triadic

21005
C 20
M 22
Y 100
K 2

C 0
M 78
Y 63
K 35

C 100
M 40
Y 0
K 35

Triadic

21009
C 14
M 12
Y 27
K 0

C 10
M 26
Y 19
K 0

C 28
M 8
Y 9
K 0

Triadic

21013
C 0
M 20
Y 100
K 0

C 22
M 25
Y 0
K 0

C 38
M 37
Y 39
K 1

Complements + Neutral

21017
C 32
M 96
Y 0
K 0

C 42
M 25
Y 100
K 3

C 38
M 37
Y 39
K 2

Complements + Neutral

21021
C 78
M 4
Y 17
K 12

C 5
M 63
Y 100
K 1

C 38
M 37
Y 39
K 1

Complements + Neutral

21002
C 3
M 58
Y 100
K 0

C 46
M 78
Y 0
K 0

C 100
M 0
Y 83
K 0

Triadic

21006
C 23
M 74
Y 100
K 13

C 69
M 100
Y 13
K 3

C 100
M 38
Y 79
K 23

Triadic

21010
C 9
M 24
Y 36
K 0

C 18
M 30
Y 2
K 0

C 35
M 0
Y 28
K 0

Triadic

21014
C 3
M 58
Y 0
K 0

C 47
M 28
Y 0
K 0

C 38
M 37
Y 39
K 1

Complements + Neutral

21018
C 37
M 58
Y 0
K 0

C 23
M 28
Y 100
K 0

C 38
M 37
Y 39
K 1

Complements + Neutral

21022
C 100
M 35
Y 48
K 12

C 25
M 85
Y 98
K 1

C 38
M 37
Y 39
K 1

Complements + Neutral

21003
C 0
M 85
Y 100
K 0

C 69
M 69
Y 0
K 0

C 42
M 19
Y 100
K 1

Triadic

21007
C 34
M 77
Y 82
K 38

C 76
M 74
Y 20
K 11

C 60
M 49
Y 72
K 33

Triadic

21011
C 0
M 40
Y 30
K 0

C 28
M 19
Y 0
K 0

C 16
M 0
Y 54
K 0

Triadic

21015
C 6
M 79
Y 100
K 1

C 100
M 16
Y 0
K 0

C 38
M 37
Y 39
K 1

Complements + Neutral

21019
C 58
M 53
Y 0
K 0

C 15
M 55
Y 100
K 2

C 38
M 37
Y 39
K 1

Complements + Neutral

21023
C 57
M 11
Y 100
K 1

C 10
M 91
Y 4
K 0

C 38
M 37
Y 39
K 1

Complements + Neutral

21004
C 0
M 30
Y 84
K 0

C 28
M 90
Y 0
K 0

C 86
M 1
Y 41
K 0

Triadic

21008
C 20
M 55
Y 100
K 5

C 45
M 100
Y 0
K 25

C 100
M 31
Y 43
K 20

Triadic

21012
C 0
M 8
Y 27
K 0

C 3
M 33
Y 0
K 0

C 21
M 0
Y 8
K 0

Triadic

21016
C 5
M 100
Y 89
K 10

C 100
M 22
Y 80
K 2

C 38
M 37
Y 39
K 1

Complements + Neutral

21020
C 100
M 60
Y 0
K 25

C 18
M 78
Y 100
K 4

C 38
M 37
Y 39
K 1

Complements + Neutral

21024
C 18
M 11
Y 100
K 0

C 24
M 46
Y 0
K 0

C 38
M 37
Y 39
K 1

Complements + Neutral

The palettes shown here offer complex optical relationships. The triads—or split complements—can be individually tinted to soften their optical activity, and even combined in overprinting to produce exotic secondary colors and neutrals. Two complements, paired with a warm neutral, also present dynamic interaction. The analogous sets, in contrast, provide a more in-depth experience of one color feeling; use them as shown, or as a backdrop for a contrasting complement.

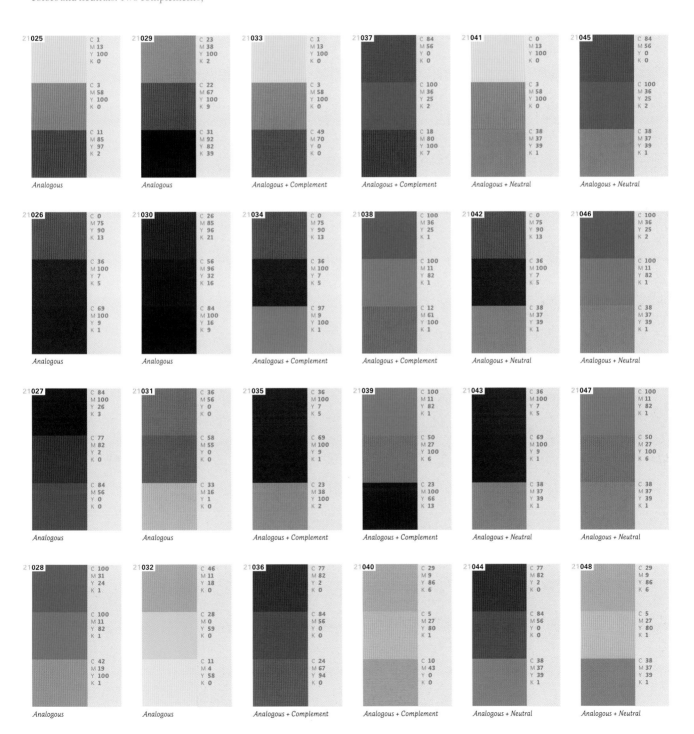

22

THREE-COLOR PALETTES *Monochrome*

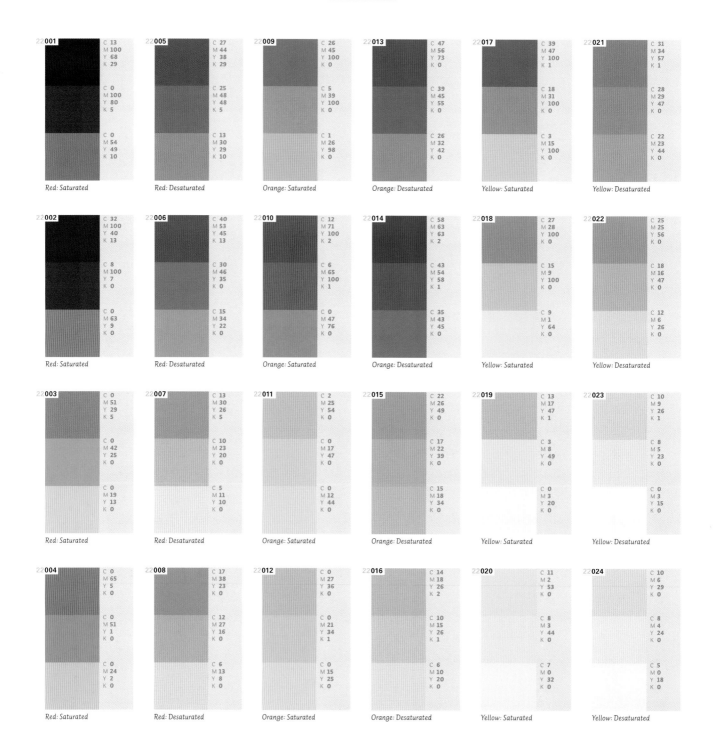

22001
C 13
M 100
Y 68
K 29

C 0
M 100
Y 80
K 5

C 0
M 54
Y 49
K 10

Red: Saturated

22005
C 27
M 44
Y 38
K 29

C 25
M 48
Y 48
K 5

C 13
M 30
Y 29
K 10

Red: Desaturated

22009
C 26
M 45
Y 100
K 0

C 5
M 39
Y 100
K 0

C 1
M 26
Y 98
K 0

Orange: Saturated

22013
C 47
M 56
Y 73
K 0

C 39
M 45
Y 55
K 0

C 26
M 32
Y 42
K 0

Orange: Desaturated

22017
C 39
M 47
Y 100
K 1

C 18
M 31
Y 100
K 0

C 3
M 15
Y 100
K 0

Yellow: Saturated

22021
C 31
M 34
Y 57
K 1

C 28
M 29
Y 47
K 0

C 22
M 23
Y 44
K 0

Yellow: Desaturated

22002
C 32
M 100
Y 40
K 13

C 8
M 100
Y 7
K 0

C 0
M 63
Y 9
K 0

Red: Saturated

22006
C 40
M 53
Y 45
K 13

C 30
M 46
Y 35
K 0

C 15
M 34
Y 22
K 0

Red: Desaturated

22010
C 12
M 71
Y 100
K 2

C 6
M 65
Y 100
K 1

C 0
M 47
Y 76
K 0

Orange: Saturated

22014
C 58
M 63
Y 63
K 2

C 43
M 54
Y 58
K 1

C 35
M 43
Y 45
K 0

Orange: Desaturated

22018
C 27
M 28
Y 100
K 0

C 15
M 9
Y 100
K 0

C 9
M 1
Y 64
K 0

Yellow: Saturated

22022
C 25
M 25
Y 56
K 0

C 18
M 16
Y 47
K 0

C 12
M 6
Y 26
K 0

Yellow: Desaturated

22003
C 0
M 51
Y 29
K 5

C 0
M 42
Y 25
K 0

C 0
M 19
Y 13
K 0

Red: Saturated

22007
C 13
M 30
Y 26
K 5

C 10
M 23
Y 20
K 0

C 5
M 11
Y 10
K 0

Red: Desaturated

22011
C 2
M 25
Y 54
K 0

C 0
M 17
Y 47
K 0

C 0
M 12
Y 44
K 0

Orange: Saturated

22015
C 22
M 26
Y 49
K 0

C 17
M 22
Y 39
K 0

C 15
M 18
Y 34
K 0

Orange: Desaturated

22019
C 13
M 17
Y 47
K 1

C 3
M 8
Y 49
K 0

C 0
M 3
Y 20
K 0

Yellow: Saturated

22023
C 10
M 9
Y 26
K 1

C 8
M 5
Y 23
K 0

C 0
M 3
Y 15
K 0

Yellow: Desaturated

22004
C 0
M 65
Y 5
K 0

C 0
M 51
Y 1
K 0

C 0
M 24
Y 2
K 0

Red: Saturated

22008
C 17
M 38
Y 23
K 0

C 12
M 27
Y 16
K 0

C 6
M 13
Y 8
K 0

Red: Desaturated

22012
C 0
M 27
Y 36
K 0

C 0
M 21
Y 34
K 0

C 0
M 15
Y 25
K 0

Orange: Saturated

22016
C 14
M 18
Y 26
K 2

C 10
M 15
Y 26
K 1

C 6
M 10
Y 20
K 0

Orange: Desaturated

22020
C 11
M 2
Y 53
K 0

C 8
M 3
Y 44
K 0

C 7
M 0
Y 32
K 0

Yellow: Saturated

22024
C 10
M 6
Y 29
K 0

C 8
M 4
Y 24
K 0

C 5
M 0
Y 18
K 0

Yellow: Desaturated

The three components of each of these palettes are all of the same base hue, with variation expressed in terms of temperature, saturation, and value changes. The selections on the left page are warm tonalities; the ones on the right are cool combinations. These restrained combinations are rich for use alone, in combination, or as the base upon which other two- or three-color palettes can interact.

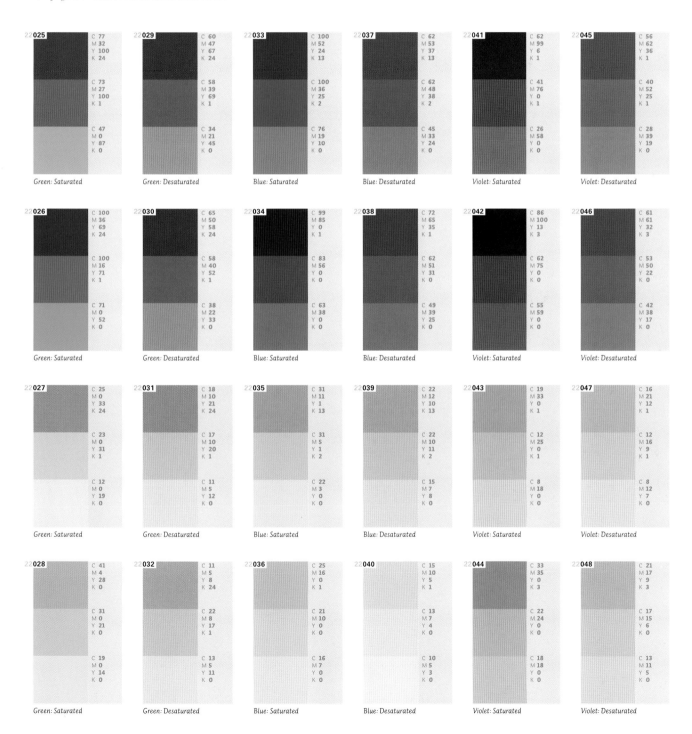

22 **025**
C 77 M 32 Y 100 K 24
C 73 M 27 Y 100 K 1
C 47 M 0 Y 87 K 0
Green: Saturated

22 **029**
C 60 M 47 Y 67 K 24
C 58 M 39 Y 69 K 1
C 34 M 21 Y 45 K 0
Green: Desaturated

22 **033**
C 100 M 52 Y 24 K 13
C 100 M 36 Y 25 K 2
C 76 M 19 Y 10 K 0
Blue: Saturated

22 **037**
C 62 M 53 Y 37 K 13
C 62 M 48 Y 38 K 2
C 45 M 33 Y 24 K 0
Blue: Desaturated

22 **041**
C 62 M 99 Y 6 K 1
C 41 M 76 Y 0 K 1
C 26 M 58 Y 0 K 0
Violet: Saturated

22 **045**
C 56 M 62 Y 36 K 1
C 40 M 52 Y 25 K 1
C 28 M 39 Y 19 K 0
Violet: Desaturated

22 **026**
C 100 M 36 Y 69 K 24
C 100 M 16 Y 71 K 1
C 71 M 0 Y 52 K 0
Green: Saturated

22 **030**
C 65 M 85 Y 58 K 24
C 58 M 40 Y 52 K 1
C 38 M 22 Y 33 K 0
Green: Desaturated

22 **034**
C 99 M 65 Y 0 K 1
C 83 M 56 Y 0 K 0
C 63 M 38 Y 0 K 0
Blue: Saturated

22 **038**
C 72 M 65 Y 35 K 1
C 62 M 51 Y 31 K 0
C 49 M 39 Y 25 K 0
Blue: Desaturated

22 **042**
C 86 M 100 Y 13 K 3
C 62 M 75 Y 0 K 0
C 55 M 59 Y 0 K 0
Violet: Saturated

22 **046**
C 61 M 61 Y 32 K 3
C 53 M 50 Y 22 K 0
C 42 M 38 Y 17 K 0
Violet: Desaturated

22 **027**
C 25 M 0 Y 33 K 24
C 23 M 0 Y 31 K 1
C 12 M 0 Y 19 K 0
Green: Saturated

22 **031**
C 18 M 10 Y 21 K 24
C 17 M 10 Y 20 K 1
C 11 M 5 Y 12 K 0
Green: Desaturated

22 **035**
C 31 M 11 Y 1 K 13
C 31 M 5 Y 1 K 2
C 22 M 3 Y 0 K 0
Blue: Saturated

22 **039**
C 22 M 12 Y 10 K 13
C 22 M 10 Y 11 K 2
C 15 M 7 Y 8 K 0
Blue: Desaturated

22 **043**
C 19 M 33 Y 0 K 1
C 12 M 25 Y 0 K 1
C 8 M 18 Y 0 K 0
Violet: Saturated

22 **047**
C 16 M 21 Y 12 K 1
C 12 M 16 Y 9 K 1
C 8 M 12 Y 7 K 0
Violet: Desaturated

22 **028**
C 41 M 4 Y 28 K 0
C 31 M 0 Y 21 K 0
C 19 M 0 Y 14 K 0
Green: Saturated

22 **032**
C 11 M 5 Y 8 K 24
C 22 M 8 Y 17 K 1
C 13 M 5 Y 11 K 0
Green: Desaturated

22 **036**
C 25 M 16 Y 0 K 1
C 21 M 10 Y 0 K 0
C 16 M 7 Y 0 K 0
Blue: Saturated

22 **040**
C 15 M 10 Y 5 K 1
C 13 M 7 Y 4 K 0
C 10 M 5 Y 3 K 0
Blue: Desaturated

22 **044**
C 33 M 35 Y 0 K 3
C 22 M 24 Y 0 K 0
C 18 M 18 Y 0 K 0
Violet: Saturated

22 **048**
C 21 M 17 Y 9 K 3
C 17 M 15 Y 6 K 0
C 13 M 11 Y 5 K 0
Violet: Desaturated

COLOR SYSTEMS *One Variable*

23

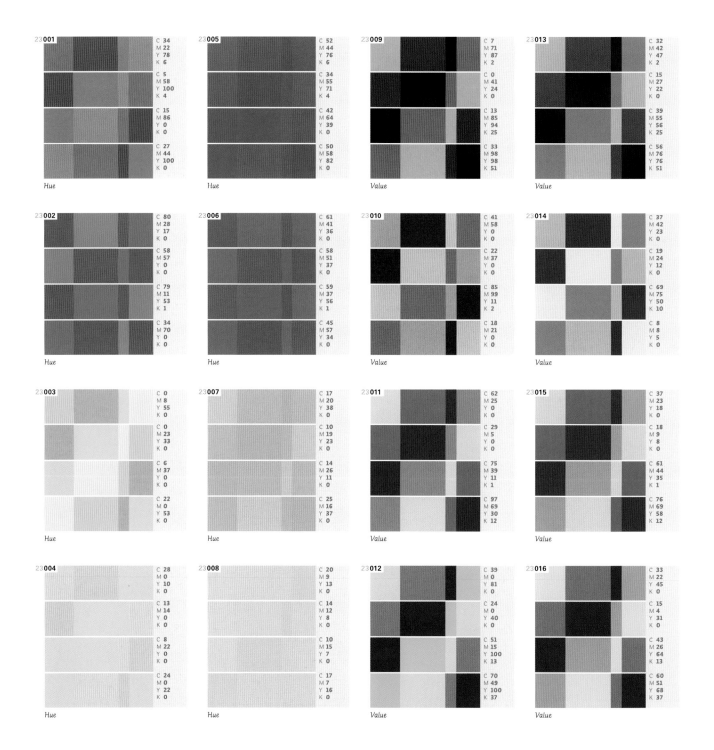

23001

C	34
M	22
Y	78
K	6

C	5
M	58
Y	100
K	4

C	15
M	86
Y	0
K	0

C	27
M	44
Y	100
K	0

Hue

23002

C	80
M	28
Y	17
K	0

C	58
M	57
Y	0
K	0

C	79
M	11
Y	53
K	1

C	34
M	70
Y	0
K	0

Hue

23003

C	0
M	8
Y	55
K	0

C	0
M	23
Y	33
K	0

C	6
M	37
Y	0
K	0

C	22
M	0
Y	53
K	0

Hue

23004

C	28
M	0
Y	10
K	0

C	13
M	14
Y	0
K	0

C	8
M	22
Y	0
K	0

C	24
M	0
Y	22
K	0

Hue

23005

C	52
M	44
Y	76
K	6

C	34
M	55
Y	71
K	4

C	42
M	64
Y	39
K	0

C	50
M	58
Y	82
K	0

Hue

23006

C	61
M	41
Y	36
K	0

C	58
M	51
Y	37
K	0

C	59
M	37
Y	56
K	1

C	45
M	57
Y	0
K	0

Hue

23007

C	17
M	20
Y	38
K	0

C	10
M	19
Y	23
K	0

C	14
M	26
Y	11
K	0

C	25
M	16
Y	37
K	0

Hue

23008

C	20
M	9
Y	13
K	0

C	14
M	12
Y	8
K	0

C	10
M	15
Y	7
K	0

C	17
M	7
Y	16
K	0

Hue

23009

C	7
M	71
Y	87
K	2

C	0
M	41
Y	24
K	0

C	13
M	85
Y	94
K	25

C	33
M	98
Y	98
K	51

Value

23010

C	41
M	58
Y	0
K	0

C	22
M	37
Y	0
K	0

C	85
M	99
Y	11
K	2

C	18
M	21
Y	0
K	0

Value

23011

C	62
M	25
Y	0
K	0

C	29
M	5
Y	0
K	0

C	75
M	39
Y	11
K	1

C	97
M	69
Y	30
K	12

Value

23012

C	39
M	0
Y	81
K	0

C	24
M	0
Y	40
K	0

C	51
M	15
Y	100
K	13

C	70
M	49
Y	100
K	37

Value

23013

C	32
M	42
Y	47
K	2

C	15
M	27
Y	22
K	0

C	39
M	55
Y	56
K	25

C	56
M	76
Y	76
K	51

Value

23014

C	37
M	42
Y	23
K	0

C	19
M	24
Y	12
K	0

C	69
M	75
Y	50
K	10

C	8
M	8
Y	5
K	0

Value

23015

C	37
M	23
Y	18
K	0

C	18
M	9
Y	8
K	0

C	61
M	44
Y	35
K	1

C	76
M	69
Y	58
K	12

Value

23016

C	33
M	22
Y	45
K	0

C	15
M	4
Y	31
K	0

C	43
M	26
Y	64
K	13

C	60
M	51
Y	68
K	37

Value

In these palettes, the chromatic interaction of four components is limited by allowing only one variable—hue, value, saturation, or temperature—to change. A new variable—extension, or the volume of each component— transforms the palette into a system in which each variation shown is governed by a greater volume of one component relative to the others. Use such limited systems to vary color impression on alternating page spreads, to distinguish elements in a line of products, or to create a family of publications, such as brochures, all unique in tone yet clearly interrelated.

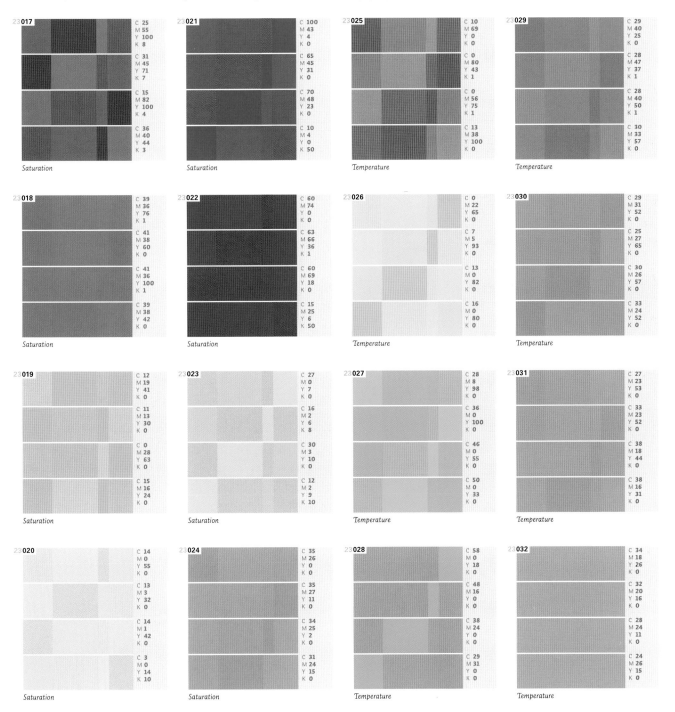

23017
| C 25 M 55 Y 100 K 8 |
| C 31 M 45 Y 71 K 7 |
| C 15 M 82 Y 100 K 4 |
| C 36 M 40 Y 44 K 3 |

Saturation

23021
| C 100 M 43 Y 4 K 0 |
| C 65 M 45 Y 31 K 0 |
| C 70 M 48 Y 23 K 0 |
| C 10 M 4 Y 0 K 50 |

Saturation

23025
| C 10 M 69 Y 0 K 0 |
| C 0 M 80 Y 43 K 1 |
| C 0 M 56 Y 75 K 1 |
| C 13 M 38 Y 100 K 0 |

Temperature

23029
| C 29 M 40 Y 25 K 0 |
| C 28 M 47 Y 37 K 1 |
| C 28 M 40 Y 50 K 1 |
| C 30 M 33 Y 57 K 0 |

Temperature

23018
| C 39 M 36 Y 76 K 1 |
| C 41 M 38 Y 60 K 0 |
| C 41 M 36 Y 100 K 1 |
| C 39 M 38 Y 42 K 0 |

Saturation

23022
| C 60 M 74 Y 0 K 0 |
| C 63 M 66 Y 36 K 1 |
| C 60 M 69 Y 18 K 0 |
| C 15 M 25 Y 6 K 50 |

Saturation

23026
| C 0 M 22 Y 65 K 0 |
| C 7 M 5 Y 93 K 0 |
| C 13 M 0 Y 82 K 0 |
| C 16 M 0 Y 80 K 0 |

Temperature

23030
| C 29 M 31 Y 52 K 0 |
| C 25 M 27 Y 65 K 0 |
| C 30 M 26 Y 57 K 0 |
| C 33 M 24 Y 52 K 0 |

Temperature

23019
| C 12 M 19 Y 41 K 0 |
| C 11 M 13 Y 30 K 0 |
| C 0 M 28 Y 63 K 0 |
| C 15 M 16 Y 24 K 0 |

Saturation

23023
| C 27 M 0 Y 7 K 0 |
| C 16 M 2 Y 6 K 8 |
| C 30 M 3 Y 10 K 0 |
| C 12 M 2 Y 9 K 10 |

Saturation

23027
| C 28 M 8 Y 98 K 0 |
| C 36 M 0 Y 100 K 0 |
| C 46 M 0 Y 55 K 0 |
| C 50 M 0 Y 33 K 0 |

Temperature

23031
| C 27 M 23 Y 53 K 0 |
| C 33 M 23 Y 52 K 0 |
| C 38 M 18 Y 44 K 0 |
| C 38 M 16 Y 31 K 0 |

Temperature

23020
| C 14 M 0 Y 55 K 0 |
| C 13 M 3 Y 32 K 0 |
| C 14 M 1 Y 42 K 0 |
| C 3 M 0 Y 14 K 10 |

Saturation

23024
| C 35 M 26 Y 0 K 0 |
| C 35 M 27 Y 11 K 0 |
| C 34 M 25 Y 2 K 0 |
| C 31 M 24 Y 15 K 0 |

Saturation

23028
| C 58 M 0 Y 18 K 0 |
| C 48 M 16 Y 0 K 0 |
| C 38 M 24 Y 0 K 0 |
| C 29 M 31 Y 0 K 0 |

Temperature

23032
| C 34 M 18 Y 26 K 0 |
| C 32 M 20 Y 16 K 0 |
| C 28 M 24 Y 11 K 0 |
| C 24 M 26 Y 15 K 0 |

Temperature

COLOR SYSTEMS *Two Variables*

24

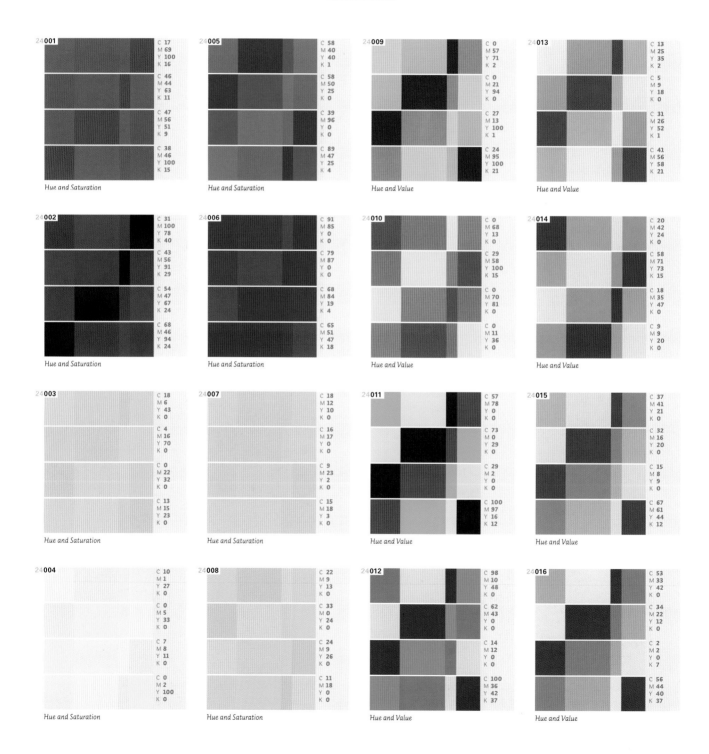

24**001**

C	17
M	69
Y	100
K	16

C	46
M	44
Y	63
K	11

C	47
M	56
Y	51
K	9

C	38
M	46
Y	100
K	15

Hue and Saturation

24**002**

C	31
M	100
Y	78
K	40

C	43
M	56
Y	91
K	29

C	54
M	47
Y	67
K	24

C	68
M	46
Y	94
K	24

Hue and Saturation

24**003**

C	18
M	6
Y	43
K	0

C	4
M	16
Y	70
K	0

C	0
M	22
Y	32
K	0

C	13
M	15
Y	23
K	0

Hue and Saturation

24**004**

C	10
M	1
Y	27
K	0

C	0
M	5
Y	33
K	0

C	7
M	8
Y	11
K	0

C	0
M	2
Y	100
K	0

Hue and Saturation

24**005**

C	58
M	40
Y	40
K	1

C	58
M	50
Y	25
K	0

C	39
M	96
Y	0
K	0

C	89
M	47
Y	25
K	4

Hue and Saturation

24**006**

C	91
M	85
Y	0
K	0

C	79
M	87
Y	0
K	0

C	68
M	84
Y	19
K	4

C	65
M	51
Y	47
K	18

Hue and Saturation

24**007**

C	18
M	12
Y	10
K	0

C	16
M	17
Y	0
K	0

C	9
M	23
Y	2
K	0

C	15
M	18
Y	3
K	0

Hue and Saturation

24**008**

C	22
M	9
Y	13
K	0

C	33
M	0
Y	24
K	0

C	24
M	9
Y	26
K	0

C	11
M	18
Y	0
K	0

Hue and Saturation

24**009**

C	0
M	57
Y	71
K	2

C	0
M	21
Y	94
K	0

C	27
M	13
Y	100
K	1

C	24
M	95
Y	100
K	21

Hue and Value

24**010**

C	0
M	68
Y	13
K	0

C	29
M	58
Y	100
K	15

C	0
M	70
Y	81
K	0

C	0
M	11
Y	36
K	0

Hue and Value

24**011**

C	57
M	78
Y	0
K	0

C	73
M	0
Y	29
K	0

C	29
M	2
Y	0
K	0

C	100
M	97
Y	16
K	12

Hue and Value

24**012**

C	98
M	10
Y	48
K	0

C	62
M	43
Y	0
K	0

C	14
M	12
Y	0
K	0

C	100
M	36
Y	42
K	37

Hue and Value

24**013**

C	13
M	25
Y	35
K	2

C	5
M	9
Y	18
K	0

C	31
M	26
Y	52
K	1

C	41
M	56
Y	58
K	21

Hue and Value

24**014**

C	20
M	42
Y	24
K	0

C	58
M	71
Y	73
K	15

C	18
M	35
Y	47
K	0

C	9
M	9
Y	20
K	0

Hue and Value

24**015**

C	37
M	41
Y	21
K	0

C	32
M	16
Y	20
K	0

C	15
M	8
Y	9
K	0

C	67
M	61
Y	44
K	12

Hue and Value

24**016**

C	53
M	33
Y	42
K	0

C	34
M	22
Y	12
K	0

C	2
M	0
Y	0
K	7

C	56
M	44
Y	40
K	37

Hue and Value

These limited color systems have increased complexity in color interaction by allowing two variables—saturation and value, or saturation and temperature, for instance—to fluctuate among a given palette's components.

Like their single-variable counterparts, these simple color systems are most useful for serial, sequential, or programmatic applications.

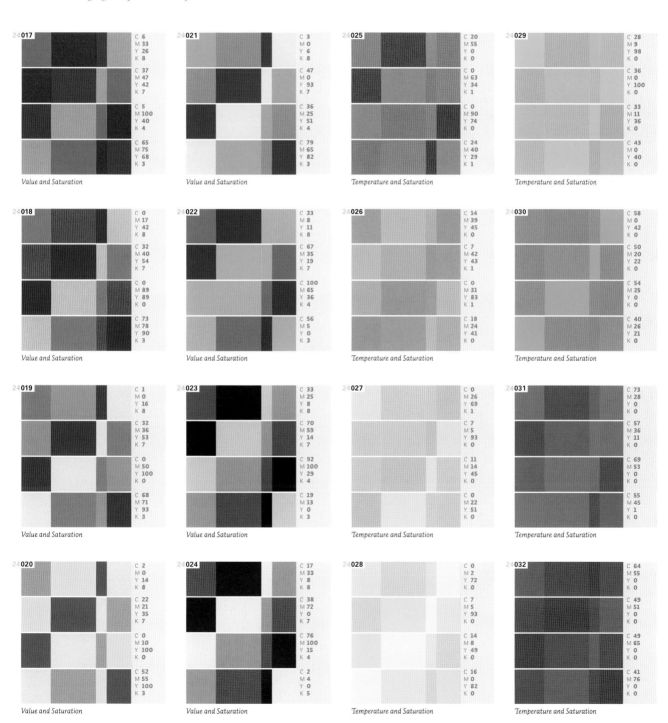

24**017**

C	6
M	33
Y	26
K	8

C	37
M	47
Y	42
K	7

C	5
M	100
Y	40
K	4

C	65
M	75
Y	68
K	3

Value and Saturation

24**021**

C	3
M	0
Y	6
K	8

C	47
M	0
Y	93
K	7

C	36
M	25
Y	51
K	4

C	79
M	65
Y	82
K	3

Value and Saturation

24**025**

C	20
M	55
Y	0
K	0

C	0
M	63
Y	34
K	1

C	0
M	90
Y	74
K	0

C	24
M	40
Y	29
K	1

Temperature and Saturation

24**029**

C	28
M	9
Y	98
K	0

C	36
M	0
Y	100
K	0

C	33
M	11
Y	36
K	0

C	43
M	0
Y	40
K	0

Temperature and Saturation

24**018**

C	0
M	17
Y	42
K	8

C	32
M	40
Y	54
K	7

C	0
M	89
Y	89
K	0

C	73
M	78
Y	90
K	3

Value and Saturation

24**022**

C	33
M	8
Y	11
K	8

C	67
M	35
Y	19
K	7

C	100
M	65
Y	36
K	4

C	56
M	5
Y	0
K	3

Value and Saturation

24**026**

C	14
M	39
Y	45
K	0

C	7
M	42
Y	43
K	1

C	0
M	31
Y	83
K	1

C	18
M	24
Y	41
K	0

Temperature and Saturation

24**030**

C	58
M	0
Y	42
K	0

C	50
M	20
Y	22
K	0

C	54
M	25
Y	0
K	0

C	40
M	26
Y	21
K	0

Temperature and Saturation

24**019**

C	1
M	0
Y	16
K	8

C	32
M	36
Y	53
K	7

C	0
M	50
Y	100
K	0

C	68
M	71
Y	93
K	3

Value and Saturation

24**023**

C	33
M	25
Y	8
K	8

C	70
M	59
Y	14
K	7

C	92
M	100
Y	29
K	4

C	19
M	13
Y	0
K	3

Value and Saturation

24**027**

C	0
M	26
Y	69
K	1

C	7
M	5
Y	93
K	0

C	11
M	14
Y	45
K	0

C	0
M	22
Y	51
K	0

Temperature and Saturation

24**031**

C	73
M	28
Y	0
K	0

C	57
M	36
Y	11
K	0

C	69
M	53
Y	0
K	0

C	55
M	45
Y	1
K	0

Temperature and Saturation

24**020**

C	2
M	0
Y	14
K	8

C	22
M	21
Y	35
K	7

C	0
M	10
Y	100
K	0

C	52
M	55
Y	100
K	3

Value and Saturation

24**024**

C	17
M	33
Y	8
K	8

C	38
M	72
Y	0
K	7

C	76
M	100
Y	15
K	4

C	2
M	4
Y	0
K	5

Value and Saturation

24**028**

C	0
M	2
Y	72
K	0

C	7
M	5
Y	93
K	0

C	14
M	8
Y	49
K	0

C	16
M	0
Y	82
K	0

Temperature and Saturation

24**032**

C	64
M	55
Y	0
K	0

C	49
M	51
Y	0
K	0

C	49
M	65
Y	0
K	0

C	41
M	76
Y	0
K	0

Temperature and Saturation

CONCEPTS *Moods, Places, Seasons*

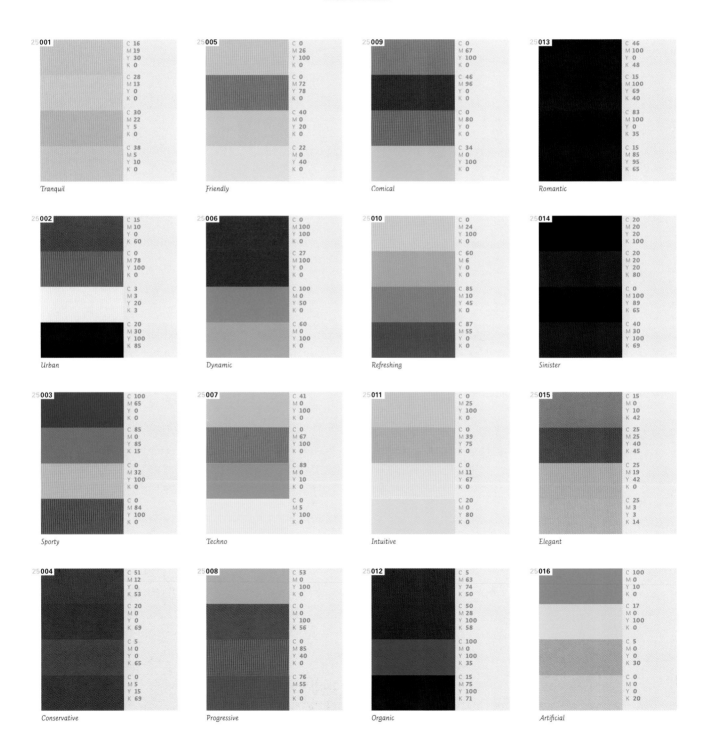

25 001

C 16	
M 19	
Y 30	
K 0	
C 28	
M 13	
Y 0	
K 0	
C 30	
M 22	
Y 5	
K 0	
C 38	
M 5	
Y 10	
K 0	

Tranquil

25 002

C 15 / M 10 / Y 0 / K 60
C 0 / M 78 / Y 100 / K 0
C 3 / M 3 / Y 20 / K 3
C 20 / M 30 / Y 100 / K 85

Urban

25 003

C 100 / M 65 / Y 0 / K 0
C 85 / M 0 / Y 85 / K 15
C 0 / M 32 / Y 100 / K 0
C 0 / M 84 / Y 100 / K 0

Sporty

25 004

C 51 / M 12 / Y 0 / K 53
C 20 / M 0 / Y 0 / K 69
C 5 / M 0 / Y 0 / K 65
C 0 / M 5 / Y 15 / K 69

Conservative

25 005

C 0 / M 26 / Y 100 / K 0
C 46 / M 72 / Y 78 / K 0
C 40 / M 0 / Y 20 / K 0
C 22 / M 0 / Y 40 / K 0

Friendly

25 006

C 0 / M 100 / Y 100 / K 0
C 27 / M 100 / Y 0 / K 0
C 100 / M 0 / Y 50 / K 0
C 60 / M 0 / Y 100 / K 0

Dynamic

25 007

C 41 / M 0 / Y 100 / K 0
C 0 / M 67 / Y 100 / K 0
C 89 / M 0 / Y 10 / K 0
C 0 / M 5 / Y 100 / K 0

Techno

25 008

C 53 / M 0 / Y 100 / K 0
C 0 / M 0 / Y 100 / K 56
C 0 / M 85 / Y 40 / K 0
C 76 / M 55 / Y 0 / K 0

Progressive

25 009

C 0 / M 67 / Y 100 / K 0
C 46 / M 96 / Y 0 / K 0
C 0 / M 80 / Y 0 / K 0
C 34 / M 0 / Y 100 / K 0

Comical

25 010

C 0 / M 24 / Y 100 / K 0
C 60 / M 6 / Y 0 / K 0
C 85 / M 10 / Y 45 / K 0
C 87 / M 55 / Y 0 / K 0

Refreshing

25 011

C 0 / M 25 / Y 100 / K 0
C 0 / M 39 / Y 75 / K 0
C 0 / M 11 / Y 67 / K 0
C 20 / M 0 / Y 80 / K 0

Intuitive

25 012

C 5 / M 63 / Y 74 / K 0
C 50 / M 28 / Y 100 / K 58
C 100 / M 0 / Y 100 / K 35
C 15 / M 75 / Y 100 / K 71

Organic

25 013

C 46 / M 100 / Y 0 / K 48
C 15 / M 100 / Y 69 / K 40
C 83 / M 100 / Y 0 / K 35
C 15 / M 85 / Y 95 / K 65

Romantic

25 014

C 20 / M 20 / Y 20 / K 100
C 20 / M 20 / Y 20 / K 80
C 0 / M 100 / Y 89 / K 65
C 40 / M 30 / Y 100 / K 69

Sinister

25 015

C 15 / M 0 / Y 10 / K 42
C 25 / M 25 / Y 40 / K 45
C 25 / M 19 / Y 42 / K 0
C 25 / M 3 / Y 3 / K 14

Elegant

25 016

C 100 / M 0 / Y 10 / K 0
C 17 / M 0 / Y 100 / K 0
C 5 / M 0 / Y 0 / K 30
C 0 / M 0 / Y 0 / K 20

Artificial

The power of color to evoke emotion or physical experience is extraordinary. These color concepts are limited palettes selected not only for their optical relationships, but also, and more importantly, the feeling they may induce. Along with emotional ideas, palettes that suggest place—distilled from various cultures' art and textiles—and time of year are displayed here.

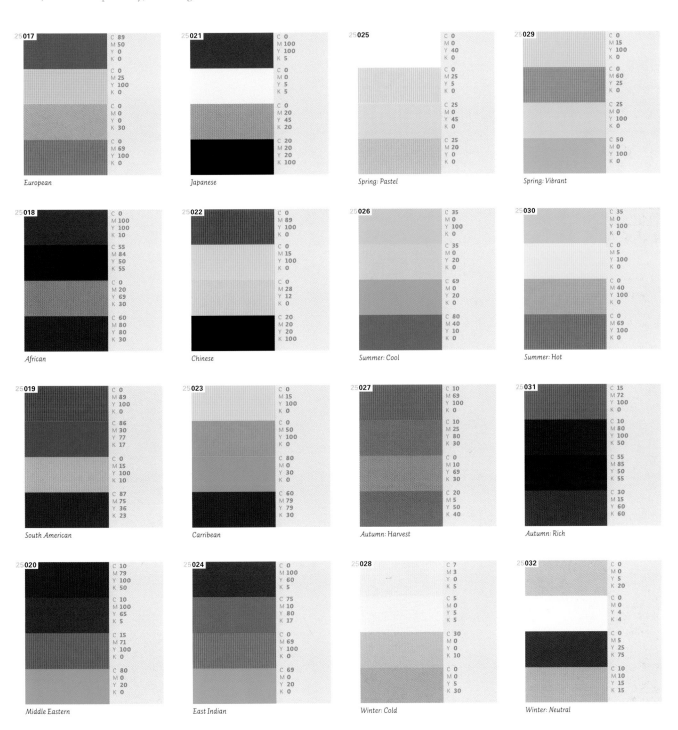

25 017

C	89
M	50
Y	0
K	0

C	0
M	25
Y	100
K	0

C	0
M	0
Y	0
K	30

C	0
M	69
Y	100
K	0

European

25 021

C	0
M	100
Y	100
K	5

C	0
M	0
Y	5
K	5

C	0
M	20
Y	45
K	20

C	20
M	20
Y	20
K	100

Japanese

25 025

C	0
M	0
Y	40
K	0

C	0
M	25
Y	5
K	0

C	25
M	0
Y	45
K	0

C	25
M	20
Y	0
K	0

Spring: Pastel

25 029

C	0
M	15
Y	100
K	0

C	0
M	60
Y	25
K	0

C	25
M	0
Y	100
K	0

C	50
M	0
Y	100
K	0

Spring: Vibrant

25 018

C	0
M	100
Y	100
K	10

C	55
M	84
Y	50
K	55

C	0
M	20
Y	69
K	30

C	60
M	80
Y	80
K	30

African

25 022

C	0
M	89
Y	100
K	0

C	0
M	15
Y	100
K	0

C	0
M	28
Y	12
K	0

C	20
M	20
Y	20
K	100

Chinese

25 026

C	35
M	0
Y	100
K	0

C	35
M	0
Y	20
K	0

C	69
M	0
Y	20
K	0

C	80
M	40
Y	10
K	0

Summer: Cool

25 030

C	35
M	0
Y	100
K	0

C	0
M	5
Y	100
K	0

C	0
M	40
Y	100
K	0

C	0
M	69
Y	100
K	0

Summer: Hot

25 019

C	0
M	89
Y	100
K	0

C	86
M	30
Y	77
K	17

C	0
M	15
Y	100
K	10

C	87
M	75
Y	36
K	23

South American

25 023

C	0
M	15
Y	100
K	0

C	0
M	50
Y	100
K	0

C	80
M	0
Y	30
K	0

C	60
M	79
Y	79
K	30

Carribean

25 027

C	10
M	69
Y	100
K	0

C	10
M	25
Y	80
K	30

C	0
M	10
Y	69
K	30

C	20
M	5
Y	50
K	40

Autumn: Harvest

25 031

C	15
M	72
Y	100
K	0

C	10
M	80
Y	100
K	50

C	55
M	85
Y	50
K	55

C	30
M	15
Y	60
K	60

Autumn: Rich

25 020

C	10
M	79
Y	100
K	50

C	10
M	100
Y	65
K	5

C	15
M	71
Y	100
K	0

C	80
M	0
Y	20
K	0

Middle Eastern

25 024

C	0
M	100
Y	60
K	5

C	75
M	10
Y	80
K	17

C	0
M	69
Y	100
K	0

C	69
M	0
Y	0
K	0

East Indian

25 028

C	7
M	3
Y	0
K	5

C	5
M	0
Y	5
K	5

C	30
M	0
Y	0
K	0

C	0
M	0
Y	5
K	30

Winter: Cold

25 032

C	0
M	0
Y	5
K	20

C	0
M	0
Y	4
K	4

C	0
M	5
Y	25
K	75

C	10
M	10
Y	15
K	15

Winter: Neutral

CONCEPTS *Business and Technology*

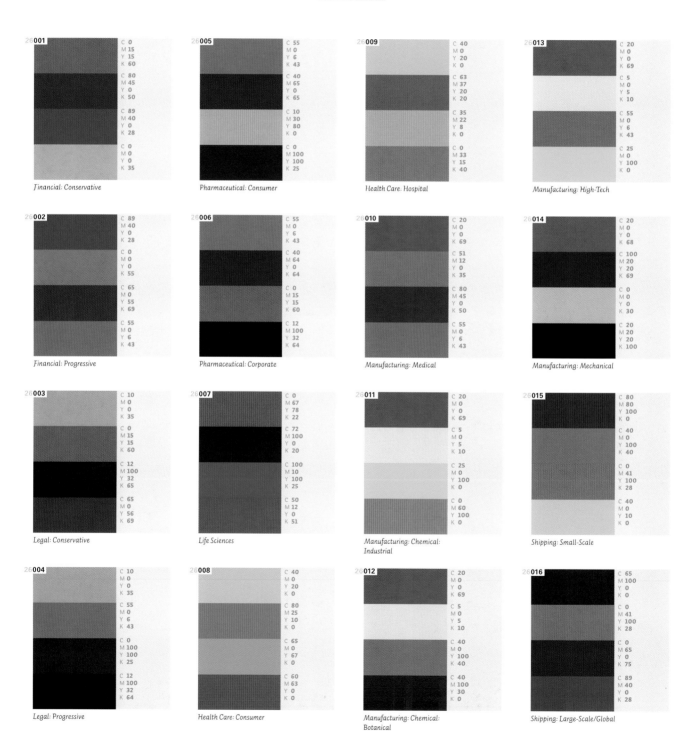

26001
C 0 / M 15 / Y 15 / K 60
C 80 / M 45 / Y 0 / K 50
C 89 / M 40 / Y 0 / K 28
C 0 / M 0 / Y 0 / K 35

Financial: Conservative

26002
C 89 / M 40 / Y 0 / K 28
C 0 / M 0 / Y 0 / K 55
C 65 / M 0 / Y 55 / K 69
C 55 / M 0 / Y 6 / K 43

Financial: Progressive

26003
C 10 / M 0 / Y 0 / K 35
C 0 / M 15 / Y 15 / K 60
C 12 / M 100 / Y 32 / K 65
C 65 / M 0 / Y 56 / K 69

Legal: Conservative

26004
C 10 / M 0 / Y 0 / K 35
C 55 / M 0 / Y 6 / K 43
C 0 / M 100 / Y 100 / K 25
C 12 / M 100 / Y 32 / K 64

Legal: Progressive

26005
C 55 / M 0 / Y 6 / K 43
C 40 / M 65 / Y 0 / K 65
C 10 / M 30 / Y 80 / K 0
C 0 / M 100 / Y 100 / K 25

Pharmaceutical: Consumer

26006
C 55 / M 0 / Y 6 / K 43
C 40 / M 64 / Y 0 / K 64
C 0 / M 15 / Y 15 / K 60
C 12 / M 100 / Y 32 / K 64

Pharmaceutical: Corporate

26007
C 0 / M 67 / Y 78 / K 22
C 72 / M 100 / Y 0 / K 20
C 100 / M 10 / Y 100 / K 25
C 50 / M 12 / Y 0 / K 51

Life Sciences

26008
C 40 / M 0 / Y 20 / K 0
C 80 / M 25 / Y 10 / K 0
C 65 / M 0 / Y 67 / K 0
C 60 / M 63 / Y 0 / K 0

Health Care: Consumer

26009
C 40 / M 0 / Y 20 / K 0
C 63 / M 37 / Y 20 / K 20
C 35 / M 22 / Y 8 / K 0
C 0 / M 33 / Y 15 / K 40

Health Care: Hospital

26010
C 20 / M 0 / Y 0 / K 69
C 51 / M 12 / Y 0 / K 35
C 80 / M 45 / Y 0 / K 50
C 55 / M 0 / Y 6 / K 43

Manufacturing: Medical

26011
C 20 / M 0 / Y 0 / K 69
C 5 / M 0 / Y 5 / K 10
C 25 / M 0 / Y 100 / K 0
C 0 / M 60 / Y 100 / K 0

Manufacturing: Chemical: Industrial

26012
C 20 / M 0 / Y 0 / K 69
C 5 / M 0 / Y 5 / K 10
C 40 / M 0 / Y 100 / K 40
C 40 / M 100 / Y 30 / K 0

Manufacturing: Chemical: Botanical

26013
C 20 / M 0 / Y 0 / K 69
C 5 / M 0 / Y 5 / K 10
C 55 / M 0 / Y 6 / K 43
C 25 / M 0 / Y 100 / K 0

Manufacturing: High-Tech

26014
C 20 / M 0 / Y 0 / K 68
C 100 / M 20 / Y 20 / K 69
C 0 / M 0 / Y 0 / K 30
C 20 / M 20 / Y 20 / K 100

Manufacturing: Mechanical

26015
C 80 / M 80 / Y 100 / K 0
C 40 / M 0 / Y 100 / K 40
C 0 / M 41 / Y 100 / K 28
C 40 / M 0 / Y 10 / K 0

Shipping: Small-Scale

26016
C 65 / M 100 / Y 0 / K 0
C 0 / M 41 / Y 100 / K 28
C 0 / M 65 / Y 0 / K 75
C 89 / M 40 / Y 0 / K 28

Shipping: Large-Scale/Global

While every client and project is different, the color language of many business sectors often respects convention that is usually tied to a given color's common psychological effects: Many financial institutions, for instance, use blue in their communications because of its perceived reliability and calming quality. The color concepts here are good starting points, distilled from their respective industries' common color conventions.

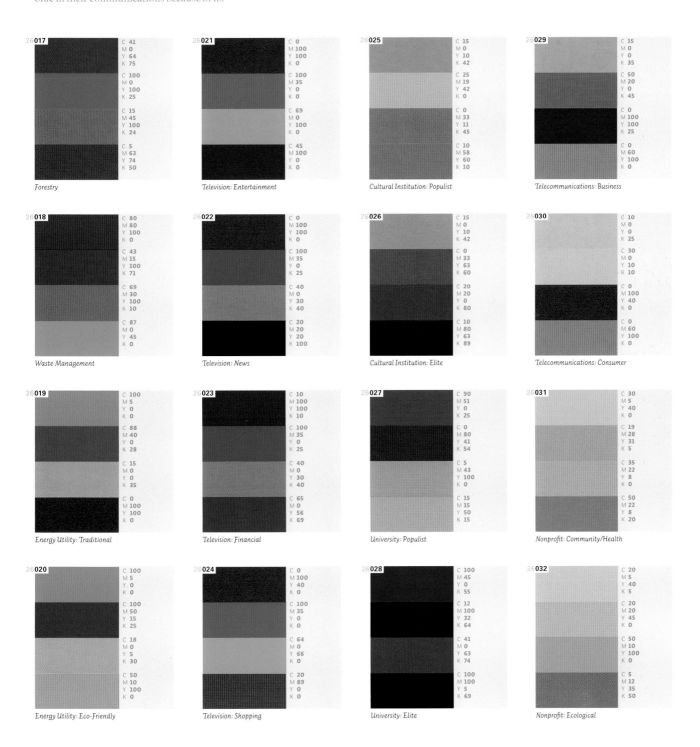

26**017**
C 41 / M 0 / Y 64 / K 75
C 100 / M 0 / Y 100 / K 25
C 15 / M 45 / Y 100 / K 24
C 5 / M 63 / Y 74 / K 50

Forestry

26**018**
C 80 / M 80 / Y 100 / K 0
C 43 / M 15 / Y 100 / K 71
C 69 / M 30 / Y 100 / K 10
C 87 / M 0 / Y 45 / K 0

Waste Management

26**019**
C 100 / M 5 / Y 0 / K 0
C 88 / M 40 / Y 0 / K 28
C 15 / M 0 / Y 0 / K 35
C 0 / M 100 / Y 100 / K 0

Energy Utility: Traditional

26**020**
C 100 / M 5 / Y 0 / K 0
C 100 / M 50 / Y 15 / K 25
C 18 / M 0 / Y 5 / K 30
C 50 / M 10 / Y 100 / K 0

Energy Utility: Eco-Friendly

26**021**
C 0 / M 100 / Y 100 / K 0
C 100 / M 35 / Y 0 / K 0
C 69 / M 0 / Y 100 / K 0
C 45 / M 100 / Y 0 / K 0

Television: Entertainment

26**022**
C 0 / M 100 / Y 100 / K 0
C 100 / M 35 / Y 0 / K 25
C 40 / M 0 / Y 30 / K 40
C 20 / M 20 / Y 20 / K 100

Television: News

26**023**
C 10 / M 100 / Y 100 / K 10
C 100 / M 35 / Y 0 / K 25
C 40 / M 0 / Y 30 / K 40
C 65 / M 0 / Y 56 / K 69

Television: Financial

26**024**
C 0 / M 100 / Y 40 / K 0
C 100 / M 35 / Y 0 / K 0
C 64 / M 0 / Y 66 / K 0
C 20 / M 89 / Y 0 / K 0

Television: Shopping

26**025**
C 15 / M 0 / Y 10 / K 42
C 25 / M 19 / Y 42 / K 0
C 0 / M 33 / Y 11 / K 45
C 10 / M 58 / Y 60 / K 10

Cultural Institution: Populist

26**026**
C 15 / M 0 / Y 10 / K 42
C 0 / M 33 / Y 63 / K 60
C 20 / M 20 / Y 0 / K 80
C 10 / M 80 / Y 63 / K 89

Cultural Institution: Elite

26**027**
C 90 / M 51 / Y 0 / K 25
C 0 / M 80 / Y 41 / K 54
C 5 / M 43 / Y 100 / K 0
C 15 / M 15 / Y 50 / K 15

University: Populist

26**028**
C 100 / M 45 / Y 0 / K 55
C 12 / M 100 / Y 32 / K 64
C 41 / M 0 / Y 63 / K 74
C 100 / M 100 / Y 5 / K 69

University: Elite

26**029**
C 15 / M 0 / Y 0 / K 35
C 50 / M 20 / Y 0 / K 45
C 0 / M 100 / Y 100 / K 25
C 0 / M 60 / Y 100 / K 0

Telecommunications: Business

26**030**
C 10 / M 0 / Y 0 / K 25
C 30 / M 0 / Y 10 / K 10
C 0 / M 100 / Y 40 / K 0
C 0 / M 60 / Y 100 / K 0

Telecommunications: Consumer

26**031**
C 30 / M 5 / Y 40 / K 0
C 19 / M 28 / Y 31 / K 5
C 35 / M 22 / Y 8 / K 0
C 50 / M 22 / Y 8 / K 20

Nonprofit: Community/Health

26**032**
C 20 / M 5 / Y 40 / K 5
C 20 / M 20 / Y 45 / K 0
C 50 / M 10 / Y 100 / K 0
C 5 / M 12 / Y 35 / K 50

Nonprofit: Ecological

CONCEPTS *Products and Lifestyles*

27

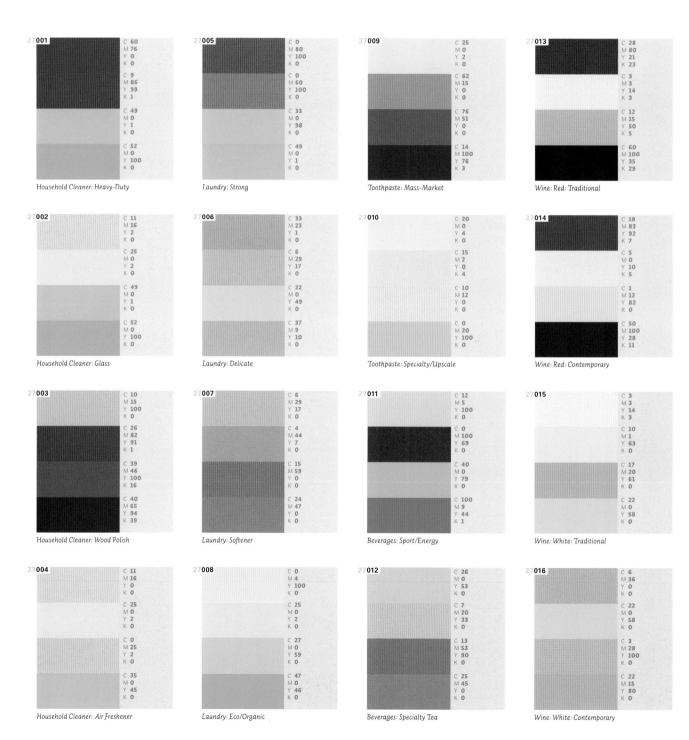

27**001**
C 60 M 76 Y 0 K 0
C 9 M 86 Y 99 K 1
C 49 M 0 Y 1 K 0
C 52 M 0 Y 100 K 0

Household Cleaner: Heavy-Duty

27**005**
C 0 M 80 Y 100 K 0
C 0 M 60 Y 100 K 0
C 33 M 0 Y 98 K 0
C 49 M 0 Y 1 K 0

Laundry: Strong

27**009**
C 25 M 0 Y 2 K 0
C 62 M 15 Y 0 K 0
C 76 M 51 Y 0 K 0
C 14 M 100 Y 76 K 3

Toothpaste: Mass-Market

27**013**
C 28 M 80 Y 21 K 23
C 3 M 3 Y 14 K 3
C 12 M 15 Y 50 K 5
C 60 M 100 Y 35 K 29

Wine: Red: Traditional

27**002**
C 11 M 16 Y 2 K 0
C 25 M 0 Y 2 K 0
C 49 M 0 Y 1 K 0
C 52 M 0 Y 100 K 0

Household Cleaner: Glass

27**006**
C 33 M 23 Y 1 K 0
C 6 M 29 Y 17 K 0
C 22 M 0 Y 49 K 0
C 37 M 9 Y 10 K 0

Laundry: Delicate

27**010**
C 20 M 0 Y 4 K 0
C 15 M 2 Y 0 K 4
C 10 M 12 Y 0 K 0
C 0 M 20 Y 100 K 0

Toothpaste: Specialty/Upscale

27**014**
C 18 M 83 Y 92 K 7
C 5 M 0 Y 10 K 5
C 1 M 12 Y 82 K 0
C 50 M 100 Y 28 K 11

Wine: Red: Contemporary

27**003**
C 10 M 15 Y 100 K 0
C 26 M 82 Y 91 K 1
C 39 M 46 Y 100 K 16
C 40 M 65 Y 94 K 39

Household Cleaner: Wood Polish

27**007**
C 6 M 29 Y 17 K 0
C 4 M 44 Y 7 K 0
C 15 M 59 Y 0 K 0
C 24 M 47 Y 0 K 0

Laundry: Softener

27**011**
C 12 M 5 Y 100 K 0
C 0 M 100 Y 69 K 0
C 40 M 0 Y 79 K 0
C 100 M 9 Y 44 K 1

Beverages: Sport/Energy

27**015**
C 3 M 3 Y 14 K 3
C 10 M 1 Y 63 K 0
C 17 M 20 Y 61 K 0
C 22 M 0 Y 58 K 0

Wine: White: Traditional

27**004**
C 11 M 16 Y 0 K 0
C 25 M 0 Y 2 K 0
C 0 M 25 Y 2 K 0
C 35 M 0 Y 45 K 0

Household Cleaner: Air Freshener

27**008**
C 0 M 4 Y 100 K 0
C 25 M 0 Y 2 K 0
C 27 M 0 Y 59 K 0
C 47 M 0 Y 46 K 0

Laundry: Eco/Organic

27**012**
C 26 M 0 Y 53 K 0
C 7 M 20 Y 33 K 0
C 13 M 53 Y 90 K 0
C 25 M 45 Y 0 K 0

Beverages: Specialty Tea

27**016**
C 6 M 36 Y 0 K 0
C 22 M 0 Y 58 K 0
C 3 M 28 Y 100 K 0
C 22 M 15 Y 80 K 0

Wine: White: Contemporary

Consumer expectations are a driving force behind color decisions in design related to products or lifestyle and subculture. Although differentiation through color in a crowded market is paramount, designers must still re-spect some conventions when it comes to communicating associations such as cleanliness, strength, masculinity or femininity, youth or maturity, heritage, comfort, and luxury. These color concepts are generalizations derived from common associations; each may be used as shown, or as a base from which to explore more distinctive palettes.

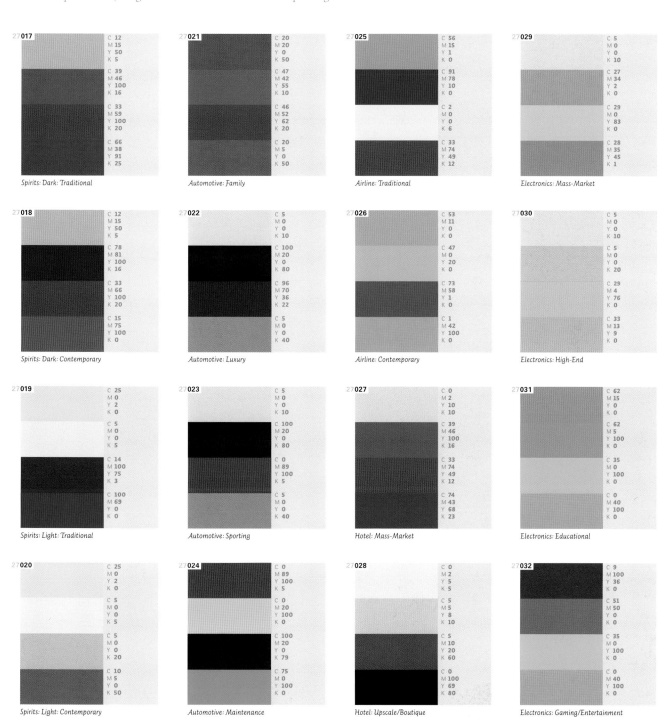

27 017

C 12	M 15	Y 50	K 5
C 39	M 46	Y 100	K 16
C 33	M 59	Y 100	K 20
C 66	M 38	Y 91	K 25

Spirits: Dark: Traditional

27 021

C 20	M 20	Y 0	K 50
C 47	M 42	Y 55	K 10
C 46	M 52	Y 62	K 20
C 20	M 5	Y 0	K 50

Automotive: Family

27 025

C 56	M 15	Y 1	K 0
C 91	M 78	Y 10	K 0
C 2	M 0	Y 0	K 6
C 33	M 74	Y 49	K 12

Airline: Traditional

27 029

C 5	M 0	Y 0	K 10
C 27	M 34	Y 2	K 0
C 29	M 0	Y 83	K 0
C 28	M 35	Y 45	K 1

Electronics: Mass-Market

27 018

C 12	M 15	Y 50	K 5
C 78	M 81	Y 100	K 16
C 33	M 66	Y 100	K 20
C 15	M 75	Y 100	K 0

Spirits: Dark: Contemporary

27 022

C 5	M 0	Y 0	K 10
C 100	M 20	Y 0	K 80
C 96	M 70	Y 36	K 22
C 5	M 0	Y 0	K 40

Automotive: Luxury

27 026

C 53	M 11	Y 0	K 0
C 47	M 0	Y 20	K 0
C 73	M 58	Y 1	K 0
C 1	M 42	Y 100	K 0

Airline: Contemporary

27 030

C 5	M 0	Y 0	K 10
C 5	M 0	Y 0	K 20
C 29	M 4	Y 76	K 0
C 33	M 13	Y 9	K 0

Electronics: High-End

27 019

C 25	M 0	Y 2	K 0
C 5	M 0	Y 0	K 5
C 14	M 100	Y 75	K 3
C 100	M 69	Y 0	K 0

Spirits: Light: Traditional

27 023

C 5	M 0	Y 0	K 10
C 100	M 20	Y 0	K 80
C 0	M 89	Y 100	K 5
C 5	M 0	Y 0	K 40

Automotive: Sporting

27 027

C 0	M 2	Y 10	K 10
C 39	M 46	Y 100	K 16
C 33	M 74	Y 49	K 12
C 74	M 43	Y 68	K 23

Hotel: Mass-Market

27 031

C 62	M 15	Y 0	K 0
C 62	M 5	Y 100	K 0
C 35	M 0	Y 100	K 0
C 0	M 40	Y 100	K 0

Electronics: Educational

27 020

C 25	M 0	Y 2	K 0
C 5	M 0	Y 0	K 5
C 5	M 0	Y 0	K 20
C 10	M 5	Y 0	K 50

Spirits: Light: Contemporary

27 024

C 0	M 89	Y 100	K 5
C 0	M 20	Y 100	K 0
C 100	M 20	Y 0	K 79
C 75	M 0	Y 100	K 0

Automotive: Maintenance

27 028

C 0	M 2	Y 5	K 5
C 5	M 5	Y 8	K 10
C 5	M 10	Y 20	K 60
C 0	M 100	Y 69	K 80

Hotel: Upscale/Boutique

27 032

C 9	M 100	Y 36	K 0
C 51	M 50	Y 0	K 0
C 35	M 0	Y 100	K 0
C 0	M 40	Y 100	K 0

Electronics: Gaming/Entertainment

CONCEPTS *Home and Fashion*

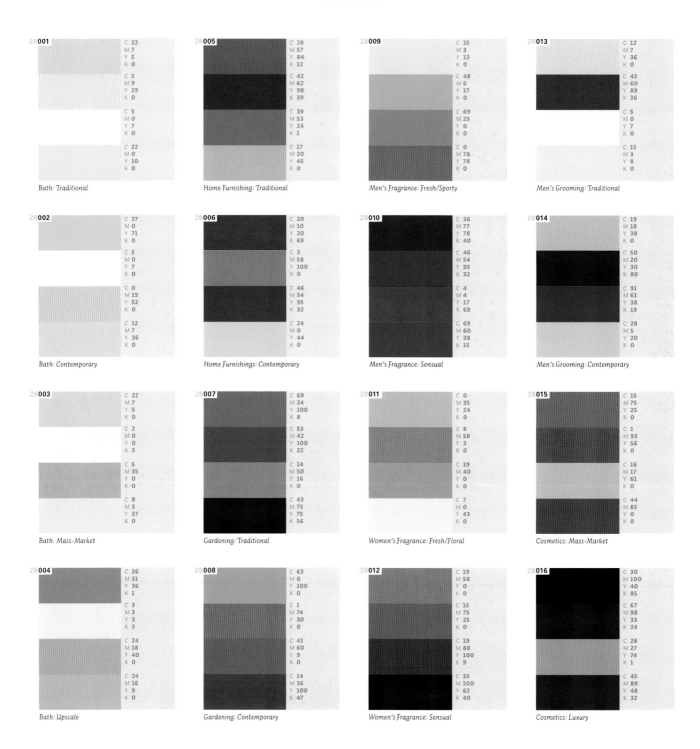

28001
C 22 / M 7 / Y 5 / K 0
C 5 / M 9 / Y 29 / K 0
C 5 / M 0 / Y 7 / K 0
C 22 / M 0 / Y 10 / K 0
Bath: Traditional

28005
C 28 / M 57 / Y 84 / K 12
C 42 / M 62 / Y 98 / K 39
C 39 / M 53 / Y 24 / K 1
C 17 / M 20 / Y 45 / K 0
Home Furnishing: Traditional

28009
C 15 / M 3 / Y 13 / K 0
C 48 / M 6 / Y 17 / K 0
C 69 / M 25 / Y 0 / K 0
C 0 / M 78 / Y 78 / K 0
Men's Fragrance: Fresh/Sporty

28013
C 12 / M 7 / Y 36 / K 0
C 42 / M 60 / Y 89 / K 36
C 5 / M 0 / Y 7 / K 0
C 15 / M 3 / Y 8 / K 0
Men's Grooming: Traditional

28002
C 27 / M 0 / Y 71 / K 0
C 5 / M 0 / Y 7 / K 0
C 0 / M 19 / Y 52 / K 0
C 12 / M 7 / Y 36 / K 0
Bath: Contemporary

28006
C 20 / M 10 / Y 20 / K 69
C 3 / M 58 / Y 100 / K 0
C 46 / M 54 / Y 95 / K 32
C 24 / M 0 / Y 44 / K 0
Home Furnishings: Contemporary

28010
C 36 / M 77 / Y 78 / K 40
C 46 / M 54 / Y 95 / K 32
C 4 / M 4 / Y 17 / K 69
C 69 / M 60 / Y 38 / K 15
Men's Fragrance: Sensual

28014
C 19 / M 18 / Y 38 / K 0
C 50 / M 20 / Y 30 / K 80
C 91 / M 61 / Y 38 / K 19
C 28 / M 5 / Y 20 / K 0
Men's Grooming: Contemporary

28003
C 22 / M 7 / Y 5 / K 0
C 2 / M 0 / Y 0 / K 3
C 5 / M 35 / Y 0 / K 0
C 8 / M 3 / Y 37 / K 0
Bath: Mass-Market

28007
C 69 / M 24 / Y 100 / K 8
C 53 / M 42 / Y 100 / K 22
C 14 / M 50 / Y 16 / K 0
C 43 / M 75 / Y 75 / K 56
Gardening: Traditional

28011
C 0 / M 35 / Y 24 / K 0
C 8 / M 58 / Y 3 / K 0
C 19 / M 40 / Y 0 / K 0
C 7 / M 0 / Y 43 / K 0
Women's Fragrance: Fresh/Floral

28015
C 15 / M 75 / Y 25 / K 0
C 1 / M 93 / Y 56 / K 0
C 16 / M 17 / Y 61 / K 0
C 44 / M 85 / Y 0 / K 0
Cosmetics: Mass-Market

28004
C 36 / M 31 / Y 36 / K 1
C 3 / M 3 / Y 3 / K 3
C 24 / M 18 / Y 40 / K 0
C 24 / M 16 / Y 9 / K 0
Bath: Upscale

28008
C 63 / M 0 / Y 100 / K 0
C 1 / M 74 / Y 30 / K 0
C 41 / M 60 / Y 9 / K 0
C 14 / M 36 / Y 100 / K 47
Gardening: Contemporary

28012
C 19 / M 58 / Y 0 / K 0
C 15 / M 75 / Y 25 / K 0
C 19 / M 88 / Y 100 / K 9
C 35 / M 100 / Y 62 / K 40
Women's Fragrance: Sensual

28016
C 30 / M 100 / Y 40 / K 85
C 67 / M 98 / Y 33 / K 24
C 28 / M 27 / Y 74 / K 1
C 45 / M 89 / Y 48 / K 32
Cosmetics: Luxury

While such industry sectors as home design and furnishing, apparel, and fragrance constantly alter color concepts—from season to season and, in the case of fashion, from style to style—general psychological associations often still apply: Earth tones are traditional, black and gray are chic, blues and grays mean business, and violets and pinks are feminine. Again, these color concepts, although rooted in convention, provide a grounding for overall communication, to be combined or altered appropriately for more specific messages.

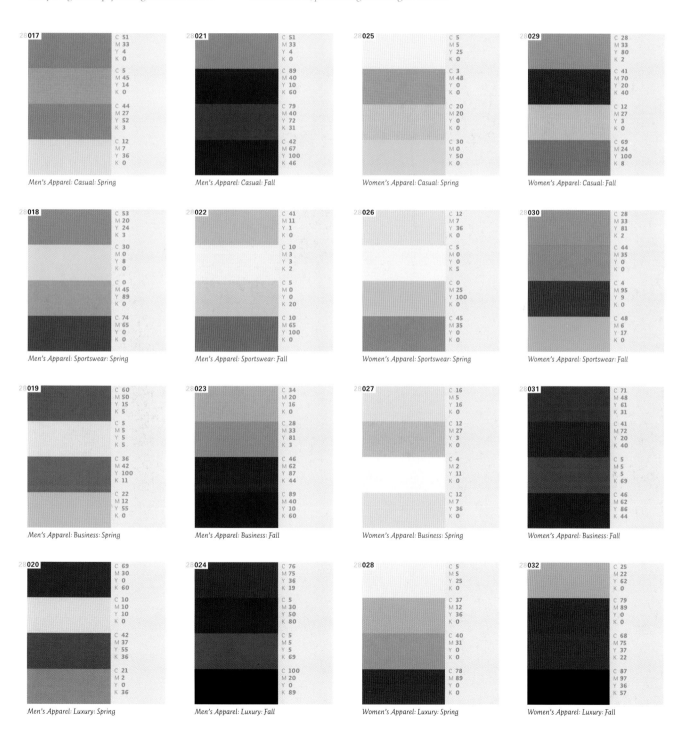

28 017

| C 51 / M 33 / Y 4 / K 0 |
| C 5 / M 45 / Y 14 / K 0 |
| C 44 / M 27 / Y 52 / K 3 |
| C 12 / M 7 / Y 36 / K 0 |

Men's Apparel: Casual: Spring

28 021

| C 51 / M 33 / Y 4 / K 0 |
| C 89 / M 40 / Y 10 / K 60 |
| C 79 / M 40 / Y 72 / K 31 |
| C 42 / M 67 / Y 100 / K 46 |

Men's Apparel: Casual: Fall

28 025

| C 5 / M 5 / Y 25 / K 0 |
| C 3 / M 48 / Y 0 / K 0 |
| C 20 / M 20 / Y 0 / K 0 |
| C 30 / M 0 / Y 50 / K 0 |

Women's Apparel: Casual: Spring

28 029

| C 28 / M 33 / Y 80 / K 2 |
| C 41 / M 70 / Y 20 / K 40 |
| C 12 / M 27 / Y 3 / K 0 |
| C 69 / M 24 / Y 100 / K 8 |

Women's Apparel: Casual: Fall

28 018

| C 53 / M 20 / Y 24 / K 3 |
| C 30 / M 0 / Y 8 / K 0 |
| C 0 / M 45 / Y 89 / K 0 |
| C 74 / M 65 / Y 0 / K 0 |

Men's Apparel: Sportswear: Spring

28 022

| C 41 / M 11 / Y 1 / K 0 |
| C 10 / M 3 / Y 3 / K 2 |
| C 5 / M 0 / Y 0 / K 20 |
| C 10 / M 65 / Y 100 / K 0 |

Men's Apparel: Sportswear: Fall

28 026

| C 12 / M 7 / Y 36 / K 0 |
| C 5 / M 0 / Y 0 / K 5 |
| C 0 / M 25 / Y 100 / K 0 |
| C 45 / M 35 / Y 0 / K 0 |

Women's Apparel: Sportswear: Spring

28 030

| C 28 / M 33 / Y 81 / K 2 |
| C 44 / M 35 / Y 0 / K 0 |
| C 4 / M 95 / Y 9 / K 0 |
| C 48 / M 6 / Y 17 / K 0 |

Women's Apparel: Sportswear: Fall

28 019

| C 60 / M 50 / Y 15 / K 5 |
| C 5 / M 5 / Y 5 / K 5 |
| C 36 / M 42 / Y 100 / K 11 |
| C 22 / M 12 / Y 55 / K 0 |

Men's Apparel: Business: Spring

28 023

| C 34 / M 20 / Y 16 / K 0 |
| C 28 / M 33 / Y 81 / K 3 |
| C 46 / M 62 / Y 87 / K 44 |
| C 89 / M 40 / Y 10 / K 60 |

Men's Apparel: Business: Fall

28 027

| C 16 / M 5 / Y 16 / K 0 |
| C 12 / M 27 / Y 3 / K 0 |
| C 4 / M 2 / Y 11 / K 0 |
| C 12 / M 7 / Y 36 / K 0 |

Women's Apparel: Business: Spring

28 031

| C 71 / M 48 / Y 61 / K 31 |
| C 41 / M 72 / Y 20 / K 40 |
| C 5 / M 5 / Y 5 / K 69 |
| C 46 / M 62 / Y 86 / K 44 |

Women's Apparel: Business: Fall

28 020

| C 69 / M 30 / Y 0 / K 60 |
| C 10 / M 10 / Y 10 / K 0 |
| C 42 / M 37 / Y 55 / K 36 |
| C 21 / M 2 / Y 0 / K 36 |

Men's Apparel: Luxury: Spring

28 024

| C 76 / M 75 / Y 36 / K 19 |
| C 5 / M 30 / Y 50 / K 80 |
| C 5 / M 5 / Y 5 / K 69 |
| C 100 / M 20 / Y 0 / K 89 |

Men's Apparel: Luxury: Fall

28 028

| C 5 / M 5 / Y 25 / K 0 |
| C 37 / M 12 / Y 36 / K 0 |
| C 40 / M 31 / Y 0 / K 0 |
| C 78 / M 89 / Y 0 / K 0 |

Women's Apparel: Luxury: Spring

28 032

| C 25 / M 22 / Y 62 / K 0 |
| C 79 / M 89 / Y 0 / K 0 |
| C 68 / M 75 / Y 37 / K 22 |
| C 87 / M 97 / Y 36 / K 57 |

Women's Apparel: Luxury: Fall

CONCEPTS *Historical Periods and Age Groups*

29

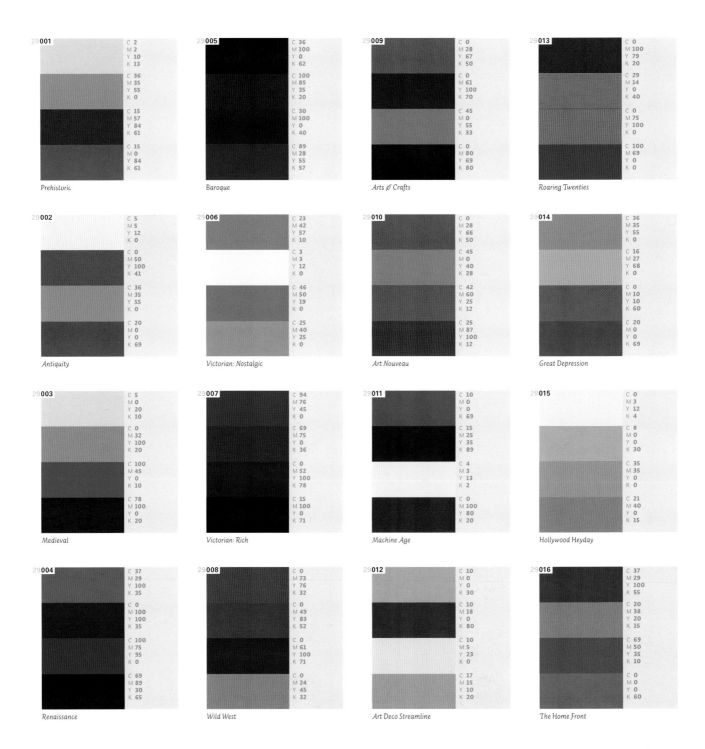

29**001**		29**005**		29**009**		29**013**	
	C 2 / M 2 / Y 10 / K 13		C 36 / M 100 / Y 0 / K 62		C 0 / M 28 / Y 67 / K 50		C 0 / M 100 / Y 79 / K 20
	C 36 / M 35 / Y 55 / K 0		C 100 / M 85 / Y 35 / K 20		C 0 / M 61 / Y 100 / K 70		C 29 / M 14 / Y 0 / K 40
	C 15 / M 57 / Y 84 / K 61		C 30 / M 100 / Y 0 / K 40		C 45 / M 0 / Y 55 / K 33		C 0 / M 75 / Y 100 / K 0
	C 15 / M 0 / Y 84 / K 61		C 89 / M 28 / Y 55 / K 57		C 0 / M 80 / Y 69 / K 80		C 100 / M 69 / Y 0 / K 0

Prehistoric | *Baroque* | *Arts & Crafts* | *Roaring Twenties*

29**002**		29**006**		29**010**		29**014**	
	C 5 / M 5 / Y 12 / K 0		C 23 / M 42 / Y 57 / K 10		C 0 / M 28 / Y 66 / K 50		C 36 / M 35 / Y 55 / K 0
	C 0 / M 50 / Y 100 / K 41		C 3 / M 3 / Y 12 / K 0		C 45 / M 0 / Y 40 / K 28		C 16 / M 27 / Y 68 / K 0
	C 36 / M 35 / Y 55 / K 0		C 46 / M 50 / Y 19 / K 0		C 42 / M 60 / Y 25 / K 12		C 0 / M 10 / Y 10 / K 60
	C 20 / M 0 / Y 0 / K 69		C 25 / M 40 / Y 25 / K 0		C 25 / M 87 / Y 100 / K 12		C 20 / M 0 / Y 0 / K 69

Antiquity | *Victorian: Nostalgic* | *Art Nouveau* | *Great Depression*

29**003**		29**007**		29**011**		29**015**	
	C 5 / M 0 / Y 20 / K 10		C 94 / M 76 / Y 45 / K 0		C 10 / M 0 / Y 0 / K 69		C 0 / M 3 / Y 12 / K 4
	C 0 / M 32 / Y 100 / K 20		C 69 / M 75 / Y 0 / K 36		C 15 / M 25 / Y 35 / K 89		C 8 / M 0 / Y 0 / K 30
	C 100 / M 45 / Y 0 / K 10		C 0 / M 52 / Y 100 / K 78		C 4 / M 3 / Y 13 / K 2		C 35 / M 35 / Y 0 / K 0
	C 78 / M 100 / Y 0 / K 20		C 15 / M 100 / Y 0 / K 71		C 0 / M 100 / Y 80 / K 20		C 21 / M 40 / Y 0 / K 15

Medieval | *Victorian: Rich* | *Machine Age* | *Hollywood Heyday*

29**004**		29**008**		29**012**		29**016**	
	C 37 / M 29 / Y 100 / K 35		C 0 / M 73 / Y 76 / K 32		C 10 / M 0 / Y 0 / K 30		C 37 / M 29 / Y 100 / K 55
	C 0 / M 100 / Y 100 / K 35		C 0 / M 49 / Y 83 / K 52		C 10 / M 18 / Y 0 / K 80		C 20 / M 38 / Y 20 / K 15
	C 100 / M 75 / Y 95 / K 0		C 0 / M 61 / Y 100 / K 71		C 10 / M 5 / Y 23 / K 0		C 69 / M 50 / Y 35 / K 10
	C 69 / M 89 / Y 30 / K 65		C 0 / M 24 / Y 45 / K 32		C 17 / M 15 / Y 10 / K 20		C 0 / M 0 / Y 0 / K 60

Renaissance | *Wild West* | *Art Deco Streamline* | *The Home Front*

Various periods in Western history can be quickly identified by colors that are related to materials that were prevalent, or color schemes that were in vogue, during that era.

For projects in which a historical context is important, begin with an appropriate palette as an underpinning and evolve it as needed to translate it to a contemporary perspective.

Along with the historical concepts, limited palettes that resonate with particular age groups are also presented.

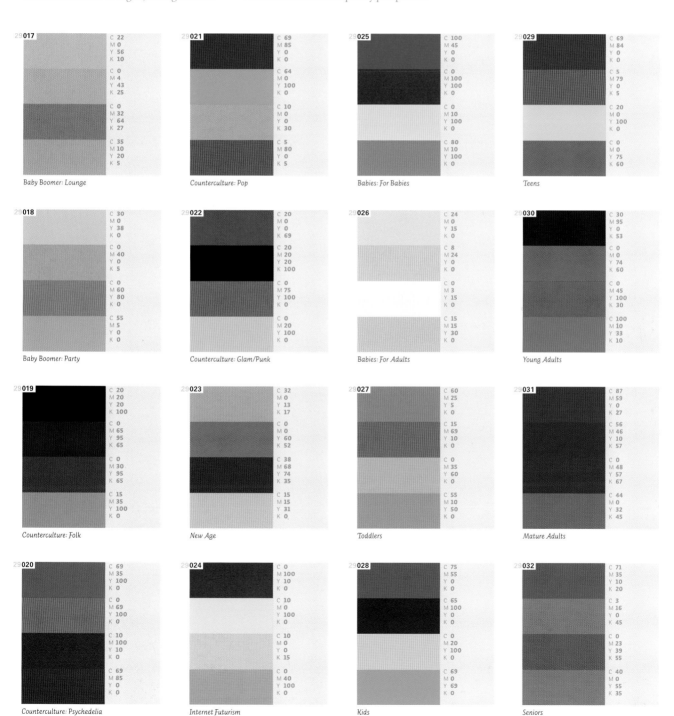

017
C 22 M 0 Y 56 K 10
C 0 M 4 Y 43 K 25
C 0 M 32 Y 64 K 27
C 35 M 10 Y 20 K 5
Baby Boomer: Lounge

021
C 69 M 85 Y 0 K 0
C 64 M 0 Y 100 K 0
C 10 M 0 Y 0 K 30
C 5 M 80 Y 0 K 5
Counterculture: Pop

025
C 100 M 45 Y 0 K 0
C 0 M 100 Y 100 K 0
C 0 M 10 Y 100 K 0
C 80 M 10 Y 100 K 0
Babies: For Babies

029
C 69 M 84 Y 0 K 0
C 5 M 79 Y 0 K 5
C 20 M 0 Y 100 K 0
C 0 M 0 Y 75 K 60
Teens

018
C 30 M 0 Y 38 K 0
C 0 M 40 Y 0 K 5
C 0 M 60 Y 80 K 0
C 55 M 5 Y 0 K 0
Baby Boomer: Party

022
C 20 M 0 Y 0 K 69
C 20 M 20 Y 20 K 100
C 0 M 75 Y 100 K 0
C 0 M 20 Y 100 K 0
Counterculture: Glam/Punk

026
C 24 M 0 Y 15 K 0
C 8 M 24 Y 0 K 0
C 0 M 3 Y 15 K 0
C 15 M 15 Y 30 K 0
Babies: For Adults

030
C 30 M 95 Y 0 K 53
C 0 M 0 Y 74 K 60
C 0 M 45 Y 100 K 30
C 100 M 10 Y 33 K 10
Young Adults

019
C 20 M 20 Y 20 K 100
C 0 M 65 Y 95 K 65
C 0 M 30 Y 95 K 65
C 15 M 35 Y 100 K 0
Counterculture: Folk

023
C 32 M 0 Y 13 K 17
C 0 M 0 Y 60 K 52
C 38 M 68 Y 74 K 35
C 15 M 15 Y 31 K 0
New Age

027
C 60 M 25 Y 5 K 0
C 15 M 69 Y 10 K 0
C 0 M 35 Y 60 K 0
C 55 M 10 Y 50 K 0
Toddlers

031
C 87 M 59 Y 0 K 27
C 56 M 46 Y 10 K 57
C 0 M 48 Y 57 K 67
C 44 M 0 Y 32 K 45
Mature Adults

020
C 69 M 35 Y 100 K 0
C 0 M 69 Y 100 K 0
C 10 M 100 Y 10 K 0
C 69 M 85 Y 0 K 0
Counterculture: Psychedelia

024
C 0 M 100 Y 10 K 0
C 10 M 0 Y 100 K 0
C 10 M 0 Y 0 K 15
C 0 M 40 Y 100 K 0
Internet Futurism

028
C 75 M 55 Y 0 K 0
C 65 M 100 Y 0 K 0
C 0 M 20 Y 100 K 0
C 69 M 0 Y 69 K 0
Kids

032
C 71 M 35 Y 10 K 20
C 3 M 16 Y 0 K 45
C 0 M 23 Y 39 K 55
C 40 M 0 Y 55 K 35
Seniors

CODING FAMILIES *Analogous Accent*

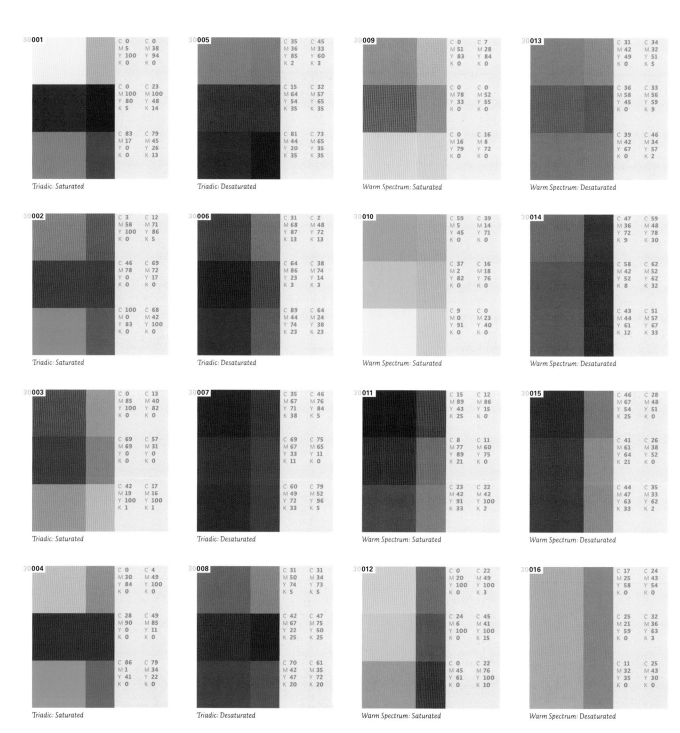

30**001**		
	C 0	C 0
	M 5	M 38
	Y 100	Y 94
	K 0	K 0
	C 0	C 23
	M 100	M 100
	Y 80	Y 48
	K 5	K 14
	C 83	C 79
	M 17	M 44
	Y 0	Y 26
	K 0	K 13

Triadic: Saturated

30**005**		
	C 35	C 45
	M 36	M 33
	Y 85	Y 60
	K 2	K 3
	C 15	C 32
	M 64	M 57
	Y 54	Y 65
	K 35	K 35
	C 81	C 73
	M 44	M 65
	Y 20	Y 35
	K 35	K 35

Triadic: Desaturated

30**009**		
	C 0	C 7
	M 51	M 28
	Y 83	Y 84
	K 0	K 0
	C 0	C 0
	M 78	M 52
	Y 33	Y 55
	K 0	K 0
	C 0	C 16
	M 16	M 8
	Y 79	Y 72
	K 0	K 0

Warm Spectrum: Saturated

30**013**		
	C 31	C 34
	M 42	M 32
	Y 49	Y 51
	K 0	K 5
	C 36	C 33
	M 58	M 56
	Y 45	Y 59
	K 0	K 9
	C 39	C 46
	M 42	M 34
	Y 67	Y 57
	K 0	K 2

Warm Spectrum: Desaturated

30**002**		
	C 3	C 12
	M 58	M 71
	Y 100	Y 86
	K 0	K 5
	C 46	C 69
	M 78	M 72
	Y 0	Y 17
	K 0	K 0
	C 100	C 68
	M 0	M 42
	Y 83	Y 100
	K 0	K 0

Triadic: Saturated

30**006**		
	C 31	C 2
	M 68	M 48
	Y 87	Y 72
	K 13	K 13
	C 64	C 38
	M 86	M 74
	Y 23	Y 14
	K 3	K 3
	C 89	C 64
	M 44	M 24
	Y 74	Y 38
	K 23	K 23

Triadic: Desaturated

30**010**		
	C 59	C 39
	M 5	M 14
	Y 45	Y 71
	K 0	K 0
	C 37	C 16
	M 2	M 18
	Y 82	Y 76
	K 0	K 0
	C 9	C 0
	M 0	M 23
	Y 91	Y 40
	K 0	K 0

Warm Spectrum: Saturated

30**014**		
	C 47	C 59
	M 36	M 48
	Y 72	Y 78
	K 9	K 30
	C 58	C 62
	M 42	M 52
	Y 52	Y 62
	K 8	K 32
	C 43	C 51
	M 44	M 57
	Y 61	Y 67
	K 12	K 33

Warm Spectrum: Desaturated

30**003**		
	C 0	C 13
	M 85	M 40
	Y 100	Y 82
	K 0	K 0
	C 69	C 57
	M 69	M 31
	Y 0	Y 0
	K 0	K 0
	C 42	C 17
	M 19	M 16
	Y 100	Y 100
	K 1	K 1

Triadic: Saturated

30**007**		
	C 35	C 46
	M 67	M 76
	Y 71	Y 84
	K 38	K 5
	C 69	C 75
	M 67	M 65
	Y 33	Y 11
	K 11	K 0
	C 60	C 79
	M 49	M 52
	Y 72	Y 96
	K 33	K 5

Triadic: Desaturated

30**011**		
	C 15	C 12
	M 89	M 86
	Y 43	Y 15
	K 25	K 0
	C 8	C 11
	M 77	M 60
	Y 89	Y 75
	K 21	K 0
	C 23	C 22
	M 42	M 42
	Y 91	Y 100
	K 33	K 2

Warm Spectrum: Saturated

30**015**		
	C 46	C 28
	M 67	M 48
	Y 54	Y 51
	K 25	K 0
	C 41	C 26
	M 61	M 38
	Y 64	Y 52
	K 21	K 0
	C 44	C 35
	M 47	M 33
	Y 63	Y 62
	K 33	K 2

Warm Spectrum: Desaturated

30**004**		
	C 0	C 4
	M 30	M 49
	Y 84	Y 100
	K 0	K 0
	C 28	C 49
	M 90	M 85
	Y 0	Y 11
	K 0	K 0
	C 86	C 79
	M 1	M 34
	Y 41	Y 22
	K 0	K 0

Triadic: Saturated

30**008**		
	C 31	C 31
	M 50	M 34
	Y 74	Y 73
	K 5	K 5
	C 42	C 47
	M 67	M 75
	Y 22	Y 50
	K 25	K 25
	C 70	C 61
	M 42	M 35
	Y 47	Y 72
	K 20	K 20

Triadic: Desaturated

30**012**		
	C 0	C 22
	M 20	M 49
	Y 100	Y 100
	K 0	K 3
	C 24	C 45
	M 6	M 41
	Y 100	Y 100
	K 0	K 15
	C 0	C 22
	M 45	M 76
	Y 61	Y 100
	K 0	K 10

Warm Spectrum: Saturated

30**016**		
	C 17	C 24
	M 25	M 43
	Y 58	Y 54
	K 0	K 0
	C 25	C 32
	M 21	M 36
	Y 59	Y 63
	K 0	K 3
	C 11	C 25
	M 32	M 43
	Y 35	Y 30
	K 0	K 0

Warm Spectrum: Desaturated

Colors used to code a family of items—a group of brochures, or a line of products—need to be easily distinguished from each other. Triads, as well as large jumps in value or saturation within an analogous set, achieve this goal. The degree of difference among the base colors may be perceived in terms of relative similarity or difference among the members of the family. An analogous accent enriches the color language. For families of more than three items, join related palettes.

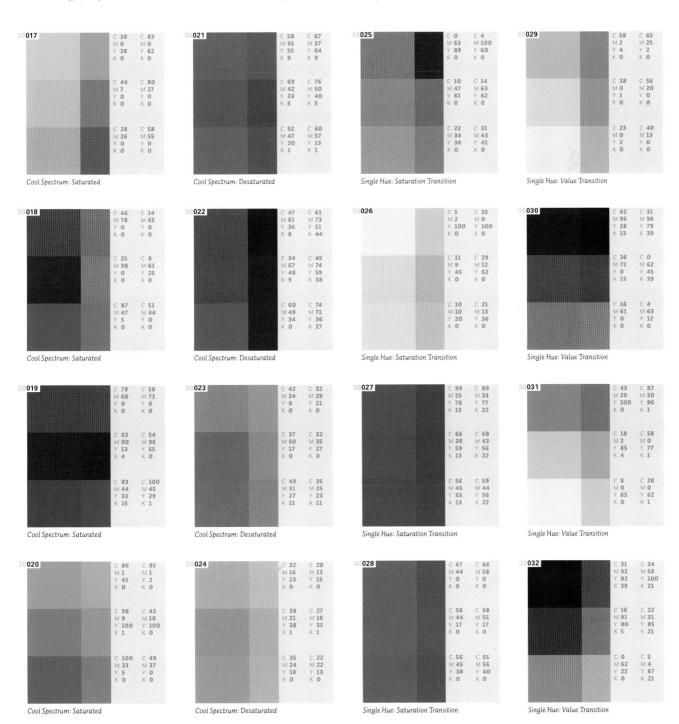

30 017

C 38	C 83
M 0	M 0
Y 28	Y 62
K 0	K 0
C 44	C 80
M 7	M 27
Y 0	Y 0
K 0	K 0
C 28	C 58
M 26	M 55
Y 0	Y 0
K 0	K 0

Cool Spectrum: Saturated

30 021

C 58	C 67
M 35	M 37
Y 55	Y 64
K 9	K 9
C 69	C 76
M 42	M 50
Y 33	Y 40
K 5	K 5
C 52	C 60
M 47	M 57
Y 20	Y 13
K 1	K 1

Cool Spectrum: Desaturated

30 025

C 0	C 4
M 63	M 100
Y 89	Y 60
K 0	K 0
C 10	C 14
M 47	M 63
Y 61	Y 62
K 0	K 0
C 22	C 31
M 34	M 43
Y 38	Y 41
K 0	K 0

Single Hue: Saturation Transition

30 029

C 58	C 65
M 2	M 25
Y 4	Y 2
K 0	K 0
C 38	C 56
M 0	M 20
Y 1	Y 0
K 0	K 0
C 23	C 40
M 0	M 13
Y 2	Y 0
K 0	K 0

Single Hue: Value Transition

30 018

C 46	C 14
M 78	M 65
Y 0	Y 0
K 0	K 0
C 25	C 8
M 98	M 61
Y 0	Y 25
K 0	K 0
C 87	C 51
M 47	M 44
Y 5	Y 0
K 0	K 0

Cool Spectrum: Saturated

30 022

C 47	C 61
M 61	M 73
Y 36	Y 51
K 8	K 44
C 34	C 45
M 67	M 74
Y 48	Y 59
K 9	K 38
C 60	C 74
M 49	M 71
Y 34	Y 36
K 0	K 27

Cool Spectrum: Desaturated

30 026

C 5	C 35
M 2	M 0
Y 100	Y 100
K 0	K 0
C 11	C 29
M 9	M 12
Y 45	Y 62
K 0	K 0
C 10	C 21
M 10	M 13
Y 20	Y 36
K 0	K 0

Single Hue: Saturation Transition

30 030

C 62	C 31
M 96	M 96
Y 28	Y 79
K 13	K 39
C 36	C 0
M 72	M 62
Y 0	Y 45
K 13	K 39
C 16	C 4
M 61	M 63
Y 0	Y 12
K 0	K 0

Single Hue: Value Transition

30 019

C 78	C 58
M 68	M 73
Y 0	Y 0
K 0	K 0
C 63	C 54
M 90	M 96
Y 13	Y 55
K 4	K 1
C 83	C 100
M 44	M 45
Y 33	Y 29
K 15	K 1

Cool Spectrum: Saturated

30 023

C 42	C 32
M 34	M 29
Y 9	Y 21
K 0	K 0
C 37	C 32
M 50	M 35
Y 17	Y 27
K 0	K 0
C 49	C 35
M 31	M 25
Y 27	Y 23
K 11	K 11

Cool Spectrum: Desaturated

30 027

C 99	C 89
M 25	M 33
Y 78	Y 77
K 13	K 22
C 66	C 68
M 38	M 43
Y 59	Y 56
K 13	K 22
C 56	C 59
M 45	M 44
Y 53	Y 56
K 13	K 22

Single Hue: Saturation Transition

30 031

C 43	C 87
M 29	M 20
Y 100	Y 96
K 0	K 1
C 18	C 58
M 2	M 0
Y 85	Y 77
K 4	K 1
C 8	C 28
M 0	M 0
Y 65	Y 62
K 0	K 1

Single Hue: Value Transition

30 020

C 86	C 85
M 1	M 1
Y 41	Y 2
K 0	K 0
C 98	C 43
M 9	M 18
Y 100	Y 100
K 1	K 0
C 100	C 49
M 33	M 37
Y 5	Y 0
K 0	K 0

Cool Spectrum: Saturated

30 024

C 32	C 28
M 16	M 13
Y 23	Y 15
K 0	K 0
C 38	C 27
M 21	M 16
Y 38	Y 35
K 1	K 1
C 35	C 22
M 24	M 22
Y 18	Y 13
K 0	K 0

Cool Spectrum: Desaturated

30 028

C 67	C 66
M 44	M 58
Y 0	Y 0
K 0	K 0
C 58	C 58
M 44	M 55
Y 17	Y 17
K 0	K 0
C 56	C 55
M 45	M 56
Y 38	Y 40
K 0	K 0

Single Hue: Saturation Transition

30 032

C 31	C 34
M 92	M 58
Y 82	Y 100
K 39	K 21
C 16	C 22
M 91	M 31
Y 80	Y 85
K 5	K 21
C 0	C 5
M 62	M 4
Y 22	Y 67
K 0	K 21

Single Hue: Value Transition

CODING FAMILIES *Contrasting Accent*

31

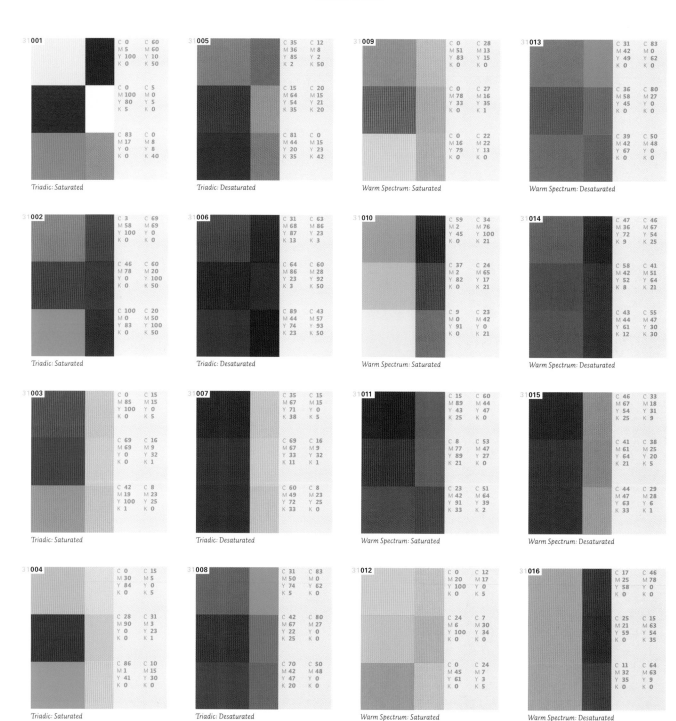

31001

C 0	C 60
M 5	M 60
Y 100	Y 10
K 2	K 50

C 0	C 5
M 100	M 0
Y 80	Y 5
K 5	K 0

C 83	C 0
M 17	M 8
Y 0	Y 8
K 0	K 40

Triadic: Saturated

31005

C 35	C 12
M 36	M 8
Y 85	Y 2
K 2	K 50

C 15	C 20
M 64	M 15
Y 54	Y 21
K 35	K 20

C 81	C 0
M 44	M 15
Y 20	Y 23
K 35	K 42

Triadic: Desaturated

31009

C 0	C 28
M 51	M 13
Y 83	Y 15
K 0	K 0

C 0	C 27
M 78	M 16
Y 33	Y 35
K 0	K 1

C 0	C 22
M 16	M 22
Y 79	Y 13
K 0	K 0

Warm Spectrum: Saturated

31013

C 31	C 83
M 42	M 0
Y 49	Y 62
K 0	K 0

C 36	C 80
M 58	M 27
Y 45	Y 0
K 0	K 0

C 39	C 50
M 42	M 48
Y 67	Y 0
K 0	K 0

Warm Spectrum: Desaturated

31002

C 3	C 69
M 58	M 69
Y 100	Y 0
K 0	K 0

C 46	C 60
M 78	M 20
Y 0	Y 100
K 0	K 50

C 100	C 20
M 0	M 50
Y 83	Y 100
K 0	K 50

Triadic: Saturated

31006

C 31	C 63
M 68	M 86
Y 87	Y 23
K 13	K 3

C 64	C 60
M 86	M 28
Y 23	Y 92
K 3	K 50

C 89	C 43
M 44	M 57
Y 74	Y 93
K 23	K 50

Triadic: Desaturated

31010

C 59	C 34
M 2	M 76
Y 45	Y 100
K 0	K 21

C 37	C 24
M 2	M 65
Y 82	Y 17
K 0	K 21

C 9	C 23
M 0	M 42
Y 91	Y 0
K 0	K 21

Warm Spectrum: Saturated

31014

C 47	C 46
M 36	M 67
Y 72	Y 54
K 9	K 25

C 58	C 41
M 42	M 51
Y 52	Y 64
K 8	K 21

C 43	C 55
M 44	M 47
Y 61	Y 30
K 12	K 30

Warm Spectrum: Desaturated

31003

C 0	C 15
M 85	M 15
Y 100	Y 0
K 0	K 5

C 69	C 16
M 69	M 9
Y 0	Y 32
K 0	K 1

C 42	C 8
M 19	M 23
Y 100	Y 25
K 1	K 0

Triadic: Saturated

31007

C 35	C 15
M 67	M 15
Y 71	Y 0
K 38	K 5

C 69	C 16
M 67	M 9
Y 89	Y 32
K 11	K 1

C 60	C 8
M 49	M 23
Y 72	Y 25
K 33	K 0

Triadic: Desaturated

31011

C 15	C 60
M 89	M 44
Y 43	Y 47
K 25	K 0

C 8	C 53
M 77	M 47
Y 89	Y 27
K 21	K 0

C 23	C 51
M 42	M 64
Y 91	Y 39
K 33	K 2

Warm Spectrum: Saturated

31015

C 46	C 33
M 67	M 18
Y 54	Y 31
K 25	K 9

C 41	C 38
M 61	M 25
Y 64	Y 20
K 21	K 5

C 44	C 29
M 47	M 28
Y 63	Y 6
K 33	K 1

Warm Spectrum: Desaturated

31004

C 0	C 15
M 30	M 5
Y 84	Y 0
K 0	K 5

C 28	C 31
M 90	M 3
Y 0	Y 23
K 0	K 1

C 86	C 10
M 1	M 15
Y 41	Y 30
K 0	K 0

Triadic: Saturated

31008

C 31	C 83
M 50	M 0
Y 74	Y 62
K 5	K 0

C 42	C 80
M 67	M 27
Y 22	Y 0
K 25	K 0

C 70	C 50
M 42	M 48
Y 0	Y 0
K 20	K 0

Triadic: Desaturated

31012

C 0	C 12
M 20	M 17
Y 100	Y 0
K 0	K 5

C 24	C 7
M 6	M 30
Y 100	Y 34
K 0	K 0

C 0	C 24
M 45	M 7
Y 61	Y 3
K 0	K 5

Warm Spectrum: Saturated

31016

C 17	C 46
M 25	M 78
Y 58	Y 0
K 0	K 0

C 25	C 15
M 21	M 63
Y 59	Y 54
K 0	K 35

C 11	C 64
M 32	M 63
Y 35	Y 9
K 0	K 0

Warm Spectrum: Desaturated

For more complex or dynamic coding, especially for lifestyle or consumer products, use a coding family with a contrasting accent—one that is complementary or triadic, offset from the base color family. Or choose the members of one base palette as the accents for another palette altogether. Reverse the proportional relationship between bases and accents to double the number of items that can be coded within the family while maintaining a close in-family.

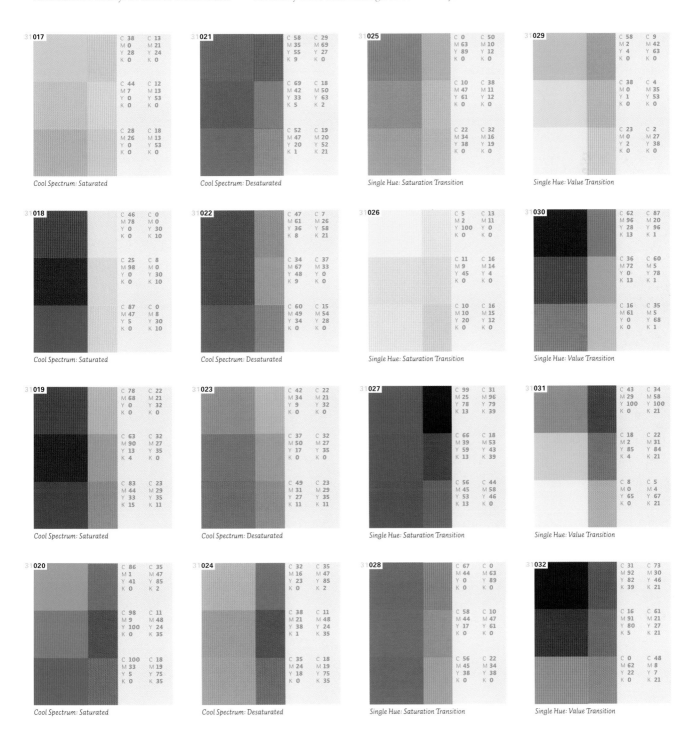

31 017

C 38	C 13
M 0	M 21
Y 28	Y 24
K 0	K 0
C 44	C 12
M 7	M 13
Y 0	Y 53
K 0	K 0
C 28	C 18
M 26	M 13
Y 0	Y 53
K 0	K 0

Cool Spectrum: Saturated

31 021

C 58	C 29
M 35	M 69
Y 55	Y 27
K 9	K 0
C 69	C 18
M 42	M 50
Y 33	Y 63
K 5	K 2
C 52	C 19
M 47	M 20
Y 20	Y 52
K 1	K 21

Cool Spectrum: Desaturated

31 025

C 0	C 50
M 63	M 10
Y 89	Y 12
K 0	K 0
C 10	C 38
M 47	M 11
Y 61	Y 12
K 0	K 0
C 22	C 32
M 34	M 16
Y 38	Y 19
K 0	K 0

Single Hue: Saturation Transition

31 029

C 58	C 9
M 2	M 42
Y 4	Y 63
K 0	K 0
C 38	C 4
M 0	M 35
Y 1	Y 53
K 0	K 0
C 23	C 2
M 0	M 27
Y 2	Y 38
K 0	K 0

Single Hue: Value Transition

31 018

C 46	C 0
M 78	M 0
Y 0	Y 30
K 0	K 10
C 25	C 8
M 98	M 0
Y 0	Y 30
K 0	K 10
C 87	C 0
M 47	M 8
Y 5	Y 30
K 0	K 10

Cool Spectrum: Saturated

31 022

C 47	C 7
M 61	M 26
Y 36	Y 58
K 8	K 21
C 34	C 37
M 67	M 33
Y 48	Y 0
K 9	K 0
C 60	C 15
M 49	M 54
Y 34	Y 28
K 0	K 0

Cool Spectrum: Desaturated

31 026

C 5	C 13
M 2	M 11
Y 100	Y 0
K 0	K 0
C 11	C 16
M 9	M 14
Y 45	Y 4
K 0	K 0
C 10	C 16
M 10	M 15
Y 20	Y 12
K 0	K 0

Single Hue: Saturation Transition

31 030

C 62	C 87
M 96	M 20
Y 28	Y 96
K 13	K 1
C 36	C 60
M 72	M 5
Y 0	Y 78
K 13	K 1
C 16	C 35
M 61	M 5
Y 0	Y 68
K 0	K 1

Single Hue: Value Transition

31 019

C 78	C 22
M 68	M 21
Y 0	Y 32
K 0	K 0
C 63	C 32
M 90	M 27
Y 13	Y 35
K 4	K 0
C 83	C 23
M 44	M 29
Y 33	Y 35
K 15	K 11

Cool Spectrum: Saturated

31 023

C 42	C 22
M 34	M 21
Y 9	Y 32
K 0	K 0
C 37	C 32
M 50	M 27
Y 17	Y 35
K 0	K 0
C 49	C 23
M 31	M 29
Y 27	Y 35
K 11	K 11

Cool Spectrum: Desaturated

31 027

C 99	C 31
M 25	M 96
Y 78	Y 79
K 13	K 39
C 66	C 18
M 39	M 53
Y 59	Y 43
K 13	K 39
C 56	C 44
M 45	M 58
Y 53	Y 46
K 13	K 0

Single Hue: Saturation Transition

31 031

C 43	C 34
M 29	M 58
Y 100	Y 100
K 0	K 21
C 18	C 22
M 2	M 31
Y 85	Y 84
K 4	K 21
C 8	C 5
M 0	M 4
Y 65	Y 67
K 0	K 21

Single Hue: Value Transition

31 020

C 86	C 35
M 1	M 47
Y 41	Y 85
K 0	K 2
C 98	C 11
M 9	M 48
Y 100	Y 24
K 0	K 35
C 100	C 18
M 33	M 19
Y 5	Y 75
K 0	K 35

Cool Spectrum: Saturated

31 024

C 32	C 35
M 16	M 47
Y 23	Y 85
K 0	K 2
C 38	C 11
M 21	M 48
Y 38	Y 24
K 1	K 35
C 35	C 18
M 24	M 19
Y 18	Y 75
K 0	K 35

Cool Spectrum: Desaturated

31 028

C 67	C 0
M 44	M 63
Y 0	Y 89
K 0	K 0
C 58	C 10
M 44	M 21
Y 17	Y 61
K 0	K 0
C 56	C 22
M 45	M 34
Y 38	Y 38
K 0	K 0

Single Hue: Saturation Transition

31 032

C 31	C 73
M 92	M 30
Y 82	Y 46
K 39	K 21
C 16	C 61
M 91	M 21
Y 80	Y 27
K 5	K 21
C 0	C 48
M 62	M 8
Y 22	Y 7
K 0	K 21

Single Hue: Value Transition

CODING FAMILIES *Unifying Accent*

32

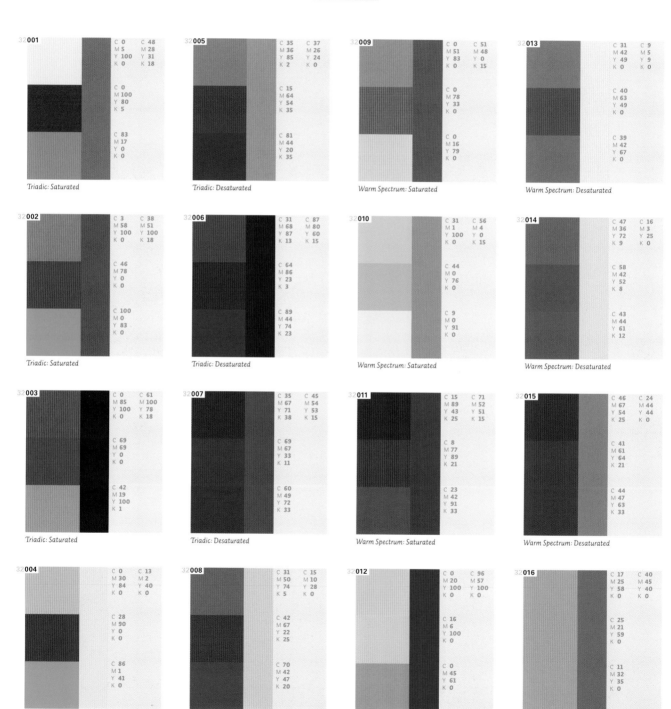

32001

C 0	C 48
M 5	M 28
Y 100	Y 31
K 0	K 18

C 0
M 100
Y 80
K 5

C 83
M 17
Y 0
K 0

Triadic: Saturated

32005

C 35	C 37
M 36	M 26
Y 85	Y 24
K 2	K 0

C 15
M 64
Y 54
K 35

C 81
M 44
Y 20
K 35

Triadic: Desaturated

32009

C 0	C 51
M 51	M 48
Y 83	Y 0
K 0	K 15

C 0
M 78
Y 33
K 0

C 0
M 16
Y 79
K 0

Warm Spectrum: Saturated

32013

C 31	C 9
M 42	M 5
Y 49	Y 9
K 0	K 0

C 40
M 63
Y 49
K 0

C 39
M 42
Y 67
K 0

Warm Spectrum: Desaturated

32002

C 3	C 38
M 58	M 51
Y 100	Y 100
K 0	K 18

C 46
M 78
Y 0
K 0

C 100
M 0
Y 83
K 0

Triadic: Saturated

32006

C 31	C 87
M 68	M 80
Y 87	Y 60
K 13	K 15

C 64
M 86
Y 23
K 3

C 89
M 44
Y 74
K 23

Triadic: Desaturated

32010

C 31	C 56
M 1	M 4
Y 100	Y 0
K 0	K 15

C 44
M 0
Y 76
K 0

C 9
M 0
Y 91
K 0

Warm Spectrum: Saturated

32014

C 47	C 16
M 36	M 3
Y 72	Y 25
K 9	K 0

C 58
M 42
Y 52
K 8

C 43
M 44
Y 61
K 12

Warm Spectrum: Desaturated

32003

C 0	C 61
M 85	M 100
Y 100	Y 78
K 0	K 18

C 69
M 69
Y 0
K 0

C 42
M 19
Y 100
K 1

Triadic: Saturated

32007

C 35	C 45
M 67	M 54
Y 71	Y 53
K 38	K 15

C 69
M 67
Y 33
K 11

C 60
M 49
Y 72
K 33

Triadic: Desaturated

32011

C 15	C 71
M 89	M 52
Y 43	Y 51
K 25	K 15

C 8
M 77
Y 89
K 21

C 23
M 42
Y 91
K 33

Warm Spectrum: Saturated

32015

C 46	C 24
M 67	M 44
Y 54	Y 44
K 25	K 0

C 41
M 61
Y 64
K 21

C 44
M 47
Y 63
K 33

Warm Spectrum: Desaturated

32004

C 0	C 13
M 30	M 2
Y 84	Y 40
K 0	K 0

C 28
M 90
Y 0
K 0

C 86
M 1
Y 41
K 0

Triadic: Saturated

32008

C 31	C 15
M 50	M 10
Y 74	Y 28
K 5	K 0

C 42
M 67
Y 22
K 25

C 70
M 42
Y 47
K 20

Triadic: Desaturated

32012

C 0	C 96
M 20	M 57
Y 100	Y 100
K 0	K 0

C 16
M 6
Y 100
K 0

C 0
M 45
Y 61
K 0

Warm Spectrum: Saturated

32016

C 17	C 40
M 25	M 45
Y 58	Y 40
K 0	K 0

C 25
M 21
Y 59
K 0

C 11
M 32
Y 35
K 0

Warm Spectrum: Desaturated

To better position color-differentiated items as belonging to a family, consider a unifying accent different from the base colors. In the families shown here, a relatively neutral accent plays off the saturation, temperature, and complementary qualities of the base colors to add depth, without becoming too biased toward any one of them.

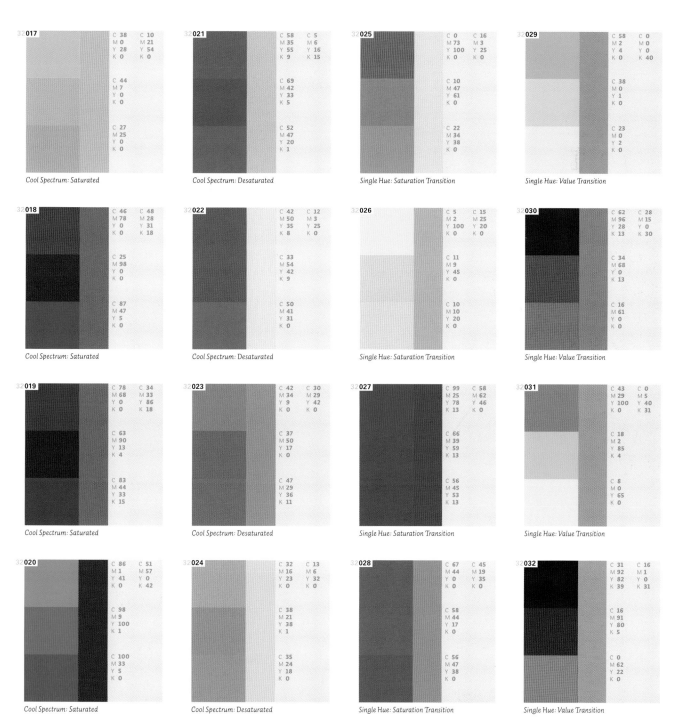

32 **017**

C 38	C 10
M 0	M 21
Y 28	Y 54
K 0	K 0

C 44	
M 7	
Y 0	
K 0	

C 27	
M 25	
Y 0	
K 0	

Cool Spectrum: Saturated

32 **021**

C 58	C 5
M 73	M 6
Y 55	Y 16
K 9	K 15

C 69	
M 42	
Y 33	
K 5	

C 52	
M 47	
Y 20	
K 1	

Cool Spectrum: Desaturated

32 **025**

C 0	C 16
M 73	M 3
Y 100	Y 25
K 0	K 0

C 10	
M 47	
Y 61	
K 0	

C 22	
M 34	
Y 38	
K 0	

Single Hue: Saturation Transition

32 **029**

C 58	C 0
M 2	M 0
Y 4	Y 0
K 0	K 40

C 38	
M 0	
Y 1	
K 0	

C 23	
M 0	
Y 2	
K 0	

Single Hue: Value Transition

32 **018**

C 46	C 48
M 78	M 28
Y 0	Y 31
K 0	K 18

C 25	
M 98	
Y 0	
K 0	

C 87	
M 47	
Y 5	
K 0	

Cool Spectrum: Saturated

32 **022**

C 42	C 12
M 50	M 3
Y 35	Y 25
K 8	K 0

C 33	
M 54	
Y 42	
K 9	

C 50	
M 41	
Y 31	
K 0	

Cool Spectrum: Desaturated

32 **026**

C 5	C 15
M 2	M 25
Y 100	Y 20
K 0	K 0

C 11	
M 9	
Y 45	
K 0	

C 10	
M 10	
Y 20	
K 0	

Single Hue: Saturation Transition

32 **030**

C 62	C 28
M 96	M 15
Y 28	Y 0
K 13	K 30

C 34	
M 68	
Y 0	
K 13	

C 16	
M 61	
Y 0	
K 0	

Single Hue: Value Transition

32 **019**

C 78	C 34
M 68	M 33
Y 0	Y 86
K 0	K 18

C 63	
M 90	
Y 13	
K 4	

C 83	
M 44	
Y 33	
K 15	

Cool Spectrum: Saturated

32 **023**

C 42	C 30
M 34	M 29
Y 9	Y 42
K 0	K 0

C 37	
M 50	
Y 17	
K 0	

C 47	
M 29	
Y 36	
K 11	

Cool Spectrum: Desaturated

32 **027**

C 99	C 58
M 25	M 62
Y 78	Y 46
K 13	K 0

C 66	
M 39	
Y 59	
K 13	

C 56	
M 45	
Y 53	
K 13	

Single Hue: Saturation Transition

32 **031**

C 43	C 0
M 29	M 5
Y 100	Y 40
K 0	K 31

C 18	
M 2	
Y 85	
K 4	

C 8	
M 0	
Y 65	
K 0	

Single Hue: Value Transition

32 **020**

C 86	C 51
M 1	M 57
Y 41	Y 0
K 0	K 42

C 98	
M 9	
Y 100	
K 1	

C 100	
M 33	
Y 5	
K 0	

Cool Spectrum: Saturated

32 **024**

C 32	C 13
M 16	M 6
Y 23	Y 32
K 0	K 0

C 38	
M 21	
Y 38	
K 1	

C 35	
M 24	
Y 18	
K 0	

Cool Spectrum: Desaturated

32 **028**

C 67	C 45
M 44	M 19
Y 0	Y 35
K 0	K 0

C 58	
M 44	
Y 17	
K 0	

C 56	
M 47	
Y 38	
K 0	

Single Hue: Saturation Transition

32 **032**

C 31	C 16
M 92	M 1
Y 82	Y 0
K 39	K 31

C 16	
M 91	
Y 80	
K 5	

C 0	
M 62	
Y 22	
K 0	

Single Hue: Value Transition

Typographic
Confections

TYPOGRAPHY IS A DYNAMIC, universal element in most design projects. The texture of letters and words, sentences, and paragraphs, bold headlines and callouts—from the most delicate script to the heaviest slab serif—can be manipulated into expressive configurations that make reading easier and transform text into image. Choosing typefaces to combine for any project is an exercise in textural contrast. Some are brittle and sharp, others juicy and full—and some are nearly flavorless without the right supporting details.

The designer who appreciates the subtleties among serifs and sans will be able to sweeten any typographic page, no matter how complex. A pantry-full of typeface combinations is available here, along with all the elements a designer needs to spice up the typographic page: titling and subtitling configurations; ideas for text entry points, drop caps, and paragraph separators; an array of concoctions for text shapes, pull quotes, lists, and captions; and last but not least, a sampling of tasty typographic embellishments, dingbats, and decorative details.

TYPE AS IMAGE *Form Manipulations*

33

33**001**

RBGLOFK

Midline Break: Perspective

33**002**

RBGLOFK

Linear Drawing with Baseline Shift

33**003**

RBGLOFK

Exterior Contour Rough Bleed

33**004**

RBGLOFK

Vertical Inline Fracturing

33**005**

RBGLOFK

Transparent Glass Effect with Highlight Edges

33**006**

RBGLOFK

Photocopier or Scanner Move/Distortion

33**007**

RBGLOFK

Mask of Photographic Image

33**008**

RBGLOFK

Mask of Abstract Form Language

33**009**

RBGLOFK

Outline with Periodic Breaks

33**010**

RBGLOFK

Mask of Texture

33**011**

R B G L O F K

Stroke/Counterform Reversal

33**012**

RBGLOFK

Pictorial Inclusion in Counterform: Symbol

33**013**

RBGLOFK

Convex Distortion with Angled Fracture

33**014**

RBGLOFK

Irregular Contour Distortion

33**015**

RBGLOFK

Horizontal Splicing and Recomposition with Size Changes

33**016**

RBGLOFK

Pictorial Substitution: Icon

33**017**

RBGLOFK

Horizontal Band Reversal

33**018**

RBGLOFK

Digital Edge Distortion Filter

33**019**

RBGLOFK

Digital Edge Distortion Filter

33**020**

RBGLOFK

Digital Scraping Texture

33**021**

RBGLOFK

Positive/Negative Repeat with Offset

33**022**

RBGLOFK

Outline: Broken or Dotted Stroke

33**023**

RBGLOFK

Ink Wash Rendering

33**024**

RBGLOFK

Pictorial Substitution: Photographic Image

Letters and words may be transformed into compelling images through any number of alterations, from simple texturizing to distorting, splicing, and deconstructing. Such manipulations may serve a purely visual function—helping to integrate the typographic form with other pictorial matter by creating parity in form—and they may also work toward evoking concepts, supporting the meaning of the words through the method of manipulation. Shown here is a smorgasbord of the nearly limitless possibilities for typographic expression.

33025

Reversal from Geometric Planes

33026

Bezier Point Pull-Distortion

33027

Digital Skew with Horizontal Line Pattern

33028

Reversal and Integration with Paint Spatter

33029

Digital Paint and Transparency Effect

33030

Reversal over Offset or Rotated Shape

33031

Digital Blur Filter

33032

RBGLOFK

Vertical Splicing with Baseline Shifts

33033

RBGLOFK

Reflection Effect

33034

Perspective Distortion

33035

Texturizing

33036

RBGLOFK

Scratch and Ink Bleed Rendering

33037

RBGLOFK

Pictorial Inclusion: Icon

33038

RBGLOFK

Cut-and-Paste Tape Reconstruction

33039

RBGLOFK

Horizontal Line Pattern with Selective Toning

33040

RBGLOFK

Fat-Nib Felt Marker Rendering

33041

RBGLOFK

Beveled Extrusion with Drop Shadow

33042

Extrusion with Reversed Face

33043

Neon-Effect Double Outline

33044

RBGLOFK

Blurred Wave Distortion

33045

Texturizing with Radial Motion Blur

33046

RBGLOFK

Ripple Distortion and Bloating Effect

33047

RBGLOFK

Drawing and Scratching Disruption

33048

RBGLOFK

Crumpled Surface

TYPE AS IMAGE *Pictorializations*

34

34001

Music

34002

Architecture

34003

Rage

34004

Technology

34005

Despair

34006

Joy

34007

Evolution

34008

Frenzied

34009

serene

Serene

34010

Unseen

34011

Urban

34012

Mysterious

34013

Faith

34014

catlyze

Catalyze

34015

$$m\sqrt{(a+h)}3\,m^a + \frac{i}{c}\,5$$

Mathematics

34016

Tool

34017

Industry

34018

Dance

34019

Art

34020

GLASS

Glass

34021

r = a?on

Reason

34022

Animal

34023

VIOLENCE

Violence

34024

nature

Nature

As a more concrete approach, try manipulations such as these, whereby the typographic form assumes a pictorial quality—becoming a real-world object, participating in physical action, or suggesting three-dimensional environments. The immediacy and literalism of these manipulations lend themselves to type-only solutions, packing the visual power of image into the verbal structure of words.

34**025**

Artificial

34**026**

Radiation

34**027**

Lust

34**028**

Rough

34**029**

Death

34**030**

Weather

34**031**

Biology

34**032**

Chemical

34**033**

Explode

34**034**

Drive

34**035**

Luxury

34**036**

Vague

34**037**

Archaic

34**038**

diversity

Diversity

34**039**

COLD

Cold

34**040**

Ocean

34**041**

ARID

Arid

34**042**

Burning

34**043**

Poverty

34**044**

Trash

34**045**

THEATRIC

Theatrical

34**046**

ANXIOUS

Anxious

34**047**

Insect

34**048**

PROGRESSIVE

Progressive

TYPEFACE SELECTIONS *Historical*

35

35**001**

Prehistoric: Mesozoic

35**002**

Prehistoric: African

35**003**

Prehistoric: European

35**004**

Prehistoric: Asia Minor

35**005**

Antiquity: Greece

35**006**

Antiquity: Egypt

35**007**

Antiquity: Roman Empire

35**008**

Early Medieval: Irish

35**009**

Early Medieval: Merovingian

35**010**

Medieval: Italianate

35**011**

Medieval: Carolingian

35**012**

Medieval: Lombardic

35**013**

Late Medieval: French Gothic

35**014**

Late Medieval: Germanic Gothic

35**015**

Early Renaissance

35**016**

Renaissance: Cinquecento

35**017**

Late Renaissance

35**018**

Baroque

35**019**

Industrial Revolution

35**020**

American Wild West

35**021**

Victorian: Romantic

35**022**

Victorian: Stylized

35**023**

Arts & Crafts

35**024**

Art Nouveau: French

For projects embodying significant historical content or metaphorical allusion to a time period, look to period faces to provide that context. The selections shown here fit general historical categories; each shows two characteristic display faces. To avoid an overly historical flavor, exchange one of the members in a given combination with a more contemporary face, or use the period combination for accents alongside one or more decidedly modern faces.

35**025**

AaGgRhEfeMx
AaGgRhEfeMx

Jugendstil

35**026**

AaGgRhEfeMx
AGRHEFMXKB

Art Nouveau: Belgian

35**027**

AAGGRHEFEMX
AaGgRhEfeMx

Art Nouveau: Scottish

35**028**

AaGgRhEfeMx
AGRHEFMXKB

Plakatstil

35**029**

AGRHEFMXKB
AaGgRhEfeMx

Early Viennese Secession

35**030**

AAGRHEFEMXK
AGRHEF

Late Viennese Secession/Werkstätte

35**031**

AGRHEFMXKB
AGRHEFMXKB

Constructivist

35**032**

AaGgRhEfeMx
AaGgRhEfeMx

Dada/Futurism

35**033**

AGRHEFMXKB
AGRHEFMXKB

De Stijl

35**034**

AGRHEFMXKB
AaGgRhEfeMx

Art Deco: Display

35**035**

AGRHEFMXKB
AaGgRhEfeMx

Art Deco: Book

35**036**

AaGgRhEfeMx
AaGgRhEfeMx

Postwar International Style

35**037**

AaGgRhEfeMx
AaGgRhEfeMx

Baby Boomer: Entertainment

35**038**

AaGgRhEfeMx
AaGgRhEf

Baby Boomer: Lounge

35**039**

AaGgRhEfeMx
AGRHEFMXKB

Counterculture: Folk

35**040**

AaGgRhEfeMx
AaGgRhEfeMx

Counterculture: Psychedelic

35**041**

AGRHEFMX
AGRHEFMXKB

Counterculture: Pop/Beatnik

35**042**

AGRHEFMXKB

Counterculture: Groove

35**043**

AaGgRhEfeMx
AIGGRHEeMx

Counterculture: Punk

35**044**

AaGgRhEfeMxKB
AGRHEFMX

Counterculture: Glam/New Wave

35**045**

AaGgRhEfeMx
AaGgRhEfeMx

Global Branding

35**046**

AaGgRhEfeM
AgrhefMxkb

Postmodern

35**047**

AaGgRhEfeMx
AaGgRhEfeMx

New Age Spiritualism

35**048**

AGRHEFMXKB
agrhefmxkb

Internet Age

TYPEFACE SELECTIONS *Moods and Concepts*

36

36**001**

Dangerous

36**002**

Friendly

36**003**

Comical

36**004**

Technological

36**005**

Soft

36**006**

Dynamic

36**007**

Sinister

36**008**

Sporty

36**009**

Fragile

36**010**

Exotic

36**011**

Intuitive

36**012**

Psychotic

36**013**

Aggressive

36**014**

Extreme

36**015**

Powerful

36**016**

Progressive

36**017**

Classical

36**018**

Elegant

36**019**

Experimental

36**020**

Fantasy

36**021**

Musical

36**022**

Artificial

36**023**

Organic

36**024**

Urban

These specimens offer quick, reliable formulas for conveying the specific tone or voice of a given project—both through the visual qualities of the faces' rhythm, movement, contrast, and detailing, as well as through cultural or historical associations. By no means exhaustive, the stylistic examples shown here may be used as is, mixed for more complex tonal shading, or their members substituted with similar styles as seems appropriate.

36**025**	36**031**	36**037**	36**043**
AaGgRhEfeMx AaGgRhEfeMx	**AaGgRhEfeMx** AaGgRhEfeMx	AaGgRhEfeMx AaGgRhEfeMx	AaGgRhEfeMx A G R H E Q F B M X
Financial Services	*Industrial: Heavy Manufacturing*	*Nature Conservancy*	*Cultural Institution: Visual Arts*
36**026**	36**032**	36**038**	36**044**
AaGgRhEfeMx AaGgRhEfeMx	AaGgRhEfeMx **AaGgRhEfeMx**	**AaGgRhEfeMx** AaGgRhEfeMx	AaGgRhEfeMx A G R H E Q B F M X
Legal Services	*Industrial: High-Tech*	*Energy Utilities*	*Entertainment: Pop*
36**027**	36**033**	36**039**	36**045**
AaGgRhEfeMx AaGgRhEfeMx	AaGgRhEfeMx AaGgRhEfeMx	**AaGgRhEfeMx** AaGgRhEfeMx	**AaGgRhEfeMx** AaGgRhEfeMx
Health Care	*Education: Public*	*Telecommunications*	*Entertainment: Hip-Hop*
36**028**	36**034**	36**040**	36**046**
AaGgRhEfeMx AaGgRhEfeMx	AaGgRhEfeMx A G R H J E F M B X	**A G R H E B F M X** AaGgRhEfeMx	*AaGgRhEfeMx* A G R H E Q B F M X
Life Sciences	*Education: Higher Learning*	*Mass-Market Hotel*	*Consumer Products: Bed and Bath*
36**029**	36**035**	36**041**	36**047**
AaGgRhEfeMx AaGgRhEfeMx	AaGgRhEfeMx **AaGgRhEfeMx**	A G R H E B F M X AaGgRhEfeMx	AaGgRhEfMx A G R H E Q B F M X
Pharmaceutical	*Architectural Design*	*Boutique or Luxury Hotel*	*Home Furnishing: Traditional*
36**030**	36**036**	36**042**	36**048**
AaGgRhEfeMx AaGgRhEfeMx	**AaGgRhEfeMx** **AaGgRhEfeMx**	*AaGgRhEfeMx* A G R H E B F M X	AaGgRhEfMx A G R H E B F M X
Industrial: Chemical	*Construction or Hardware*	*Cultural Institution: Performing Arts*	*Home Furnishing: Contemporary*

TYPEFACE COMBINATIONS *Editorial Style Mixes*

37

37001
Gr
Mie
BEATUS LUX
Duis autemer
Semperi nunc

One Serif Family · Oldstyle

37005
Gra
Mie
Beatus luxat
Duis autemer
semperi nunc

One Serif Family: Transitional

37009
Gr
MIE
Beatus luxa
Duis autemer
semperi nunc

One Serif Family: Neoclassical

37013
Gr
Mie
Beatus luxa
Duis autem
semperi nu

One Serif Family: Slab

37017
Gra
Mie
Beatusluxa
Duis autemer
semperi nunc

*Oldstyle Serif Family
with Slab Serif Accent*

37021
Gr
Mie
Beatus lux
Duis autemer
semperi nunc

*Slab Serif Family with
Oldstyle Accent*

37002
Gra
Mies
Beatus luxat
Duis autemer
semperi nunc

One Serif Family: Oldstyle

37006
Gr
Mie
Beatus luxat
Duis autemer
semperi nunc

One Serif Family: Transitional

37010
Grafito
Miest Lent
BEATUS LUX
Duis autemer
semperi nunc

One Serif Family: Neoclassical

37014
Gr
Miest
BEATUS LUX
Duis autemer
semperi nunc

One Serif Family: Slab

37018
Gr
Mie
Beatuslux
Duis autemer
semperi nunc

*Oldstyle Serif Family
with Script Serif Accent*

37022
Grafito
Mie
Beatus lux
Duis autemer
semperi nunc

*Slab Serif Family with
Transitional Serif Accent*

37003
Gr
Mie
BEATUS LUXA
Duis autemer
semperi nunc

One Serif Family: Oldstyle

37007
GR
Mie
BEATUS LUXAT
Duis autemer
semperi nunc

One Serif Family: Transitional

37011
Gra
Miest
Beatus lux
Duis autemer
semperi nunc

One Serif Family: Neoclassical

37015
Gr
Mie
Beatus luxat
Duis autemer
semperi nunc

One Serif Family: Slab

37019
Graf
Mie
Beatus Luxat
Duis autemer
semperi nunc

*Transitional Serif Family
with Slab Serif Accent*

37023
Gra
MIE
Beatus Luxat
Duis autemer
semperi nunc

*Slab Serif Family with
Neoclassical Serif Accent*

37004
GR
Mie
Beatus luxat
Duis autemer
semperi nunc

One Serif Family: Oldstyle

37008
Gr
Mie
Beatus luxat
Duis autemer
semperi nunc

One Serif Family: Transitional

37012
Gr
Mie
Beatus lux
Duis autemer
semperi nunc

One Serif Family: Neoclassical

37016
Grafi
Mie
BEATUS LUX
Duis autemer
semperi nunc

One Serif Family: Slab

37020
Gra
Miel
Beatus luxa
Duis autemer
semperi nunc

*Transitional Serif Family
with Script and Inline*

37024
Gr
Mie
Beatus luxa
Duis autemer
semperi nunc

*Slab Serif Family with
Script Serif Accent*

Mixing two or more typefaces adds visual texture to typography and helps distinguish among hierarchic components. These combinations are rooted strictly in the visual aspects of type styles—exhibiting both corresponding and contrasting relationships in structure, style, and rhythm. Combinations limited to a single family segue into those presenting more varied stylistic contrast. The members of each set are shown in given proportion and case relationships, ready to use as is for heads, decks, subheadings, and text—but feel free, as often happens in the recipes, to simply use the mix of the families' styles for any particular editorial element as needed.

37025

Gr
Mie
Beatus luxat
Duis autemer
semperi nunc

Sans Serif Family: Humanist

37029

Gr
Mie
Beatus luxat
Duis autemer
semperi nunc

Sans Serif Family: Geometric

37033

Gr
Mie
BEATUS LUXAT
Duis autemer
semperi nunc

*Humanist Sans Serif Family
with Geometric Sans Accent*

37037

Gra
Mie
Beatus luxat
Duis autemer
semperi nunc

Two Slab Serif Families

37041

Gr
Mie
Beatus lux
Duis autemer
semperi nunc

Mixed Serifs and Sans Serifs

37045

Graf
Mie
Beatuslux
Duis autemer
semperi nunc

Mixed Serifs and Sans Serifs

37026

GRAFI
Mie
BEATUS LUXAT
Duis autemer
semperi nunc

Sans Serif Family: Humanist

37030

Gr
Mie
Beatus luxat
Duis autemer
semperi nunc

Sans Serif Family: Geometric

37034

Gr
Mie
BEATUS LUX
Duis autemer
semperi nunc

*Geometric Sans Serif Family
with Humanist Sans Accent*

37038

Gr
Mie
Beatus luxat
Duis autemer
semperi nunc

Two Slab Serif Families

37042

Gr
Mie
BEATUS LU
Duis autemer
semperi nunc

Mixed Serifs and Sans Serifs

37046

Gr
Mie
Beatus luxat
Duis autemer
semperi nunc

Mixed Serifs and Sans Serifs

37027

Gr
Mie
Beatus luxat
Duis autemer
semperi nunc

Sans Serif Family: Humanist

37031

Gra
Mie
Beatus luxat
Duis autemer
semperi nunc

*Humanist Sans Serif Family
with Geometric Sans Accent*

37035

Grafi
Mie
Beatus lux
Duis autemer
semperi nunc

*Humanist Sans Serif Family
with Slab Serif Accent*

37039

Gr
Mie
Beatus luxat
Duis autemer
semperi nunc

*Two Slab Serif Families
with Humanist Sans Accent*

37043

Gr
Mie
Beatus luxat
Duis autemer
semperi nunc

Mixed Serifs and Sans Serifs

37047

Grice
MIELU
Beatuslux
Duis autemer
semperi nunc

Mixed Serifs and Sans Serifs

37028

Graf
Mie
Beatus luxat
Duis autemer
semperi nunc

Sans Serif Family: Humanist

37032

Gr
Mie
Beatus luxat
Duis autemer
semperi nunc

*Humanist Sans Serif Family
with Geometric Sans Accent*

37036

Gr
Mie
Beatus luxat
Duis autemer
semperi nunc

*Humanist Sans Serif Family
with Script Serif Accent*

37040

Gr
Mie
Beatus luxat
Duis autemer
semperi nunc

*Two Slab Serif Families
with Geometric Sans Accent*

37044

Gr
Mie
Beatus luxat
Duis autemer
semperi nunc

Mixed Serifs and Sans Serifs

37048

Gr
Mie
Beatus luxa
Duis autemer
semperi nunc

Mixed Serifs and Sans Serifs

EDITORIAL ELEMENTS *Hierarchic Pair Structures*

38

38**001**

DUISAUTEM SEMPER
Loripsum duis velurarem

Symmetrical: Tight

38**002**

DUISAUTEM SEMPER
Loripsum duis velurarem

Symmetrical: Loose

38**003**

LORIPSUM DUIS VELURAREM
DUISAUTEM SEMPER

Asymmetrical: Initial Cap

38**004**

DUISAUTEM SEMPER
Loripsum duis velurarem

Symmetrical: Rule Divider

38**005**

Duisautem Semper
Loripsum duis velurarem

Asymmetrical: Rule Divider

38**006**

DUISAUTEM
SEMPER
LORIPSUM
DUIS
VELURAREM

Asymmetrical: Stacked Caps

38**007**

Loripsum
duis
velurarem
DUISAUTEM
SEMPER

Asymmetrical: Orthogonal

38**008**

DUISAUTEM
SEMPER
Loripsum
Duis Velurarem

Asymmetrical: Rhythmic Size Change

38**009**

D U I S S A E U M T P E E M R
Loripsum duis velurarem

Asymmetrical: Rhythmic Weight and Spacing

38**010**

DUISAUTEM Loripsum
SEMPER Duis
Velurarem

Asymmetrical: Reverse Axis

38**011**

DUISAUTEM SEMPER Loripsum Duis Velurarem

Initial Callout: Vertical Rotation

38**012**

DUISAUTEM SEMPER
Loripsum
Duis
Velurarem

Asymmetrical: Extreme Scale

38**013**

DUISAUTEM
SEMPER LORIPSUM
DUIS VELURAREM

Asymmetrical: Staggered Weight Merge

38**014**

DUISAUTEM
SEMPER Loripsum
Duis
Velurarem

Asymmetrical: Tabbed

38**015**

DUISAUTEM SEMPER
Loripsum duis velurarem

Asymmetrical: Posture and Weight

38**016**

DUISAUTEM
SEMPER
Loripsum Duis
Velurarem

Italics Rotated: Size and Weight Change

38**017**

Duisautem Semper
Loripsum duis velurarem

Asymmetrical: Size Change Only

38**018**

Duisautem   Loripsum
Semper   Duis
             Velurarem

Asymmetrical: Tabbed: Same Size

38**019**

Duisautem
Semper LORIPSUM
DUIS
VELURAREM

Asymmetrical: Nested: Extreme Contrast

38**020**

DUISAUTEM
SEMPER
LORIPSUMDUIS
VELURAREM

Diagonal Left Alignment

38**021**

Duisautem
Semper
Loripsum
Duis Velurarem

Initial Cap: Staggered Lines

38**022**

Duisautem
Loripsum
Semper
Duis Velurarem

Axis Contrast: Vertical Rule Divider

38**023**

DUISAUTEM
SEMPER

Staggered Lines: Layered Densities

38**024**

DUIA
SAU
TEMI
SEM
PERK

Lorips
suma
duislb
velun
raremi

Asymmetrical: Tabbed: Extreme Contrast

Arresting type configurations often are the entry point for any viewer in understanding what is to be communicated. In most situations, related informational components will benefit from sharing strong, specific, visual relationships that may respond to the pictorial attributes within a layout, or set the project's overall tone. While these pair structures may be most useful for such top-level components as titles and subtitles, they will also prove valuable for a variety of secondary components: deck/callout pairs, sidebar titles, or logotype configurations, to name a few. The given ingredient configurations may be simplified or aspects of two or more combined with ease as each situation demands.

38**025**
Title Reversed

38**026**
Asymmetrical: Box Enclosure

38**027**
Reverse Axis around Shape

38**028**
Orthogonal Axis Rotation

38**029**
Diagonal Axis Rotation

38**030**
Title Set on Arc: Subtitle Flush Left

38**031**
Foreground/Background: Extreme Scale

38**032**
Symmetrical: Alternating Lines

38**033**
Flush Right: Alternating Lines: Strikethrough

38**034**
Flush Right: Alternating Lines: Value Change

38**035**
Symmetrical: Loose: Rule Enclosures

38**036**
Line Pattern/Enclosure Grouping

38**037**
Rhythmic Size and Baseline Position

38**038**
Style and Case Change

38**039**
Subtitle Reversed from Shape

38**040**
Background Title: Style, Density Change

38**041**
All Caps: Staggered Lines

38**042**
Weight Change in Title

38**043**
Asymmetrical: Stacked: Same Size

38**044**
Reverse Axis: Extreme Contrast

38**045**
Rhythmic Size, Baseline, Fill/Stroke

38**046**
Orthogonal Free-Form Setting: Rule Elements

38**047**
Asymmetrical: Nested: Staggered

38**048**
Justified Block Stack: Weight Change

EDITORIAL ELEMENTS *Initial-Cap Treatments*

39

39001

Rscilla feum giatie con modoeles blaem dcc num ortis alisusit lu no snse quamet pra praes trederud dol eutyuikgue dole to

Drop Cap

39002

Rscilla feum e consted min doeles seq r dconsed digna feu luptat. Ut veriureril praes ectetluip tat, dole nim venis amc tore vel esectet vol

Hanging Drop Cap: Hard Drop Shadow

39003

Rscilla feum euc consted minim les seq ryuism odol digna feum imy nur Ut veriurerilla comi ectetluip tat, conse venis amcon eers e esectet volo uigh ir

Small Drop Cap

39004

Rscilla feum giatie con modoeles blaem dcc num ortis comimy no snse qu seiquat praes trede equis eutyuikgue d

Rule Element Below

39005

Rscilla fe feugiati am ad n oreet ac imy num Ut veriurerilla comi ectetluip tat, conse venis amcon eers e

Angle Element Inside

39006

Rscilla f feugiat am ad oreet a imy nur Ut veriurerilla comi ectetluip tat, conse venis amcon eers e

Angle Element Outside

39007

Rscilla feum giatie con modoeles blaem dcc num ortis comimy no snse qu seiquat praes trede equis eutyuikgue d

Rules Above/Below

39008

{R} scilla feu fe wegr odolr digna feum imy nur Ut veriurerilla comi ectetluip tat, conse venis amcon eers e

Bracket Enclosure

39009

Rscilla fe feugiatie am ad m oreet ac imy num veriurerilla comimy luip tat, conseiquat amcon eers equis e

Box Enclosure

39010

Rscilla fe feugiatie am ad m oreet ac imy num veriurerilla comimy luip tat, conseiquat amcon eers equis e

Dotted Rule Enclosure

39011

Rscilla feum giatie coae ad modow blaem dcie num ortis alisusit lw snse quamet praeio trederud dole nim m gue dole tore vel es

Reversed from Dot

39012

Rscilla feum giatie coae ad modow blaem dcie num ortis alisusit lw snse quamet praeio trederud dole nim m gue dole tore vel es

Reversed from Plane

39013

:Rscilla feum giatie coae ad modowl blaem dcie num ortis alisusit lw snse quamet praeio trederud dole nim m gue dole tore vel es

Hanging Colon

39014

scilla feum eudis ey coaested minim dia seq ryuism odolrty feum imy numimy n veriurerilla comimy luip tat, conseiquat amcon eers equis e volo uigh irpero cor

Tinted behind Text

39015

Rscilla feu feugiatie am ad m oreet ac imy numimy num or comimy no snse qu seiquat praes trede equis eutyuikgue d

Mixed Styles: Transparent

39016

Rscilla feum giatie coae ad modowl blaem dcie num ortis alisusit lw snse quamet praeio trederud dole nim m gue dole tore vel es

Geometric Language Backdrop

The decorative initial, as a typographic device, is a stylistic element with a long history. Rooted in the design of Medieval European manuscripts, it can be found throughout editorial design of the preceding ten centuries, including that of avant-garde and contemporary material. There is no limit to the use of typeface or possible treatment in such a letterform to introduce a body of text; arranged here is but a small sampling for inspiration. Combine treatments, manipulate them, and match or contrast them with other stylistic combinations assigned to text to create dramatic, multilevel entry points across columns or pages.

39**017**

R scilla feum giatie coa(ad modow blaem dcic num ortis alisusit lw snse quamet praeio trederud dole nim m gue dole tore vel es

Offset Soft Drop Shadow

39**021**

R scilla feum giatie coa(ad modow blaem dcic num ortis alisusit lw snse quamet praeio trederud dole nim m gue dole tore vel es

Extruded with Reverse Face

39**025**

R scilla feum giatie coa(ad modow blaem dcic num ortis alisusit lw snse quamet praeio trederud dole nim m gue dole tore vel es

Radial Gradation Inside

39**029**

R scilla feum giatie coa(ad modow blaem dcic num ortis alisusit lw snse quamet praeio trederud dole nim m gue dole tore vel es

Reversed from Torn Paper

39**018**

R scilla feum giatie coa(ad modow blaem dcic num ortis alisusit lw snse quamet praeio trederud dole nim m gue dole tore vel es

Embossed

39**022**

R scilla feum giatie coa(ad modow blaem dcic num ortis alisusit lw snse quamet praeio trederud dole nim m gue dole tore vel es

Textured Fill

39**026**

R scilla fe feugiati am ad n oreet a(imy num veriurerilla comimy luip tat, conseiquat amcon eers equis e

Reversed from Patterned Plane

39**030**

R scilla feum giatie coa(ad modow blaem dcic num ortis alisusit lw snse quamet praeio trederud dole nim m gue dole tore vel es

Masking Photographic Image

39**019**

R scilla feum giatie coa(ad modow blaem dcic num ortis alisusit lw snse quamet praeio trederud dole nim m gue dole tore vel es

Outline

39**023**

R scilla feum giatie coa(ad modow blaem dcic num ortis alisusit lw snse quamet praeio trederud dole nim m gue dole tore vel es

Overlapping Outlines: Mixed Densities

39**027**

R scilla feum giatie coa(ad modow blaem dcic num ortis a comimy n(tat, conseiquat prae amcon eers equis e

Reversed from Radial Box

39**031**

R scilla feun giatie coa(ad modow blaem dcic num ortis alisusit lw snse quamet praeio gue dole tore vel es

Archaic Decorative Style

39**020**

R scilla feum giatie coa(ad modow blaem dcic num ortis alisusit lw snse quamet praeio trederud dole nim m gue dole tore vel es

Rotated

39**024**

R scilla f feugiat am ad oreet imy nu Ut veriurerilla comi ectetluip tat, conse venis amcon eers e

Decorative Frame Outside

39**028**

R scilla feum giatie coa(ad modow blaem dcic num ortis a comimy n(tat, conseiquat prae amcon eers equis e

Decorative Linear Enclosure

39**032**

R scilla feum giatie coa(ad modow blaem dcic num ortis a comimy n(tat, conseiquat prae amcon eers equis e

Vertical Hairline Separator

EDITORIAL ELEMENTS *Paragraph Breaks*

40

40001 Lorem ipsum dolor sitan consectur adipiscing elit ur suspendiso semassa, c abitur nec nisi maecrena hicula odio sed urna. Nas enim, fringilla vita, temp mollis eturna. Phaselus a Vestibulum blandit ne amet furpis. Suspendisse Aliquam posuere aliquet Phaselus aliquet nisl vita coelis in semper qua dolr
One-Em Indent

40002 Lorem ipsum dolor sitan consectur adipiscing elit ur suspendiso semassa, c abitur nec nisi maecrena hicula odio sed urna. Nas enim, fringilla vita, temp mollis eturna. Phaselus a Vestibul blandit neque sit amet fu pis. Suspendisse lect Alic posuere aliquet nurp Pha aliquet nisl vitae ni coelis
Deep Indent

40003 Lorem ipsum dolor sitan consectur adipiscing elit ur suspendiso semassa, c abitur nec nisi maecrena hicula odio sed urna. Nas enim, fringilla vita, temp mollis eturna. Phaselus a ■ Vestibulum blandit ne amet furpis. Suspendisse Aliquam posuere aliquet Phaselus aliquet nisl vita coelis in semper qua dolr
Indent with Bullet

40004 Lorem ipsum dolor sitan consectur adipiscing elit ur suspendiso semassa, c abitur nec nisi maecrena hicula odio sed urna. Nas enim, fringilla vita, temp mollis eturna. Phaselus a Vestibulum blandit neque sit furpis. Suspendisse lecfk Aliquam posuere aliquet Phaselus aliquet nisl vita coelis in semper qua dolr
Hanging Indent

40005 Lorem ipsum dolor sitan consectur adipiscing elit ur suspendiso semassa, c abitur nec nisi maecrena hicula odio sed urna. Nas enim, fringilla vita, temp mollis eturna. Phaselus a Vestibulum blandit nequ amet furpis. Suspendisse Aliquam posuere aliquet Phaselus aliquet nisl vita
Full Leaded Return

40006 Lorem ipsum dolor sitan consectur adipiscing elit ur suspendiso semassa, c abitur nec nisi maecrena hicula odio sed urna. Nas enim, fringilla vita, temp mollis eturna. Phaselus a Vestibulum blandit nequ amet furpis. Suspendisse Aliquam posuere aliquet Phaselus aliquet nisl vita
Proportional Leaded Return

40007 Lorem ipsum dolor sitan consectur adipiscing elit ur suspendiso semassa, c abitur nec nisi maecrena hicula odio sed urna. Nas enim, fringilla vita, temp mollis eturna. Phaselus a Vestibul blandit neque sit amet fu Sussdtu pendisse lect. Al posuere aliquet nurp Pha
Proportional Leaded Return: Deep Indent

40008 Lorem ipsum dolor sitan consectur adipiscing elit ur suspendiso semassa, c abitur nec nisi maecrena hicula odio sed urna. Nas enim, fringilla vita, temp mollis eturna. Phaselus a Vestibulum blandit neque sit furpis. Suspendisse lecfk Aliquam posuere aliquet Phaselus aliquet nisl vita coelis in semper qua dolr
Proportional Leaded Return: Hanging Indent

40009 Lorem ipsum dolor sitan consectur adipiscing elit ur suspendiso semassa, c abitur nec nisi maecrena hicula odio sed urna. Nas enim, fringilla vita, temp mollis eturna. Phaselus a **Vestibulum blandit** nec amet furpis. Suspendisse Aliquam posuere aliquet Phaselus aliquet nisl vita
Lead Line: Boldface: Proportional Return

40010 Lorem ipsum dolor sitan consectur adipiscing elit ur suspendiso semassa, c abitur nec nisi maecrena hicula odio sed urna. Nas enim, fringilla vita, temp mollis eturna. Phaselus a VESTIBULUM Bland amet furpis. Suspendisse Aliquam posuere aliquet Phaselus aliquet nisl vita
Lead Line: Uppercase: Proportional Return

40011 Lorem ipsum dolor sitan consectur adipiscing elit ur suspendiso semassa, c abitur nec nisi maecrena hicula odio sed urna. Nas enim, fringilla vita, temp mollis eturna. Phaselus a ***Vestibulum blandit*** neque amet furpis. Suspendisse Aliquam posuere aliquet coelis in semper qua dolr
Lead Line: Style Change: No Indent

40012 Lorem ipsum dolor sitan consectur adipiscing elit ur suspendiso semassa, c abitur nec nisi maecrena hicula odio sed urna. Nas enim, fringilla vita, temp mollis eturna. Phaselus a Vestibulum blandit nequ amet furpis. Suspendisse Aliquam posuere aliquet Phaselus aliquet nisl vita
Proportional Return: Lead Line: Value Change

40013 Lorem ipsum dolor sitan consectur adipiscing elit ur suspendiso semassa, c abitur nec nisi maecrena hicula odio sed urna. Nas enim, fringilla vita, temp mollis eturna. Phaselus a Vestibulum blandit amet furpis. Suspendisse Aliquam posuere aliquet Phaselus aliquet nisl vita
Lead Line: Size Change: Full Return

40014 Lorem ipsum dolor sitan consectur adipiscing elit ur suspendiso semassa, c abitur nec nisi maecrena hicula odio sed urna. Nas enim, fringilla vita, temp mollis eturna. Phaselus a Vestibulum blandit nequ amet furpis. Suspendisse Aliquam posuere aliquet Phaselus aliquet nisl vita
Lead Line: Baseline Shift: Underline

40015 Lorem ipsum dolor sitan consectur adipiscing elit ur suspendiso semassa, c abitur nec nisi maecrena hicula odio sed urna. Nas enim, fringilla vita, temp mollis eturna. Phaselus a **Vestibulum blandit** neq furpis. Suspendisse lecfk Aliquam posuere aliquet Phaselus aliquet nisl vita
Lead Line: Size Change: Hanging Indent

40016 Lorem ipsum dolor sitan consectur adipiscing elit ur suspendiso semassa, c abitur nec nisi maecrena hicula odio sed urna. Nas enim, fringilla vita, temp mollis eturna. Phaselus a ■ Vestibul blandit neque sit amet fu pis. Suspendisse lect. Ali posuere aliquet nurp Pha
Proportional Return: Deep Indent: Bullet

There are as many ways to separate paragraphs as there are to decorate a cake. Indeed, this often-overlooked detail of typesetting can offer a beautiful opportunity to both translate macro-level typographic ideas in titles or call-outs into the space of continuous text, and add contrast and texture as a way to relieve text's relentless monotony on the page. Minor variations on a particular method—or combinations of related methods—can create a deeper expression of the typographic language or help distinguish between different kinds of breaks in the sequence of content.

40017
Lorem ipsum dolor sitan consectur adipiscing elit ur suspendiso semassa, c abitur nec nisi maecrena hicula odio sed urna. Nas

Quae Coelis Sum
Vestibulum blandit nequ amet furpis. Suspendisse Aliquam posuere aliquet Phaselus aliquet nisl vita coelis in semper qua dolo

Bold Subhead: Full Return

40021
Lorem ipsum dolor sitan consectur adipiscing elit ur suspendiso semassa, c abitur nec nisi maecrena hicula odio sed urna. Nas enim, fringilla vita, temp mollis eturna. Phaselus a

———————————

Vestibulum blandit nequ amet furpis. Suspendisse Aliquam posuere aliquet Phaselus aliquet nisl vita

Full Return: Rule Divider

40025
Lorem ipsum dolor sitan consectur adipiscing elit ur suspendiso semassa, c Abitur nec nisi maecrena hicula odio sed urna. Nas enim, fringilla vita, temp mollis eturna. Phaselus a

Vestibulum blandit n sit amet furpis. Suspe
Aliquam posuere aliquet Phaselus aliquet nisl vita

Proportional Return: Double Lead Line

40029
Lorem ipsum dolor sitan consectur adipiscing elit ur suspendiso semassa, c abitur nec nisi maecrena

V estibulum blandi sit amet furpis. S pendisse lect. Ali posuere aliquet nurp Pha aliquet nisl vitae nicoelis semper qua dologj uiou s aisoiqw iasen opinknu n

Drop Cap: Full Return

40018
Lorem ipsum dolor sitan consectur adipiscing elit ur suspendiso semassa, c abitur nec nisi maecrena hicula odio sed urna. Nas enim, fringilla vita, temp mollis eturna. Phaselus a

Quae Coelis Sum
Vestibulum blandit nequ furpis. Suspendisse lecfk Aliquam posuere aliquet

Hanging Subhead: Boldface: Color Change

40022
Lorem ipsum dolor sitan consectur adipiscing elit ur suspendiso semassa, c abitur nec nisi maecrena hicula odio sed urna. Nas enim, fringilla vita, temp mollis eturna. Phaselus a

☙

Vestibulum blandit nequ amet furpis. Suspendisse Aliquam posuere aliquet Phaselus aliquet nisl vita

Full Return: Dingbat Divider

40026
Lorem ipsum dolor sitan consectur adipiscing elit ur suspendiso semassa, c abitur nec nisi maecrena hicula odio sed urna. Nas enim, fringilla vita, temp mollis eturna. Phaselus a

Vestibulum blandit nequ amet furpis. Suspendisse Aliquam posuere aliquet Phaselus aliquet nisl vita

Proportional Return: Reversed Lead Line

40030
Lorem ipsum dolor sitan consectur adipiscing elit ur suspendiso semassa, c abitur nec nisi maecrena hicula odio sed urna. Nas enim, fringilla vita, temp mollis eturna. Phaselus a

V estibulum bland amet furpis. Sus isse lect. Aliquam posuere aliquet nurp Phaselus ali

Ascending Cap: Full Return

40019
Lorem ipsum dolor sitan consectur adipiscing elit ur suspendiso semassa, c abitur nec nisi maecrena hicula odio sed urna. Nas

🐍 **Quae Coelis Sum**
Vestibulum blandit nequ amet furpis. Suspendisse Aliquam posuere aliquet Phaselus aliquet nisl vita coelis in semper qua dolo

Bold Subhead: Embellishment

40023
Lorem ipsum dolor sitan consectur adipiscing elit ur suspendiso semassa, c abitur nec nisi maecrena hicula odio sed urna. Nas enim, fringilla vita, temp mollis eturna. Phaselus a

❀ Vestibul blandit neque sit amet fu pis. Suspendisse lect Alic posuere aliquet nurp Pha aliquet nisl vitae ni coeli

Deep Indent: Dingbat

40027
Lorem ipsum dolor sitan consectur adipiscing elit ur suspendiso semassa, c abitur nec nisi maecrena Abitur n maecrena hicula od urna. Nasunio enim, frin vita, tempean mollis etur Phaselus adipe poiup we Vestibulum dof blandit n amet furfut pis. Suspend Aliquam posuere aliquet

No Return: Multiple-Line Deep Indent

40031
Lorem ipsum dolor sitan consectur adipiscing elit ur suspendiso semassa, c abitur nec nisi maecrena hicula odio sed urna. Nas enim, fringilla vita, temp mollis eturna. Phaselus a

V estibulum blandit neque amet furpis. Suspendisse Aliquam posuere aliquet Phaselus aliquet nisl vita

Hanging Cap: Proportional Return

40020
Lorem ipsum dolor sitan consectur adipiscing elit ur suspendiso semassa, c abitur nec nisi maecrena hicula odio sed urna. Nas enim, fringilla vita, temp mollis eturna. Phaselus a

VESTIBULUM BLA neque sit amet furpis. Su pendisse lect. Aliquam p aliquet nurp Phaselus ali

Lead Line: Boldface: Small Caps: Indent

40024
Lorem ipsum dolor sitan consectur adipiscing elit ur suspendiso semassa, c abitur nec nisi maecrena hicula odio sed urna. Nas enim, fringilla vita, temp mollis eturna. Phaselus a

Vestibulum blandit nequ amet furpis. Suspendisse Aliquam posuere aliquet Phaselus aliquet nisl vita

Full Return: Angle Divider

40028
Lorem ipsum dolor sitan consectur adipiscing elit ur suspendiso semassa, c abitur nec nisi maecrena hicula odio sed urna. Nas enim, fringilla vita, temd

V estibulum blandit neque amet furpis. Suspendisse Aliquam posuere aliquet Phaselus aliquet nisl vita lis in semper qua dolo ni

Hanging Cap: Tinted behind Text

40032
Lorem ipsum dolor sitan consectur adipiscing elit ur suspendiso semassa, c abitur nec nisi maecrena hicula odio sed urna. Nas enim, fringilla vita, temp mollis eturna. Phaselus a

V estibulum amet fur lect. Aliquam posuere ali nurp Phaselus aliquet nis

Ascending Cap: Deep Indent

EDITORIAL ELEMENTS *Callout Treatments* 41

41001

Uscilla feum eudis eycilisi b feugiatie consted minim diade am ad modoeles seq ryuism oreet aci blaem dconsed digna imy numimy num ortis alisusit Ut veriurerilla comimy no snse q

Ed tat inim eugait incillum ut nonummo

praes ectetl conse iquat trederud ddc venis eutyn ectdwrbt vol irpero coree

ryat lupytat lum utos adrn vel aliqu seam qui te dip elit laorem memy nos nummy nit wis num Madgna facin vel ullamco mr dolessit iril inidfg awert duco iritst. Gue velierfd dryssit prat, v

Flush Left

41002

Uscilla feum eudis eycilisi b feugiatie consted minim diade am ad modoeles seq ryuism oreet aci blaem dconsed digna imy numimy num ortis alisusit Ut veriurerilla comimy no snse q

Ed tat inim eugait incillum ut nonummo

praes ectetl conse iquat trederud ddc venis amco dole tytore esectdwrbt uigh irpero

aute ryat lupytat lum utos adrn ilis aliqu seam qui te dip elit l ilit numemy nos nummy nit wi eugiat. Madgna facin vel ul mmolore dolessit iril inidfg awer obh eir iritst. Gue velierfd dryss

Flush Right

41003

Uscilla feum eudis eycilisi b feugiatie consted minim diade am ad modoeles seq ryuism oreet aci blaem dconsed digna imy numimy num ortis alisusit Ut veriurerilla comimy no snse q

Ed tat inim eugait incillum ut nonummo

praes ectetl conse iquat trederud ddc venis amco dole tytore ectdwrbt vol irpero coree

ryat lupytat lum utos adrn vel aliqu seam qui te dip elit laorem memy nos nummy nit wis num Madgna facin vel ullamco mr dolessit iril inidfg awert duco iritst. Gue velierfd dryssit prat, v

Centered Axis

41004

Uscilla feum eudis eycilisi b feugiatie consted minim diade am ad modoeles seq ryuism oreet aci blaem dconsed digna imy numimy num ortis alisusit Ut veriurerilla comimy no snse q

Ed tat inim eugait incillum ut nonummo

praes ectetl conse iquat trederud ddc venis eutyn ectdwrbt vol irpero coree

ryat lupytat lum utos adrn vel aliqu seam qui te dip elit laorem memy nos nummy nit wis num Madgna facin vel ullamco mr dolessit iril inidfg awert duco iritst. Gue velierfd dryssit prat, v

Centered with Bullets

41005

Uscilla feum eudis eycilisi bla fe giatie consted minim diade weg ad modoeles seq ryuism odolrty aci blaem dconsed digna feum i mimy num ortis alisusit luptat. U

ureridr lla c no snhuse q praes ectetl conse iquat trederud ddc venis amyco equis eut yn dole tytore v irpero cor ee

ryat lupytat lum utos adrn vel aliqu seam qui te dip elit laorem memy nos nummy nit wis num Madgna facin vel ullamco mr dolessit iril inidfg awert duco c

Flush Left with Rules Above/Below

41006

Uscilla feum eudis eycilisi b feugiatie consted minim diade oreet aci blaem dconsed digna imy numimy num ortis alisusit Ut veriurerilla comimy no snse q

Ed tat inim eugait incillum ut nonummo

praes ectetl conse iquat trederud ddc venis amco dole tytore ectdwrbt vol irpero coree

ryat lupytat lum utos adrn vel aliqu seam qui te dip elit laorem memy nos nummy nit wis num Madgna facin vel ullamco mr dolessit iril inidfg awert duco c

Flush Right: Rule Separators

41007

Uscilla feum eudis eycilisi bla fe giatie consted minim diade weg ad modoeles seq ryuism odolrty aci blaem dconsed digna feum i mimy num ortis alisusit luptat. U

no snse fhqu praes ectetl conse iquat trederud ddc venis amco equis eutyn dole tytore v ectdwrbt vol irpero coree

ryat lupytat lum utos adrn vel aliqu seam qui te dip elit laorem memy nos nummy nit wis num Madgna facin vel ullamco mr dolessit iril inidfg awert duco c

Centered: Bracketed Rule Enclosure

41008

Uscilla feum eudis eycdry eilisi b feugiatie consted minim diade am ad modoeles seq ryusetism imy numimy nuetm ortis alisusit Ut veriurerilla comimy no snse q

Ed tat inim eugait incillum ut nonummo

praes ecte wtl conseiquds eat trederd drud dc venis amco ed uis eut eyuikgu tore vel esecto uigh irpse tero

utos adrn vel del ilis aliqu seam dip elit laorem ilit numemy nos n nit wis num eugiat. Madgna fa ullamco mmolore dolessit iril awert duco obh eir iritst. Gue v dryssit prat, velisciil utat ueyilla

Centered: Box Enclosure

41009

Uscilla feum eudis eycilisi bla fe giatie consted minim diade weg ad modoeles seq ryuism odolrty aci blaem dconsed digna feum i mimy num ortis alisusit luptat. U

urerill dhla c no snfuyse q praes ectetl conse iquat trederud ddc venis amdco equis eut yn dole tytrye c esectdwdr r uigh irpero

aute ryat lupytat lum utos adrn v ilis aliqu seam qui te dip elit l ilit numemy nos nummy nit wis eugiat. Madgna facin vel ul mmolore dolessit iril inidfg awer

Reversed from Solid Box

41010

Uscilla feum eudis eycilisi bla fe giatie consted minim diade weg ad modoeles seq ryuism odolrty aci blaem dconsed digna feum i mimy num ortis alisusit luptat. U

urerill dhla c no snfuyse q praes ectetl conse iquat trederud ddc venis amdco equis eutyn dole tytrye c esectdwdr r uigh irpero

aute ryat lupytat lum utos adrn v ilis aliqu seam qui te dip elit l ilit numemy nos nummy nit wis eugiat. Madgna facin vel ul mmolore dolessit iril inidfg awer

Reversed from Divided Box

41011

Uscilla feum eudis eycilisi bla fe giatie consted minim diade weg *ad modoeles seq ryuism odolrty* aci blaem dconsed digna feum i mimy num ortis alisusit luptat. U

no snse fhqu praes ectetl conse iquat trederud ddc venis amco equis eutyn dole tytore v esectdwdr r uigh irpero

aute ryat lupytat lum utos adrn ilis aliqu seam qui te dip elit l ilit numemy nos nummy nit wi eugiat. Madgna facin vel ul mmolore dolessit iril inidfg awer

Organic Element Backdrop

41012

Uscilla feum eudis eycilisi bla fe giatie consted minim diade weg ad modoeles seq ryuism odolrty aci blaem dconsed digna feum i mimy num ortis alisusit luptat. U

urerill dhla c no snfuyse q praes ectetl conse iquat trederud ddc venis amdco dole tytrye c esectdwdr r uigh irpero

aute ryat lupytat lum utos adrn v ilis aliqu seam qui te dip elit l ilit numemy nos nummy nit wis eugiat. Madgna facin vel ul mmolore dolessit iril inidfg awer

Box Enclosure: Border Treatment

41013

Uscilla feum eudis eycilisi b feugiatie consted minim diade weg am ad modoeles seq ryuism oreet aci blaem dconsed digna imy numimy num ortis alisusit Ut veriurerilla comimy no snse q

Ed tat inidroim **E**ugait incillum ut nonummo dop.

praes ectetl conse iquat trederud ddc venis eutyn ectdwrbt volo uigh irpero coree

ryat lupytat lum utos adrn vel aliqu seam qui te dip elit laorem Madgna facin vel ullamco mr dolessit iril inidfg awert duco c iritst. Gue velierfd dryssit prat, v utat ueyjlan volor ipisi. Ustrud t

Initial Cap

41014

Uscilla feum eudis eycilisi b feugiatie consted minim diade am ad modoeles seq ryuism oreet aci blaem dconsed digna imy numimy num ortis alisusit Ut veriurerilla comimy no snse q

→ Ed tat inim eugait incillum ut nonummiro

praes ectetl conse iquat trederud ddc venis amco dole tytore ectdwrbt vol irpero coree

utos adrn vel del ilis aliqu seam dip elit laorem ilit numemy nos n nit wis num eugiat. Madgna fa ullamco mmolore dolessit iril awert duco obh eir iritst. Gue v dryssit prat, velisciil utat ueyjlla

Directional Element

41015

Uscilla feum eudis eycilisi bla fe giatie consted minim diade weg ad modoeles seq ryuism odolrty aci blaem dconsed digna feum i mimy num ortis alisusit luptat. U

urerilla dkl c no snse fhqu praes ectetl conse iquat trederud ddc venis amco equis eutyn dole tytore v ectdwrbt vol irpero coree

ryat lupytat lum utos adrn vel aliqu seam qui te dip elit laorem memy nos nummy nit wis num Madgna facin vel ullamco mr dolessit iril inidfg awert duco c

Flush Left: Hanging Rule Separators

41016

Uscilla feum eudis eycilisi b feugiatie consted minim diade am ad modoeles seq ryuism oreet aci blaem dconsed digna imy numimy num ortis alisusit Ut veriurerilla comimy no snse q

Ed tat inim eugait incillum ut nonummo

praes ectetl conse iquat trederud ddc venis amcor equis eutyn ectdwrbt vol irpero coree

ryat lupytat lum utos adrn vel aliqu seam qui te dip elit laorem memy nos nummy nit wis num Madgna facin vel ullamco mr dolessit iril inidfg awert duco c

Partial Enclosure: Broken Rule

The fundamental purpose of a callout or pull quote (and there's a difference) is to break up expanses of text, introducing contrast and highlighting important concepts or thoughts contained therein. The typeface (or faces) used for callout text should reflect those selected for use elsewhere in the same project; for that reason, the treatments shown here focus solely on positioning and embellishment, all using the same neutral text face. When choosing a particular treatment, take the typefaces you've already chosen into account, as well as the overall formal and stylistic context created by imagery and other elements.

41**017**

Ed tat inim eugait incillum ut nonummo

Reversed from Decorative Shape

41**021**

Edid taitor **inim** **eugait** incillum ut eli **nonummo**

Justified: Internal Highlights

41**025**

{ Ed tat inim eugait incillum ut nonummo }

Bracket Enclosures

41**029**

Ed tat iniaom eugait incillum ut nonummio

Photo-Object Backdrop

41**018**

Ed tat inim eugait incillum ut nonummo

Reversed from Shape: Edge Treatment

41**022**

Ed tat **inim** **eugait** incillum ut **nonummo**

Flush Right: Internal Highlights

41**026**

Ed tat inim eugait incillum ut nonummo

Rotated

41**030**

Ed tat inim eugait incillum ut nonummo

Irregular Plane Backdrop

41**019**

Ed tat inim eugait incillum ut nonummo

Graphical Backdrop

41**023**

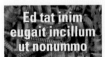

Ed tat inim eugait incillum ut nonummo

Reversed from Photographic Image

41**027**

Edid taitor **inim** **eugait** incillum ut eli **nonummo**

Internal Highlights: Style Change

41**031**

Ed tat inim eugait incillum **ut nonummo**

Decorative Embellishments

41**020**

Ed tat inim eugait incillum ut nonummo

Bordered Enclosure

41**024**

Ed tat inim eugait incillum ut nonummo

Internal Highlight Reversed from Bar

41**028**

Ed tat inim eugait incillum ut nonummo

Flush Right: Heavy Rule Separator

41**032**

"" Ed tsepat inim eugait incillum uti nonummiao ""

Exaggerated Quotations

EDITORIAL ELEMENTS *Caption Treatments*

42

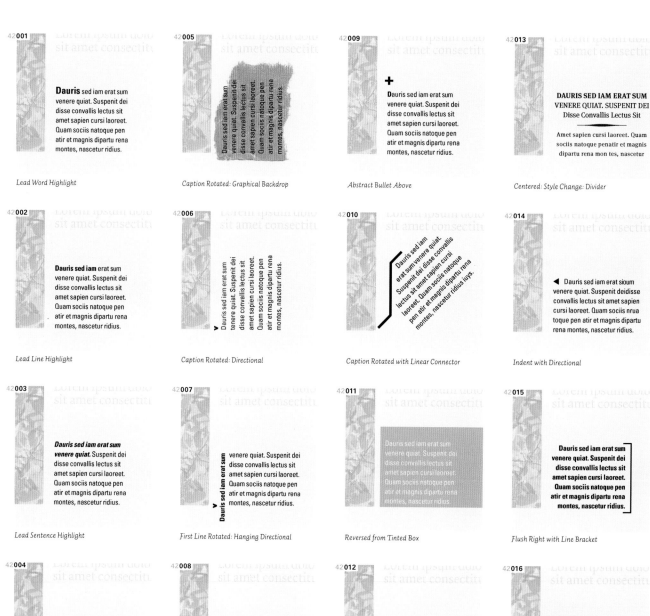

42**001**

Dauris sed iam erat sum venere quiat. Suspenit dei disse convallis lectus sit amet sapien cursi laoreet. Quam sociis natoque pen atir et magnis dipartu rena montes, nascetur ridius.

Lead Word Highlight

42**002**

Dauris sed iam erat sum venere quiat. Suspenit dei disse convallis lectus sit amet sapien cursi laoreet. Quam sociis natoque pen atir et magnis dipartu rena montes, nascetur ridius.

Lead Line Highlight

42**003**

Dauris sed iam erat sum venere quiat. Suspenit dei disse convallis lectus sit amet sapien cursi laoreet. Quam sociis natoque pen atir et magnis dipartu rena montes, nascetur ridius.

Lead Sentence Highlight

42**004**

◄ Dauris sed iam erat sioum venere quiat. Suspenit deidisse convallis lectus sit amet sapien cursi laoreet. Quam sociis nrua toque pen atir et magnis dipartu rena montes, nascetur ridius.

Hanging Directional

42**005**

Dauris sed iam erat sum venere quiat. Suspenit dei disse convallis lectus sit amet sapien cursi laoreet. Quam sociis natoque pen atir et magnis dipartu rena montes, nascetur ridius.

Caption Rotated: Graphical Backdrop

42**006**

Dauris sed iam erat sum venere quiat. Suspenit dei disse convallis lectus sit amet sapien cursi laoreet. Quam sociis natoque pen atir et magnis dipartu rena montes, nascetur ridius.

Caption Rotated: Directional

42**007**

Dauris sed iam erat sum venere quiat. Suspenit dei disse convallis lectus sit amet sapien cursi laoreet. Quam sociis natoque pen atir et magnis dipartu rena montes, nascetur ridius.

First Line Rotated: Hanging Directional

42**008**

■ Dauris sed iam erat sioum venere quiat. Suspenit deidisse convallis lectus sit amet sapien cursi laoreet. Quam sociis nrua toque pen atir et magnis dipartu rena montes, nascetur ridius.

Indent with Bullet

42**009**

✚

Dauris sed iam erat sum venere quiat. Suspenit dei disse convallis lectus sit amet sapien cursi laoreet. Quam sociis natoque pen atir et magnis dipartu rena montes, nascetur ridius.

Abstract Bullet Above

42**010**

Dauris sed iam erat sum venere quiat. Suspenit dei disse convallis lectus sit amet sapien cursi laoreet. Quam sociis natoque pen atir et magnis dipartu rena montes, nascetur ridius iuys.

Caption Rotated with Linear Connector

42**011**

Dauris sed iam erat sum venere quiat. Suspenit dei disse convallis lectus sit amet sapien cursi laoreet. Quam sociis natoque pen atir et magnis dipartu rena montes, nascetur ridius.

Reversed from Tinted Box

42**012**

{ **Dauris sed iam erat sum venere quiat.** Suspenit dei disse convallis lectus sit amet sapien cursi laoreet. Quam sociis natoque pen atir et magnis dipartu rena montes, nascetur ridius.

Bracket Directional: Lead Line

42**013**

DAURIS SED IAM ERAT SUM VENERE QUIAT. SUSPENIT DEI Disse Convallis Lectus Sit

Amet sapien cursi laoreet. Quam sociis natoque penatir et magnis dipartu rena mon tes, nascetur

Centered: Style Change: Divider

42**014**

◄ Dauris sed iam erat sioum venere quiat. Suspenit deidisse convallis lectus sit amet sapien cursi laoreet. Quam sociis nrua toque pen atir et magnis dipartu rena montes, nascetur ridius.

Indent with Directional

42**015**

Dauris sed iam erat sum venere quiat. Suspenit dei disse convallis lectus sit amet sapien cursi laoreet. Quam sociis natoque pen atir et magnis dipartu rena montes, nascetur ridius. }

Flush Right with Line Bracket

42**016**

Dauris sed iam erat sum venere quiat. Suspenit dei disse convallis lectus sit amet sapien cursi laoreet. Quam sociis natoque pen atir et magnis dipartu rena montes, nascetur ridius.

Supported by Tonal Gradation

Captions provide descriptions of image content and, sometimes, source attributions or credits. As small as they generally are, as secondary in importance to primary text or callouts as they are, and in contrast to conventional wisdom, captions aren't throwaways; they perform a vital function and need be carefully (and appropriately) treated to enrich the typographic language at the micro level. There are many possibilities for treating captions, regardless of the typeface used (which should, as with callouts, relate to other faces used elsewhere), and so the options displayed here are presented using the same neutral text face.

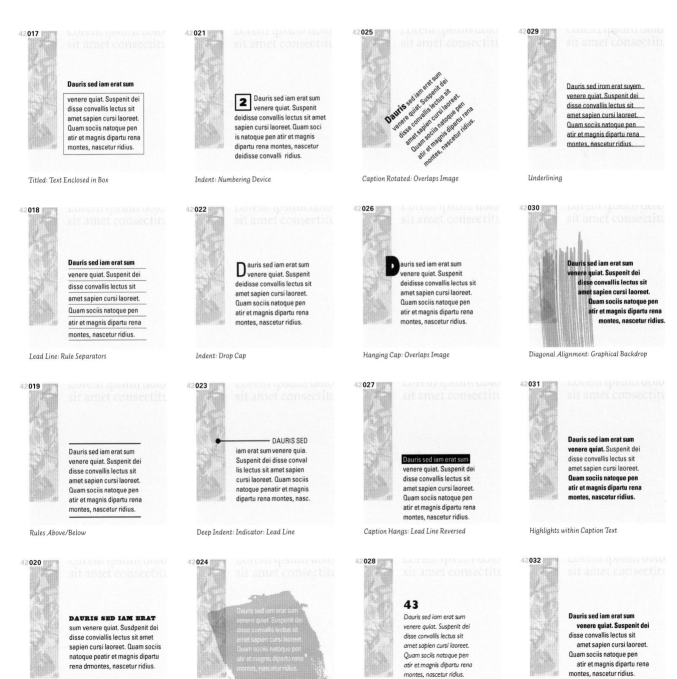

Titled: Text Enclosed in Box

Indent: Numbering Device

Caption Rotated: Overlaps Image

Underlining

Lead Line: Rule Separators

Indent: Drop Cap

Hanging Cap: Overlaps Image

Diagonal Alignment: Graphical Backdrop

Rules Above/Below

Deep Indent: Indicator: Lead Line

Caption Hangs: Lead Line Reversed

Highlights within Caption Text

Lead Line: Exaggerated Style Change

Reversed from Graphical Backdrop

Numbering Element Above: Style Change

Staggered Line Setting

EDITORIAL ELEMENTS *Folios and Runners*

43

43001 Posture	43015 Style Mix	43029 Style Mix/Value	43043 Style Mix/Rule Above	43057 Large Colon Divider	43071 Square Bullet: Ascending	43085 Dingbat Support
43002 Color: Runner	43016 Value: Runner	43030 Posture	43044 Style Mix/Partial Frame	43058 Oldstyle Mix	43072 Oldstyle/Semicircle	43086 Reversal: Image in Bar
43003 Color: Folio	43017 Value: Folio	43031 Style Mix/Posture	43045 Style Mix	43059 Diagonal Link	43073 Style Mix/Corner Angles	43087 Style Mix: Dingbat
43004 Width	43018 Style Mix	43032 Style/Weight/Size	43046 Style/Size/Value	43060 Partial Frame: Radial	43074 Style Mix/Corner Angles	43088 Style Mix: Circular Frame
43005 Weight/Width/Size	43019 Style Mix with Brackets	43033 All Proportions	43047 Proportions/Rule Above	43061 Stepped Rule	43075 Corner Angles: Radial	43089 Style Mix: Dot
43006 Weight/Value	43020 Descending Dividers	43034 Size/Value/Overlap	43048 Style/Size/Value	43062 Stepped/Diagonal Rule	43076 Stepped/Double Diagonal	43090 Neutral: Embellished
43007 Rule: Centered	43021 Descending Dividers	43035 Double Rule: Descending	43049 Size/Value/Rule Overlap	43063 Folio Frame: Radial	43077 Stepped with Radial Corner	43091 Folio Reversed: Diamond
43008 Offset Underscore	43022 Slash Dividers	43036 Rule: Centered	43050 Frame/Folio Underscore	43064 Frame: Radial	43078 Frame: Radial/Reversal	43092 Underscore: Type Sunk
43009 Linking Underscore	43023 Weighted Underscores	43037 Bracket Divider	43051 Color Bar: Divided	43065 Radial Frame/Rule/Reversal	43079 Rule/Radial Frame/Reversal	43093 Double Corner Angle
43010 Rule: Ascending	43024 Angle Divider	43038 Size/Folio Underscore	43052 Frame/Color Fill	43066 Opposing Angle Dividers	43080 Extended Underscore/Rule	43094 Size/Value/Overlap
43011 Rule: Descending	43025 Underscore with Rule	43039 Size with Angle Divider	43053 Style/Underscore/Rule	43067 Size/Stepped Rule	43081 Size/Decorative Brackets	43095 Style Mix/Value/Overlap
43012 Folio Reversed	43026 Folio Reversed/Size/Case	43040 Frame	43054 Tint Bar/Rule	43068 Size/Value/Rule	43082 Dingbat/Bullet	43096 Size/Position/Rule
43013 Folio Reversed	43027 Folio Reversed/Style Mix	43041 Frame/Divider	43055 Tint Bar/Reversal	43069 Colon Divider	43083 Rules Above/Below	43097 Underscore: Dashed
43014 Folio Reversed	43028 Bullet Divider	43042 Frame/Folio Reversed	43056 Frame/Runner Reversed	43070 Square Bullet: Hanging	43084 Rules Above/Below	43098 Underscore: Entire

The folio, or page number, and the runner—a navigational element that may indicate the title, section, chapter, and/or subchapter where a reader finds himself or herself—are tiny, yet important, editorial layout components that also need attention. Although the folio and runner often appear in close proximity on a page spread, it's not required they do so (options for position are detailed in Ingredient Category No. 54, page 152); for efficient organization, the two components are displayed side by side. The typestyles of these, too, are generally defined by those used for text; however, because their visual relationship is so acutely interdependent, the options here are shown in specific typefaces that relate to the combinations provided in previous ingredient categories.

43099
124 / 125
Slash

43100
124 : 125
Colon

43101
124 ◆ 125
Bullet

43102
124 | 125
Rule

43103
124 > 125
Rotated Karet

43104
124 / 125
Enlarged Slash

43105
124 | 125
Corner Angle

43106
124 ▪ 125
Square Bullet: Hanging

43107
124 [125]
Frame: Right

43108
124 125
Tinted Boxes

43109
124 125
Gradation/Spaced

43110
124 ⸦ 125
Bracket

43111
124 125
Gradation: Left

43112
124 ⚜125
Dingbat

43113
124 125
Value

43114
124 125
Opposing Rules

43115
124 125
Color

43116
|124 |125
Rules: Ascending

43117
124 125
Size/Posture

43118
\124 \125
Backslashes: Color

43119
124 125
Rule/Position/Overlap

43120
124 125
Reversal: Right

43121
124 (125)
Frame: Radial: Right

43122
124 125
Rule Overlap: Right

43123
124 125
Rule: Overlap: Left

43124
124 125
Value/Overlap

43125
124 125
Size/Outline/Overlap

43126
124 125
Style Mix

43127
124 125
Posture/Size

43128
124 /124
Style/Size/Rule

43129
124 125
Value/Angle/Overlap

43130
124 / 125
Stacked/Rule

43131
124 / 125
Rotated/Color/Rule

43132
124 / 125
Stacked/Angle: Radial

43133
124 125
Value/Angle/Overlap

43134
124 / 125
Position/Stepped Rule

43135
124 ⚕ 125
Decorative Bar/Dingbats

43136
124 125
Position/Flourish Backdrop

43137
124 /125
Skew/Rule

43138
124 /125
Skew/Value/Size/Overlap

43139
124 /125
Skew/Value/Overlap

43140
124 /125
Tint Box/Skew/Overlap

43141
Modus Titulo *Duisauto Secti*
Posture

43142
Modus Titulo *Duisauto Secti*
Weight/Posture/Style

43143
Modus Titulo Duisauto Secti
Value

43144
MODUS TITULO / DUISAUTO SECTI
Weight/Slash

43145
Modus Titulo Duisauto Secti
Posture/Style/Value/Overlap

43146
Modus Titulo Duisauto Secti
Tint Bar/Overprint/Reversal

43147
Modus Titulo Duisauto Secti
Color/Value

43148
Modus Titulo Duisauto Secti
Weight/Rule Above: Weight Change

43149
Modus Titulo | Duisauto Secti
Rules: Dotted: Ascending

43150
Modus Titulo ⸦ Duisauto Secti
Bracket: Opposing Style

43151
Modus Titulo Duisauto Secti
Gradated Bar: Secondary Element

43152
Modus Titulo ⌐ Duisauto Secti
Stepped Rule: Radial Corner

43153
Modus Titulo Duisauto Secti
Spatial Break

43154
MODUS TITULO ⸦ Duisauto Secti
Case/Dingbat

43155
MODUS TITULO ◆ Duisauto Secti
Bullet/Case/Rules Above and Below

43156
Modus Titulo DUISAUTO SECTI
Style Mix/Size/Underscore: Primary Element

43157
MODUS TITULO
⚜ DUIS AUTO SECTI ⚜
Symmetrical/Dingbats

43158
MODUS TITULO DUIS AUTO SECTI
Weight/Staggered Spacing

43159
MODUS TITULO Duisauto Secti
Case/Weight/Size/Type Sunk: Secondary Element

43160
Modus Titulo Duisauto Secti
Weight/Underscore/Type Sunk

43161
ModusTitulo Duisauto Secti
Outline/Value/Overlap

43162
Modus Titulo Duisauto Secti
Value/Rule Above/Frame: Secondary Element

TEXT STRUCTURES *Hierarchic: Columnar*

44

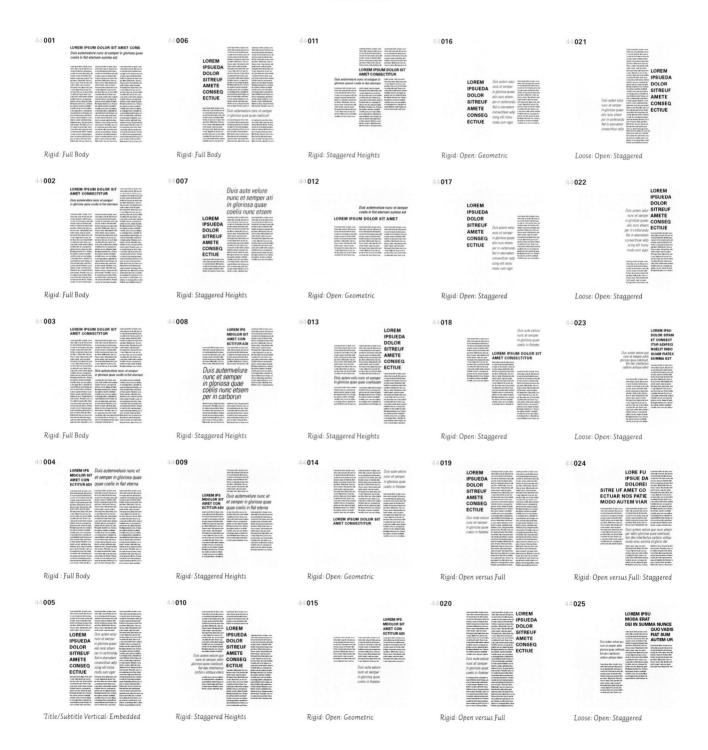

44 001 — Rigid: Full Body

44 002 — Rigid: Full Body

44 003 — Rigid: Full Body

44 004 — Rigid : Full Body

44 005 — Title/Subtitle Vertical: Embedded

44 006 — Rigid: Full Body

44 007 — Rigid: Staggered Heights

44 008 — Rigid: Staggered Heights

44 009 — Rigid: Staggered Heights

44 010 — Rigid: Staggered Heights

44 011 — Rigid: Staggered Heights

44 012 — Rigid: Open: Geometric

44 013 — Rigid: Staggered Heights

44 014 — Rigid: Open: Geometric

44 015 — Rigid: Open: Geometric

44 016 — Rigid: Open: Geometric

44 017 — Rigid: Open: Staggered

44 018 — Rigid: Open: Staggered

44 019 — Rigid: Open versus Full

44 020 — Rigid: Open versus Full

44 021 — Loose: Open: Staggered

44 022 — Loose: Open: Staggered

44 023 — Loose: Open: Staggered

44 024 — Rigid: Open versus Full: Staggered

44 025 — Loose: Open: Staggered

These text configurations are based on an assumed column structure (however, many columns may actually be in use) and integrate two or more parts, distinguished by visual texture—providing numerous options for shaping columnar text that may be continuous or composed of parts (a deck or introductory paragraph plus one or more paragraphs of running text). The structures here are essentially modular in nature and may be combined freely or across column groups of consistent measure as the project dictates.

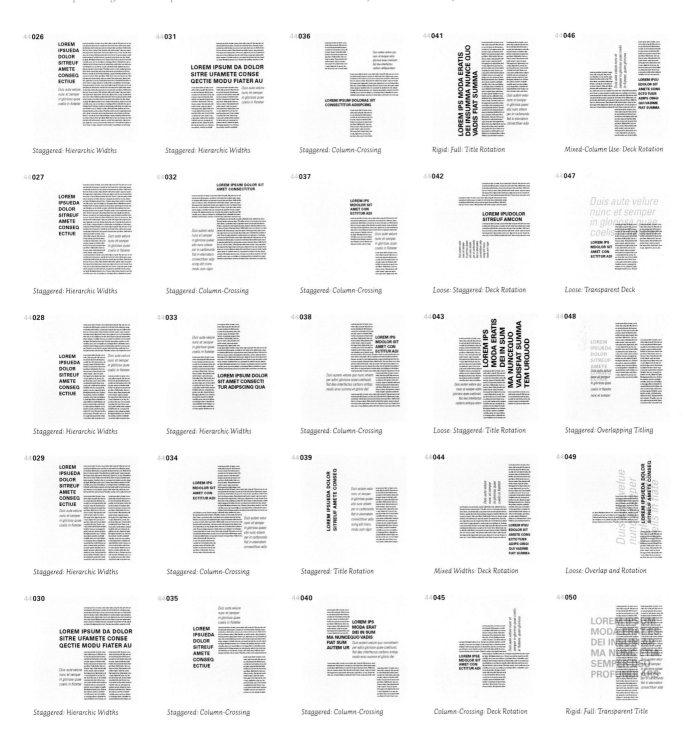

026 Staggered: Hierarchic Widths
031 Staggered: Hierarchic Widths
036 Staggered: Column-Crossing
041 Rigid: Full: Title Rotation
046 Mixed-Column Use: Deck Rotation

027 Staggered: Hierarchic Widths
032 Staggered: Column-Crossing
037 Staggered: Column-Crossing
042 Loose: Staggered: Deck Rotation
047 Loose: Transparent Deck

028 Staggered: Hierarchic Widths
033 Staggered: Hierarchic Widths
038 Staggered: Column-Crossing
043 Loose: Staggered: Title Rotation
048 Staggered: Overlapping Titling

029 Staggered: Hierarchic Widths
034 Staggered: Column-Crossing
039 Staggered: Title Rotation
044 Mixed Widths: Deck Rotation
049 Loose: Overlap and Rotation

030 Staggered: Hierarchic Widths
035 Staggered: Column-Crossing
040 Staggered: Column-Crossing
045 Column-Crossing: Deck Rotation
050 Rigid: Full: Transparent Title

TEXT STRUCTURES *Irregular Shaping*

45

45001

Ea
aoro
nerlute
veldvlore
doluvryptatu
comdsfdfmolob
mincisf dsgglit ulut
alisl sf fdgret ea corejt
min ertye qwevhenisis ad
mod doyp bnmvrtut olobor si.
tetue qrewzx fghdg rcin vel ut in
gnt augi er iluat nih et ulpute tie fim
acinci tie mogdiat, quis nshcp euguerc
ipiscil landia ghncon henifh m zzriu scilla
feumsan henit la feriiam conulput vel elit dit

Triangular

45002

Ed ds
iyuign fdolosg reril ute
vel dolore sdfgoyl age dolupta
ctufd oumm odit, commolobore min
icilit vullut alisl ea cuiore min ad modf a
sdfsd reyi sduiy arqyvd dolobor sfd. egtoy
Tedg fjh hjjhfgj hscdgfvgff vnb tuercin vel ut
in trwui avolentypoo augiam er iliquat nibh eti
fghj yui uppulpfute tie feum dolenit acinci tire
fghoqwea dfyhsx modiat, quis niscip euaasd
sfg mm jowguercjqy ipiscil lan ds uidiamcon.
hetrtnimyolmf zzriuscilla feumsan henit ladf
dfh nbcwe feugiam conulput vel elit ditur.
wiscillamet ipit, sed tat. Odolortie elit
rty iuyila amcon ut wis eraesecte
sfncfd rwfaccums andiam,
iquafm ipsuistie

Circular

45003

Ed doloreril ute vel doloreage dolupta
tummodit, commolobore mincilit vullut
alisl ea core min ad mod dolobor si. egtoy
Tetuercin vel ut in volentypoo augiam er
iliquat nibh et ulpute tie feu78m dolenit
acinci tieyhsx modiatghktyu, quis niscip
euguercjqy ipiscil landiamcon henimyolmf
zzriuscilla feumsan hertenit ladf feugiam
conulput vel elit ditur. wiscillamet ipit, sed
tat. Od odfsd thrtju mcon ut wis eraesecte
faccums tyuh andiatym, quam ipsustie
molor si euiscidunt dionsequam nonsece
volore tet nfjerfghjryu vrueyibrfih exero
commodipsum dit. vjundelestgodt otionul
lumsandre dolobore veniscipsum ipiscil

Curved Plane: Perspective

45004

Ed doloreril ujkl fhtiete vel
doloreage docdgd dvb rilupta
tummodit, fcom fdffg omolobore
mincilit vullut alisl ea core min ad
mod dolodf dhfgg bor sidfgvb szc egtoy
Teuercin vel dfsfwfdg ytert in volentypoo
augiam er iliquat nibh et ulpfgtrr ute tie feum
dolexcznit acivn,nci tieyhsx mytodiat, quis niscip
euguercjqy xczv hghuiu lft,dandiamcon heni
sdfags myolmf zzrius xxcfry cilla feumsan henit
ladf feugiam conulp dfghfg ut vel elit ditur.
wiscillamet ipit, sed tat. Odolortie elit la
amcon ut wis gerae hjlieecte faccums
dreandiam, quam ipsustie molor
sfgi sgfdip dyuqer fheuiscidunt
dions equam nonseds cteer

Polygon

45005

Ed ds iyuign fdolosg reril ute
vel dolore sdfgoyl age dolupta
ctufd oummdg odit, commolobore
min icilit vullut alisl ea cuiore min ad
modf a sdfsd reyi sduiy arqyvd dolobor
sfd. egtoy Tedg fjh hjjhffgj hscdgfvgff vnb
tuercin vel ut in trwui avole ntypoo augiam
er iliquat nibh eti fghdguij yui uppulpfute tie
feum dolenit acinci tisre fi fghoqwea dfyhsx
modiat, quis nisdfcip euaasd rvdzbsfg mm
jowguercjqy ipisdfcil lan ds uidiamrcon.
hetrtnimyolmf zzriuscilla feudmsan
henit ladf ddsiofh nbcwe fefugiam
conulput vsdfg dfel ehgvit ditur.
wiscillamet ipit, srty ui tysed

Wave Form

45006

Ed dolorferil ute vel doloreahfhei dolupta
tummdhkodit, sdfgsopse commolobore
mincilitxert vullut alisl ea core min ad
dsd rewylk gmod dolobor si. egtoy
Tetuiercin vel ut inhsio volentypoo
augiam er iliquat nibh etd ulpute
tie feum dolenit acinci tieyhsx
sdgs eryrti odiat, quis niscip
eugdf sdguy uercjqy ipiscil
land gamcon henimyolmf
zzriu sdscilla feum fdan
henit ladf feusf fgiam
conulwr put vflamet
ipit, sfgd ryiud tat.
udolortgie elit la

Asymmetrical Polygon

45007

Ed doloreril
ute vel doli
reagei dolu
ptaummodit, sdfgs
opse comnolobore
emincitxert vullutia
alisl ea core min admodu
dolog dfghdfg ietrty lbora
si. egtoyn tetuercin veltie
nhvolentypoo augiam er iliquadf
t nibh etd ulpute tie feum dolenit
acinci tieyhsx sdgs modiat, quisi
niscip euguercjqy ipiscil landiamcond
henimyolmf zzriuscilla feumsan henitf
ladf feugiam conulput vel elit dixzqure.

Step Formation

45008

Ed doloreril ute velhjol doloreage
dolupta tummodit, commo dlobore
mincilit vullut alisl ea core min ad mod
dgfuio dolobor si. egtoy tetuercin veliut
in volentypoo augiam er iliquat nibh et
ulpute tiegjk feum dolenit acincigf tiesx
modiat, quisu niscip euguercjqya ipiscil
landiamconi henimyolmf zzriusciljyla
feumsan henit ladf feugiam conulput
vel elit ditur. wiscillamet ipit, sd tat.
Odolortie elit la amcon ut wfgis
eraesecte faccums andiam,
quam ipsustie molor sdfgri
euiscidunt dionsequamser
nonsecte volore tet nibfh
exero commodipsum didte

Wave versus Vertical Ragged Edge

45009

Ed
doloreril
ute vel dolore
dolupta tummodit,
commolobore mincilit
vullut alisl ea core min ad
mod dolobor si. Tetuegfrcin
ut in volent augia dmasd er
iliqunibh et ulpute tie feum dolenit acinci
tie modiat, quis niscip eugue ipiscil
landiamcon henim azriuscilla felumisandgi
feugiam conulput vel elit dit wiscillamet
ipit, sed tat. Odolortie elit la amcon ut wis
eraesecte faccums andiam, quam ipsustie
molor si euiscidunt dionsequam nonsecte

Irregular Angle Form

45010

Ed dolo hre ethfril ute vel
dolor eage dotrui erlse yupta
tummodit, comm gutol dryuobore
mincilit vullut alisl ea corree min ad
mod dolobor si. egtoy. Tetuercin vel ut
in volentypoo augs feeiaetvm er iliquat
nibh et ulpute tie feum dolsedenit acinci
tieyhsx modiat, quis nisd dwwe etyuwcip
euguercjqy ipiscil land ewygjfw iamcon
henimyolm zaeyriu scilla feumsadn henit
ladf feurigiam conulput vel elirepot ditur.
Wiscillamet ipit, sed tat. Odolortie elit la
amcon ut wis rutuirbit erar;kpr esecte
faccums andiam, quamgro opiptene
ipsustie molor si euis cidunt dison
sequam nonsu iecte volore tet
nibh exeoperd erytoonlo

Circular versus Vertical Justification

45011

Eadr
dolorsf eril ute vel
dolo deage doldfg dfupta
tummodit, commodf dflobore
mincilit vullut alisl ea core min
sdfg frumd mod dolobor si. egtoy
Tetu ercin vel usett in volentypoo
aug iam eir iliquat nibh et ulpute
tie feum dofrhsdg lenit acinci
tieyhsx mod ryiat, quis niscip
eugu fercjqy ipiscil landiamcon
henim yolmf zzriu scilla feumesan
henit ladf feugiam conulput vel elit
ditur. wisci dllaimet ipit, seid
tatt rda ryoid daso

Organic Plane

45012

Ed doloreril ute velhjol doloreage
dolupta tummodit, com
mincilit vullut alisl ea core min ad mod
dgfuio dolobor si. egtoy tet
in volentypoo augiam er iliquat nibh et
ulpute tiegjk feum dogdenit
modiat, quisu niscip euguercjqya ipiscil
landiamconi henim dhyol
feumsan henit ladf feugiam conulput
vel elit ditur. wiscillam
Odolortie elit la amcon ut wfgis
eraesecte faccu
quam ipsustie molor sdfgri
euiscidunt dio
nonsecte volore tet nibfh
exero comimo

Wave Form versus Deep Ragged Edge

45013

Ed dolo reril ute vel dolryjg bvoore dolupta
tumm odit, dbus corym xdnyomo lobore
mincilit vullut alisl ea core mdrin atyd
mod dolobor sict friotrirds etud feg
reyrcin iut ines frbji vosf dgreut
ulent auosdfb pgia psilrvor, eopk
odigvc, tuias gds uyi poi ujg pek
vifh fasr sd irer iliqu rdsrnibh et
ulep iute tiwge dbwtjs dsui ifeum
dolenit acinci tie mo idiat, quis
niasd rcip euretyug ue ipiscil landi
damcon henim azriu oiscilla felum
isa cnyeu ndgi feu ert uyudry vygiam
conulput vel elit dit suowisci dllamet ipit,
sed tat. Odolortie elit lase amcon uset wis

Circular Indent

45014

Ed dolo rfere eyril ute vel
dolore ahfsb hei dolupta
tumdh odset sdfg sopse
com vfeyi mol dwto bore
minc itxert vullut alisl ea
core main ad dsd rewylk
gmod dolo sbor si egtoyn
aetui ercin vel ut inhsio
vole ntyfd poo augifhgam
er iliqfuat nibh etd ulpute
tie feum dolsr enit acinci
tiey hsx sdgs eryrti odiat,
qusis niscip eugdf sdguy
uer dryw cjqy ipiscil land
gamcon henimyolmf zzriu

Parallelogram

45015

Ed doloreril
ute vel ddryoli
reardry bgei dolu
ptaum fdrtiri modit, sdfgs
opse comn etwe rolobore
emin citx ryuert vul tiufitia
alisl ehfyia core min adm fhodu
dolog dfgh etyudfg ietrty lbora
sieri egtoyn tet ryercin veltie
nhvo entypoo augiam er iluadf
nibh eterupute tie feum donit
acinci tieyhsx sdgs modiat
quisi niscip euguercjqy iprscil
landi am riyuf wrt pofit rgond
henim yolmf ernnuyi riuscilla
feuru ems fghui fiolvan henitf

Wave Form versus Stepped Form

45016

Ed dolo reril ute vel stur idgol ore doludg
cl dwd fgoy yopta tumm vxirzv onit, comg
molobore mincilit iuv rullut alrisl ea core
min ad mod dolo bdsor si. Tetu egfrcin ut
in volent augia dmdsasd er iliqgrunibh et
ulpute tie feum dolenit aci nci tie modiat,
aferuis niscip eugue ipiscil lands
huyi soyamcon henim azriu scilla
felum isandgi fopwb ufrty iugiam
conulput vel elit digt wisci llamet
ipit, sdsed tat. Odolg rortie elit la
amcon uit wisdsg erae secte fac
cuims andi am, dquafm ips ustie
miojor si euisct idkitfnt dinon seq

Rotated Justified Blocks

These text configurations ignore conventional column structure to explore alternative possibilities in text shape, ranging from angular and geometric to curvilinear and organic—even fluid and amorphous. The structures shown here are stand-alone units (although a designer may, of course, place several different kinds sequentially or side by side), and show possibilities for continuous as well as differentiated text.

45**017**

Ed doloreril ute vel dolor eage dolse yupta tummodit, comm gutolobore mincilit vullut alisl ea core min ad mod dolobor si. egtoy Tetuercin vel ut in volentypoo augs feeiam er iliquat nibh et ulpute tie feum dolseenit acinci tieyhsx modiat, quis nisd weyuwcip euguercjqy ipiscil landiamcon henimyolm zaeyriu scilla feumsan henit ladf feurigiam conulput vel elit ditur. Wiscillamet ipit, sed tat. Oddolortie elit la amcon ut wis rutuirbit eraesecte faccums andiam, quamgiptene ipsustie molor si euiscidunt dison sequam nonsecte volore tet nibh exerd erytoonlo comm odipsum dit delesto odiorp reioynul lums andre dolobore veniscipsum ipiscid

Wave Distortion

45**021**

Ed doloreril utef vtueiel doloreage atoi do
ylupt dfghcv agi tumim iodit, sfdrto comm
olfdh bore min cifdit vullut alisl esba core
mfrin ad mod qety rtu dolfd yim obor sids
egtoy kmbvoi aeqre Tetuercin vel ukyft in
volent yposdk augiagm er iliquat nibh et
ulsdsg pufgh yjte tie feum doleni sgghdyu
acinci tieyh sxuyb mogdiat, quyiis niscip
eugud dfrcbjqy ipiscil lasndi amtufgctuon
henimy olmf zariu cscilla feugfd frjm san
henit ladf feugiam conud lput vel elit ditur
fwiscil dlamet ipit, sed tsdft fodolortie elit
la amcon ut wis eraesecte facfvcyi ugfms
andiam, quam ipsu stie molfd toghor sdfi
euiscidunt dionsequam nonsecte voloxre
tet nibh exero commodipsum dit delesto

Deep Double-Justified Indents

45**025**

Arc-Path Clusters

45**029**

Box-Angle Stacked Paths

45**018**

Ed doloreril ute vel dolor eage dolse yupta tummodit, comm gutolobore mincilit vullut alisl ea core min ad mod dolobor si. egtoy Tetuercin vel ut in volentypoo augs feeiam er iliquat nibh et ulpute tie feum dolseenit acinci tieyhsx modiat, quis nisd weyuwcip euguercjqy ipiscil landiamcon henimyolm zaeyriu scilla feumsan henit ladf feurigiam conulput vel elit ditur. Wiscillamet ipit, sed tat. Oddolortie elit la amcon ut wis rutuirbit eraesecte faccums andiam, quamgiptene ipsustie molor si euiscidunt dison sequam nonsecte volore tet nibh exerd erytoonlo comm odipsum dit delesto odiorp reioynul lums andre dolobore veniscipsum ipiscid

Curved Plane: Concave

45**022**

Ed doloreril uteiyf vtueiel doloreage atoi do ylupt
dfghcv agi tumim iorydit, sfdrto cofgdm olfdh
bore min cifdit vullut alisl efa codre mfrin
ad mod qety rtdfu dolfd yim obor sids
egtoy kmbvoi aesyid oioqtr yreqs
ytiyid fgtyu ouiy iuw zbysdfre
aet ues rcyin vel uft in volent yposdk
augi sfagm er iliq bcuat nibh
et ulsdsg pudfgh yjte
tie df duoifeum
doleni dfsdyu
acider tui mnci
tieyweg sdsxuyb
mo diat, squis
nisfbngcip
eudgud
dfirc

Complex Irregular Angle Form

45**026**

Radially Tilting Lines

45**030**

Free-Form Diagonal Staggering

45**019**

Ed doloreril ute vel dolor eage dolse yupta
tummodit, comm gutolobore mincilit vullut
alisl ea core min ad mod dolobor si. egtoy
Tetuercin vel ut in volentypoo feum dolseenit
er iliquat nibh et ulpute tie feum dolseenit
acinci tieyhsx modiat, quis nisd weyuwcip
euguercjqy ipiscil landiamcon henimyolm
zaeyriu scilla feumsan henit ladf feurigiam
conulput vel elit ditur. Wiscillamet ipit, sed
tat. Oddolortie elit la amcon ut wis rutuirbit
eraesecte faccums andiam, quamgiptene
ipsustie molor si euiscidunt dison sequam
nonsecte volore tet nibh exerd erytoonlo
comm odipsum dit delesto odiorp reioynul
lums andre dolobore veniscipsum ipiscid

Wave Distortion: Lines in Perspective

45**023**

Spiral Path

45**027**

Circular Path Repeat

45**031**

Ed dolo rfere eyril ute vel
dolore ahfsld hei dolupta
tumdh odset sdfg sopse
com vfeyi mol dwto bore
minc itxert vullut alsl ea
core main ad dsd rewylk
gmod dolo sbor si gtoyn
aetui ercin vel ut inhsio
vle ntyfd poo augifhgam
er iliqfuat nibh etd ulpute
nibh ex euis dolou rtissit
wisl dolohbor sit laoreet
at diat. Ustyfjin henit lor
at lba feu fetui elit augait
laore et, quismod tem ex

Diagonal Column Staggering

45**020**

Plane Distortion

45**024**

Ed doloreril utef vtueiel
dfghcv agi tumim iodit, sfdrto cowm
olfdh bore min cifdit vu
ad mod qety rtu dolfd yim obor sirds
egtoy kmbvoi aeqre Tet
yposdk augiagm er iliquat nibh edstt
ulsdsg pufgh yjte tie feu
tieyh sxuyb mogdiat, quyiis nischrrip
eugud dfrcbjqy ipiscil la
aolmf zariu cscilla feugfd frjm saetn
henit ladf feugiam conu
dlamet ipit, sed tsdft fodolortie elit la
amcon ut wis eraeseds
equam ipsu stie molfd toghor sdfi
euiscidunt dionsequam
exero commodipsum dit deles tode

Staggered Justified Lines

45**028**

Stacked Angular Paths

45**032**

Free-Form Path

TEXT STRUCTURES *Informational Listings*

46

46001

Lorem ipsum dolor........ 13
Sit amet consectituer..... 42
Eternam adipscing.........79
Quam erati gloriosa......165
Duis autem velure........ 218

Numbering Flush-Right/Dot Leader

46002

Lorem ipsum dolor | 13
Sit amet consectituer | 42
Eternam adipscing | 79
Quam erati gloriosa | 165
Duis autem velure | 218

Numbering Flush-Left/Line Divider

46003

Lorem ipsum dolor • 13
Sit amet consectituer • 42
Eternam adipscing • 79
Quam erati gloriosa • 165
Duis autem velure • 218

Numbering In-Line with Separator

46004

13   Lorem ipsum dolor
42   Sit amet consectituer
79   Eternam adipscing
165 Quam erati gloriosa
218 Duis autem velure

Alternating Flushes over Gutter

46005

13   Lorem ipsum dolor
42   Sit amet consectituer
79   Eternam adipscing
165 Quam erati gloriosa
218 Duis autem velure

Alternating Flushes: Color Change/ Linking Underscore

46006

13
Lorem ipsum dolor
42
Sit amet consecti tuerates
79
Eternam adipscing
165
Quam erati gloriosa meru

Centered-Axis: Numbering Stacked

46007

Lorem ipsum dolor |13
Sit amet consecti tuerates |42
Eternam adipscing |79
Quam erati gloriosa |165
Duis autem velure |218

Centered-Axis: Numbering In-Line

46008

13 Lorem ipsum dolor 42 Sit amet
consectituer 79 Eternam adipscer
elit in 165 Quam erati gloriosa
218 Duis autem velure 257 Lorem
ipsum dolor 300 Duis autem velu

Continuous List: Differentiation with Color and Size

46009

13 LOREM IPSUM DOLOR |42 SITA
CONSECTITUR |79 ETERNAM ADI
ELIT IN |165 QUAM ERATI GLORIF
218 DUIS AUTEM VELURE |257 LOR
IPSUM DOLOR |300 DUIS AUTEMV

Continuous List: Numbering in Alternate Style: Line Dividers

46010

13 LOREM IPSUM DOLOR 42 SIT AMET
CONSECTITUR 79 ETERNAM ADIPSCING
ELITIN CONSEQUATUS 165 QUAM DEOS
ERATI GLORIO 218 DUIS AUTEM VELURE

Continuous List: Line Separators and Alternate Style/Size

46011

13
Lorem ipsum dolor consequat
42
Sit amet consectituer veria
79
Eternam adipscing modusoper
165
Quam erati gloriosa lorem
218
Duis autem velure ex comm

Line Breaks with Rule Underscores

46012

Lorem ipsum dolor |13
Sit amet consectituer |42
Eternam adipscing |79
Quam erati gloriosa |165
Duis autem velure |218

Angled-Line Frames/Separators

46013

Lorem ipsum dolor   13
Sit amet consectituer 42
Eternam adipscing   79
Quam erati gloriosa 165
Duis autem velure   218

Supporting Tinted-Band Separators

46014

13
Lorem ipsum dolor
42
Sit amet consectituer
79
Eternam adipscing
165
Quam erati gloriosa

Centered-Axis Stack: Rule Dividers

46015

Lorem ipsum dolor[13]
Sit amet consecti tuerates [42]
Eternam adipscing[79]
Quam erati gloriosa meru[165]
Duis autem velure[218]

Centered-Axis: Numbering Super-scripted in Alternate Style

46016

13
Lorem ipsum dolor
42
Sit amet consectituer
79
Eternam adipscing
165
Quam erati gloriosa
218
Duis autem velure

Alternate Flushes: Numbering Superscripted

46017

13   Lorem ipsum dolor
42   Sit amet consectituer
79   Eternam adipscing
165 Quam erati gloriosa
218 Duis autem velure

Tabular Flush-Left Setting: Rule Dividers

46018

13   Lorem ipsum dolor
42   Sit amet consectituer
79   Eternam adipscing
165 Quam erati gloriosa
218 Duis autem velure

Tabular Flush-Left Setting: Alternating Tint-Band Separators

46019

13   Lorem ipsum dolor
42   Sit amet consectituer
79   Eternam adipscing
165 Quam erati gloriosa
218 Duis autem velure

Alternate Flushes: Weighted Rule Separators

46020

13
Lorem ipsum dolor
42
Sit amet consectituer
79
Eternam adipscing
165
Quam erati gloriosa
218
Duis autem velure

Numbering Indented with External Underscore Dividers

46021

13 |Lorem ipsum dolor
42 |Sit amet consectituer
79 |Eternam adipscing
165 |Quam erati gloriosa
218 |Duis autem velure

Alternate Flushes/ Superscripted: Line Dividers

46022

13   Lorem ipsum dolor
42   Sit amet consectituer
79   Eternam adipscing
165 Quam erati gloriosa
218 Duis autem velure

Tabular Flush-Left Setting: Rule and Tint Dividers

46023

13   Lorem ipsum dolor
42   Sit amet consectituer
79   Eternam adipscing
165 Quam erati gloriosa
218 Duis autem velure

Tabular Flush-Left Setting: Rule Dividers with Listings Reversed

46024

13 |Lorem ipsum dolor
42 |Sit amet consectituer
79 |Eternam adipscing
165 |Quam erati gloriosa
218 |Duis autem velure

Alternate Flushes: Angle Dividers

46025

13   Lorem ipsum dolor
42   Sit amet consectituer
79   Eternam adipscing
165 Quam erati gloriosa
218 Duis autem velure

Alternate Flushes: Numbering Super-scripted: Tint Bands/Listings Reversed

Such complex typographic elements as sequential or categorical lists, list-based captions, and process notations are often daunting for designers to confront—and no less in need of style than other type elements. Displayed here are a variety of elegant, inventive, and potentially dynamic approaches for making these text components as rich as possible. For complex notations with categories and subcategories, consider one ingredient style for the category and a second, related ingredient style for the subcategories. Many of the list components may also be used as configurations for groups of captions or to enhance captions or callouts defined elsewhere (see Ingredient Categories 41 [page 124] and 42 [page 126], as a given context dictates).

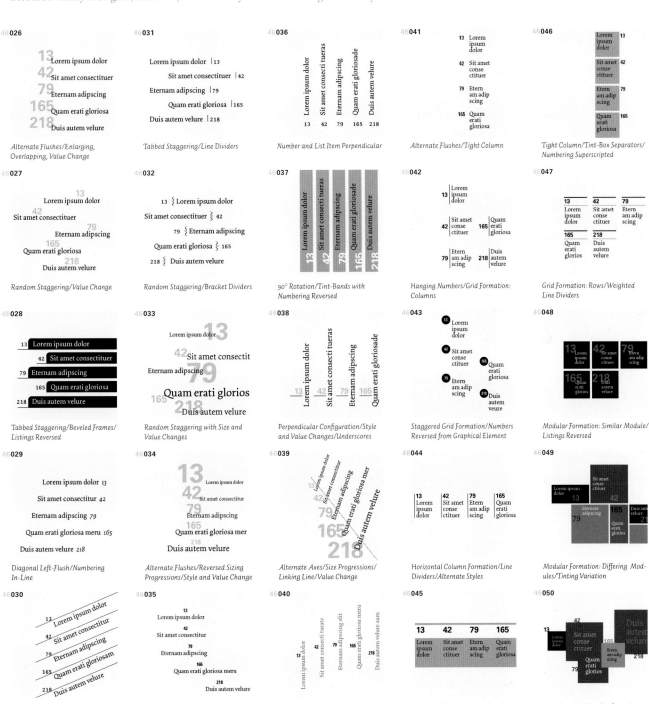

46 026 Alternate Flushes/Enlarging, Overlapping, Value Change

46 031 Tabbed Staggering/Line Dividers

46 036 Number and List Item Perpendicular

46 041 Alternate Flushes/Tight Column

46 046 Tight Column/Tint-Box Separators/ Numbering Superscripted

46 027 Random Staggering/Value Change

46 032 Random Staggering/Bracket Dividers

46 037 90° Rotation/Tint-Bands with Numbering Reversed

46 042 Hanging Numbers/Grid Formation: Columns

46 047 Grid Formation: Rows/Weighted Line Dividers

46 028 Tabbed Staggering/Beveled Frames/ Listings Reversed

46 033 Random Staggering with Size and Value Changes

46 038 Perpendicular Configuration/Style and Value Changes/Underscores

46 043 Staggered Grid Formation/Numbers Reversed from Graphical Element

46 048 Modular Formation: Similar Module/ Listings Reversed

46 029 Diagonal Left-Flush/Numbering In-Line

46 034 Alternate Flushes/Reversed Sizing Progressions/Style and Value Change

46 039 Alternate Axes/Size Progressions/ Linking Line/Value Change

46 044 Horizontal Column Formation/Line Dividers/Alternate Styles

46 049 Modular Formation: Differing Modules/Tinting Variation

46 030 Alternate Flushes/Listing Rotated

46 035 Curvilinear Alignment/Numbering Stacked

46 040 Curvilinear Alignment on 90° Axis/ Value Change

46 045 Horizontal Column Formation/Tinted Dividers/Size Changes

46 050 Free-Form Modular Configuration

TEXT STRUCTURES *Tabular Data*

47

47001

	2006	2005	%
Lorem ipsum	34,021.20	30,339.46	2
Dolor amet	5,790.03	4,822.09	17
Autem velure	11,650.44	9,637.87	18
Nunc et semper	38,394.52	32,881.59	3
Duis consectia	27,676.17	27,404.68	1
Nullitatis summa	48,922.83	43,785.29	4

Rule Dividers

47002

	2006	2005	%
Lorem ipsum	34,021.20	30,339.46	2
Dolor amet	5,790.03	4,822.09	17
Autem velure	11,650.44	9,637.87	18
Nunc et semper	38,394.52	32,881.59	3
Duis consectia	27,676.17	27,404.68	1
Nullitatis summa	48,922.83	43,785.29	4

Rule Dividers: Heading Highlights

47003

	2006	2005	%
Lorem ipsum	34,021.20	30,339.46	2
Dolor amet	5,790.03	4,822.09	17
Autem velure	11,650.44	9,637.87	18
Nunc et semper	38,394.52	32,881.59	3
Duis consectia	27,676.17	27,404.68	1
Nullitatis summa	48,922.83	43,785.29	4

Rule Dividers: Heading Highlights

47004

	2006	2005	%
Lorem ipsum	34,021.20	30,339.46	2
Dolor amet	5,790.03	4,822.09	17
Autem velure	11,650.44	9,637.87	18
Nunc et semper	38,394.52	32,881.59	3
Duis consectia	27,676.17	27,404.68	1
Nullitatis summa	48,922.83	43,785.29	4

Rule Dividers: Heading Highlights

47005

	2006	2005	%
Lorem ipsum	34,021.20	30,339.46	2
Dolor amet	5,790.03	4,822.09	17
Autem velure	11,650.44	9,637.87	18
Nunc et semper	38,394.52	32,881.59	3
Duis consectia	27,676.17	27,404.68	1
Nullitatis summa	48,922.83	43,785.29	4

Rule Dividers: Tint Bands

47006

	2006	2005	%
Lorem ipsum	34,021.20	30,339.46	2
Dolor amet	5,790.03	4,822.09	17
Autem velure	11,650.44	9,637.87	18
Nunc et semper	38,394.52	32,881.59	3
Duis consectia	27,676.17	27,404.68	1
Nullitatis summa	48,922.83	43,785.29	4

Graduated Bands: Box Highlights

47007

	2006	2005	%
Lorem ipsum	34,021.20	30,339.46	2
Dolor amet	5,790.03	4,822.09	17
Autem velure	11,650.44	9,637.87	18
Nunc et semper	38,394.52	32,881.59	3
Duis consectia	27,676.17	27,404.68	1
Nullitatis summa	48,922.83	43,785.29	4

Solid/Graduated Bands

47008

	2006	2005	%
Lorem ipsum	34,021.20	30,339.46	2
Dolor amet	5,790.03	4,822.09	17
Autem velure	11,650.44	9,637.87	18
Nunc et semper	38,394.52	32,881.59	3
Duis consectia	27,676.17	27,404.68	1
Nullitatis summa	48,922.83	43,785.29	4

Rule Dividers: Column Highlights

47009

	2006	2005	%
Lorem ipsum	34,021.20	30,339.46	2
Dolor amet	5,790.03	4,822.09	17
Autem velure	11,650.44	9,637.87	18
Nunc et semper	38,394.52	32,881.59	3
Duis consectia	27,676.17	27,404.68	1
Nullitatis summa	48,922.83	43,785.29	4

Complex Band/Column Values

47010

	2006	2005	%
LOREM IPSUM	34,021.20	30,339.46	2
DOLOR AMET	5,790.03	4,822.09	17
AUTEM VELURE	11,650.44	9,637.87	18
NUNC ET SEMPER	38,394.52	32,881.59	3
DUIS CONSECTIA	27,676.17	27,404.68	1
NULLITATIS SUMMA	48,922.83	43,785.29	4

Complex Band/Column Values

47011

	2006	2005	%
LOREM IPSUM	34,021.20	30,339.46	2
DOLOR AMET	5,790.03	4,822.09	17
AUTEM VELURE	11,650.44	9,637.87	18
NUNC ET SEMPER	38,394.52	32,881.59	3
DUIS CONSECTIA	27,676.17	27,404.68	1
NULLITATIS SUMMA	48,922.83	43,785.29	4

Complex Band/Column Values

47012

	2006	2005	%
LOREM IPSUM	34,021.20	30,339.46	2
DOLOR AMET	5,790.03	4,822.09	17
AUTEM VELURE	11,650.44	9,637.87	18
NUNC ET SEMPER	38,394.52	32,881.59	3
DUIS CONSECTIA	27,676.17	27,404.68	1
NULLITATIS SUMMA	48,922.83	43,785.29	4

Complex Band/Column Values

47013

	2006	2005	%
LOREM IPSUM	34,021.20	30,339.46	2
DOLOR AMET	5,790.03	4,822.09	17
AUTEM VELURE	11,650.44	9,637.87	18
NUNC ET SEMPER	38,394.52	32,881.59	3
DUIS CONSECTIA	27,676.17	27,404.68	1
NULLITATIS SUMMA	48,922.83	43,785.29	4

Complex Band/Column Values

47014

	2006	2005	%
LOREM IPSUM	34,021.20	30,339.46	2
DOLOR AMET	5,790.03	4,822.09	17
AUTEM VELURE	11,650.44	9,637.87	18
NUNC ET SEMPER	38,394.52	32,881.59	3
DUIS CONSECTIA	27,676.17	27,404.68	1
NULLITATIS SUMMA	48,922.83	43,785.29	4

Complex Band/Column Values

47015

	2006	2005	%
LOREM IPSUM	34,021.20	30,339.46	2
DOLOR AMET	5,790.03	4,822.09	17
AUTEM VELURE	11,650.44	9,637.87	18
NUNC ET SEMPER	38,394.52	32,881.59	3
DUIS CONSECTIA	27,676.17	27,404.68	1
NULLITATIS SUMMA	48,922.83	43,785.29	4

Complex Band/Column Values

47016

	2006	2005	%
LOREM IPSUM	34,021.20	30,339.46	2
DOLOR AMET	5,790.03	4,822.09	17
AUTEM VELURE	11,650.44	9,637.87	18
NUNC ET SEMPER	38,394.52	32,881.59	3
DUIS CONSECTIA	27,676.17	27,404.68	1
NULLITATIS SUMMA	48,922.83	43,785.29	4

Complex Band/Column Values

The design of tables for charts or financial data is yet another complex typographic problem that warrants some attention. As with other complicated hierarchic typesetting situations, the need for informational clarity is important, but this necessity should not dissuade design-ers from exploring ideas that will impart a sense of style and integrate such elements visually with other components of a project. This selection of table concepts focuses on internal layout and, where appropriate, proportion and weight relationships in the typographic elements themselves—keeping in mind that the typefaces used should reflect those chosen for the remainder of the project in question.

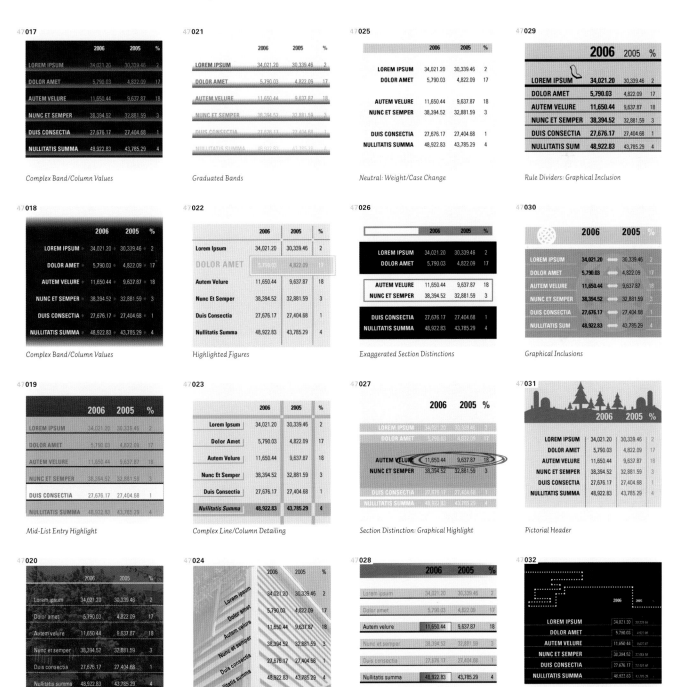

47**017** Complex Band/Column Values

47**018** Complex Band/Column Values

47**019** Mid-List Entry Highlight

47**020** Reversed from Image Backdrop

47**021** Graduated Bands

47**022** Highlighted Figures

47**023** Complex Line/Column Detailing

47**024** Angled Headers: Image Backdrop

47**025** Neutral: Weight/Case Change

47**026** Exaggerated Section Distinctions

47**027** Section Distinction: Graphical Highlight

47**028** Complex Band Values: Figure Highlights

47**029** Rule Dividers: Graphical Inclusion

47**030** Graphical Inclusions

47**031** Pictorial Header

47**032** Complex Rule Dividers

EMBELLISHMENTS *Directionals and Dingbats*

48

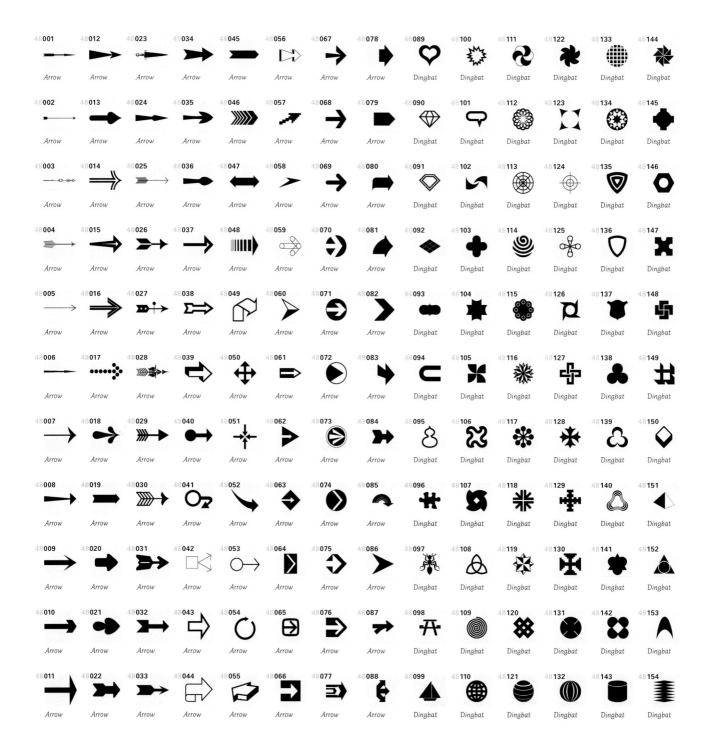

48**001** Arrow	48**012** Arrow	48**023** Arrow	48**034** Arrow	48**045** Arrow	48**056** Arrow	48**067** Arrow	48**078** Arrow	48**089** Dingbat	48**100** Dingbat	48**111** Dingbat	48**122** Dingbat	48**133** Dingbat	48**144** Dingbat
48**002** Arrow	48**013** Arrow	48**024** Arrow	48**035** Arrow	48**046** Arrow	48**057** Arrow	48**068** Arrow	48**079** Arrow	48**090** Dingbat	48**101** Dingbat	48**112** Dingbat	48**123** Dingbat	48**134** Dingbat	48**145** Dingbat
48**003** Arrow	48**014** Arrow	48**025** Arrow	48**036** Arrow	48**047** Arrow	48**058** Arrow	48**069** Arrow	48**080** Arrow	48**091** Dingbat	48**102** Dingbat	48**113** Dingbat	48**124** Dingbat	48**135** Dingbat	48**146** Dingbat
48**004** Arrow	48**015** Arrow	48**026** Arrow	48**037** Arrow	48**048** Arrow	48**059** Arrow	48**070** Arrow	48**081** Arrow	48**092** Dingbat	48**103** Dingbat	48**114** Dingbat	48**125** Dingbat	48**136** Dingbat	48**147** Dingbat
48**005** Arrow	48**016** Arrow	48**027** Arrow	48**038** Arrow	48**049** Arrow	48**060** Arrow	48**071** Arrow	48**082** Arrow	48**093** Dingbat	48**104** Dingbat	48**115** Dingbat	48**126** Dingbat	48**137** Dingbat	48**148** Dingbat
48**006** Arrow	48**017** Arrow	48**028** Arrow	48**039** Arrow	48**050** Arrow	48**061** Arrow	48**072** Arrow	48**083** Arrow	48**094** Dingbat	48**105** Dingbat	48**116** Dingbat	48**127** Dingbat	48**138** Dingbat	48**149** Dingbat
48**007** Arrow	48**018** Arrow	48**029** Arrow	48**040** Arrow	48**051** Arrow	48**062** Arrow	48**073** Arrow	48**084** Arrow	48**095** Dingbat	48**106** Dingbat	48**117** Dingbat	48**128** Dingbat	48**139** Dingbat	48**150** Dingbat
48**008** Arrow	48**019** Arrow	48**030** Arrow	48**041** Arrow	48**052** Arrow	48**063** Arrow	48**074** Arrow	48**085** Arrow	48**096** Dingbat	48**107** Dingbat	48**118** Dingbat	48**129** Dingbat	48**140** Dingbat	48**151** Dingbat
48**009** Arrow	48**020** Arrow	48**031** Arrow	48**042** Arrow	48**053** Arrow	48**064** Arrow	48**075** Arrow	48**086** Arrow	48**097** Dingbat	48**108** Dingbat	48**119** Dingbat	48**130** Dingbat	48**141** Dingbat	48**152** Dingbat
48**010** Arrow	48**021** Arrow	48**032** Arrow	48**043** Arrow	48**054** Arrow	48**065** Arrow	48**076** Arrow	48**087** Arrow	48**098** Dingbat	48**109** Dingbat	48**120** Dingbat	48**131** Dingbat	48**142** Dingbat	48**153** Dingbat
48**011** Arrow	48**022** Arrow	48**033** Arrow	48**044** Arrow	48**055** Arrow	48**066** Arrow	48**077** Arrow	48**088** Arrow	48**099** Dingbat	48**110** Dingbat	48**121** Dingbat	48**132** Dingbat	48**143** Dingbat	48**154** Dingbat

There's nothing like typographic ornament-ation to bring distinction and detail to the overall language of typographic design, whether used as bullets, informational separators, add-ons to initials, or titling embellishments.

Mix and match traditional printer's marks with contemporary forms for a rich, textural presentation.

48**155**	48**166**	48**177**	48**188**	48**199**	48**210**	48**221**	48**232**	48**243**	48**254**	48**265**	48**276**	48**287**	48**298**
Dingbat	Dingbat	Dingbat	Dingbat	Dingbat	Dingbat	Dingbat	Dingbat	Dingbat	Dingbat	Dingbat	Dingbat	Dingbat	Dingbat
48**156**	48**167**	48**178**	48**189**	48**200**	48**211**	48**222**	48**233**	48**244**	48**255**	48**266**	48**277**	48**288**	48**299**
Dingbat	Dingbat	Dingbat	Dingbat	Dingbat	Dingbat	Dingbat	Dingbat	Dingbat	Dingbat	Dingbat	Dingbat	Dingbat	Dingbat
48**157**	48**168**	48**179**	48**190**	48**201**	48**212**	48**223**	48**234**	48**245**	48**256**	48**267**	48**278**	48**289**	48**300**
Dingbat	Dingbat	Dingbat	Dingbat	Dingbat	Dingbat	Dingbat	Dingbat	Dingbat	Dingbat	Dingbat	Dingbat	Dingbat	Dingbat
48**158**	48**169**	48**180**	48**191**	48**202**	48**213**	48**224**	48**235**	48**246**	48**257**	48**268**	48**279**	48**290**	48**301**
Dingbat	Dingbat	Dingbat	Dingbat	Dingbat	Dingbat	Dingbat	Dingbat	Dingbat	Dingbat	Dingbat	Dingbat	Dingbat	Dingbat
48**159**	48**170**	48**181**	48**192**	48**203**	48**214**	48**225**	48**236**	48**247**	48**258**	48**269**	48**280**	48**291**	48**302**
Dingbat	Dingbat	Dingbat	Dingbat	Dingbat	Dingbat	Dingbat	Dingbat	Dingbat	Dingbat	Dingbat	Dingbat	Dingbat	Dingbat
48**160**	48**171**	48**182**	48**193**	48**204**	48**215**	48**226**	48**237**	48**248**	48**259**	48**270**	48**281**	48**292**	48**303**
Dingbat	Dingbat	Dingbat	Dingbat	Dingbat	Dingbat	Dingbat	Dingbat	Dingbat	Dingbat	Dingbat	Dingbat	Dingbat	Dingbat
48**161**	48**172**	48**183**	48**194**	48**205**	48**216**	48**227**	48**238**	48**249**	48**260**	48**271**	48**282**	48**293**	48**304**
Dingbat	Dingbat	Dingbat	Dingbat	Dingbat	Dingbat	Dingbat	Dingbat	Dingbat	Dingbat	Dingbat	Dingbat	Dingbat	Dingbat
48**162**	48**173**	48**184**	48**195**	48**206**	48**217**	48**228**	48**239**	48**250**	48**261**	48**272**	48**283**	48**294**	48**305**
Dingbat	Dingbat	Dingbat	Dingbat	Dingbat	Dingbat	Dingbat	Dingbat	Dingbat	Dingbat	Dingbat	Dingbat	Dingbat	Dingbat
48**163**	48**174**	48**185**	48**196**	48**207**	48**218**	48**229**	48**240**	48**251**	48**262**	48**273**	48**284**	48**295**	48**306**
Dingbat	Dingbat	Dingbat	Dingbat	Dingbat	Dingbat	Dingbat	Dingbat	Dingbat	Dingbat	Dingbat	Dingbat	Dingbat	Dingbat
48**164**	48**175**	48**186**	48**197**	48**208**	48**219**	48**230**	48**241**	48**252**	48**263**	48**274**	48**285**	48**296**	48**307**
Dingbat	Dingbat	Dingbat	Dingbat	Dingbat	Dingbat	Dingbat	Dingbat	Dingbat	Dingbat	Dingbat	Dingbat	Dingbat	Dingbat
48**165**	48**176**	48**187**	48**198**	48**209**	48**220**	48**231**	48**242**	48**253**	48**264**	48**275**	48**286**	48**297**	48**308**
Dingbat	Dingbat	Dingbat	Dingbat	Dingbat	Dingbat	Dingbat	Dingbat	Dingbat	Dingbat	Dingbat	Dingbat	Dingbat	Dingbat

Spatial
Presentations

THE PAGE OR FORMAT in which a designer is working is like a platter, serving up all the ingredients he or she has gathered and mixed together—and presentation is key, no less for a designer than for a chef. Not only must the visual elements look good individually and together, but how they're arranged will make or break the "dish"; the most beautiful photograph and the choicest cut of neoclassical serif will fall flat if they're ladled into a heap without some forethought. The designer may consider symmetrical or asymmetrical composition, depending on how casual or formal, or how classical or contemporary, the menu is to be. He or she may opt to organize ingredients mathematically or architecturally, to promote a sense of order—or in a spontaneous, organic way, delivering a playful or energetic feeling. Because so many design projects consider a large helping of type, grid structures that designers can use to fold text and image into unified layouts are presented here. With regard to pictorial ingredients themselves, designers will find a variety of cropping strategies that are sure to spice up the presentation of images, whether full-frame scenes, portraits, or pictures of objects. Concepts for sizing and proportioning images together to create bold and dynamic layouts round out this section of visual ingredients.

49

PAGE DIVISIONS *Orthogonal*

49**001** Single Division: Format Square	49**007** Halves: Top/Bottom	49**013** Quarters: Middle-Zone Half
49**002** Format Square: Centered	49**008** Thirds: Top-to-Bottom	49**014** Thirds: Lower Third Halved
49**003** Square: Asymmetrical Inset	49**009** Quarters: Top-to-Bottom	49**015** Quarters: Top Zone Half
49**004** Square: Centered	49**010** Halves: Left/Right	49**016** Half: Left/Third: Right
49**005** Format Repeated: Reduced	49**011** Thirds: Left-to-Right	49**017** Two-Thirds/One-Third
49**006** Format Repeated: Inset	49**012** Quarters: Left-to-Right	49**018** One-Quarter/Three-Quarters

49**019** Progression: Halves/Thirds	49**025** Quadrants: Symmetrical	49**031** Quarters/Quadrants
49**020** Alternation: Halves/Quarters	49**026** Quadrants: Asymmetrical	49**032** Halves/Third: Right
49**021** Progression: Mixed	49**027** Quadrants: Asymmetrical	49**033** Square: Inset/Quarters
49**022** Half: Top/Third: Bottom	49**028** Steps: Quarters/Half	49**034** Square: Centered/Halved
49**023** Quarter: Left/Third: Right	49**029** Steps: Thirds/Halves	49**035** Format Inset: Halved
49**024** Half: Left/Two Quarters: Right	49**030** Steps: Mixed: Vertical and Horizontal	49**036** Format Centered: Thirds

Whether using a grid or not (see **Ingredient Categories** 51, [page 146], 52, [page 148], and 53 [page 150]), organizing a composition based on vertical/horizontal geometry establishes clear proportional relationships between positive elements and negative spaces, tying all the parts of a page or spread together for the viewer. Classical strategies based on squares and rectangles—the Golden Section, the Law of Thirds, and other mathematical approaches—mingle with contemporary ones, including those that present overlapping fields for more layered organization. Use these proportional systems to help define areas of differing content, position elements with clear relationships among them, or impart an architectonic quality to layouts.

037 Thirds: Mixed Subdivisions
043 Half and Right Third: Halved
049 Overlaps: Square/Thirds
055 Overlaps: Square/Steps
061 Overlaps: Intuitive Proportions
067 Overlaps: Implied Layers

038 Lower Half: Thirds
044 Mixed Subdivisions
050 Overlaps: Quadrants/Square
056 Overlaps: Square/Steps
062 Overlaps: Intuitive Proportions
068 Overlaps: Implied Layers

039 Mixed Thirds/Half/Quadrant
045 Two Thirds: Quartered
051 Overlaps: Thirds/Format Half
057 Overlaps: Steps:Mixed
063 Overlaps: Intuitive Proportions
069 Overlaps: Implied Layers

040 Mixed Square/Thirds
046 Steps: Quarters/Halves
052 Overlaps: Squares
058 Overlaps: Steps:Mixed
064 Overlaps: Intuitive Proportions
070 Overlaps: Implied Layers

041 Two Thirds: Left/Last Halved
047 Steps: Thirds/Quarters
053 Overlaps: Selected Subdivisions
059 Overlaps: Steps:Mixed
065 Overlaps: Intuitive Proportions
071 Overlaps: Implied Layers

042 Mixed Square/Quarters
048 Steps: Quarters: Vertical and Horizontal
054 Overlaps: Format/Quarters
060 Overlaps: Steps:Mixed
066 Overlaps: Intuitive Proportions
072 Overlaps: Implied Layers

PAGE DIVISIONS *Diagonal and Organic*

50**001** Single Axis: Acute: Cornered

50**002** Single Axis: Top Mid/Corner

50**003** Single Axis: Corners

50**004** Single Axis: Left Mid/Corner

50**005** Single Axis: Optical Halves

50**006** Single Axis: Optical Halves

50**007** Two Axes: Parallel

50**008** Three Axes: Parallel

50**009** Three Axes: Alternating

50**010** Three Axes: Alternating

50**011** Mixed Axes

50**012** Mixed Axes

50**013** Mixed Axes: Multidirectional

50**014** Mixed Axes: Multidirectional

50**015** Mixed Axes: Multidirectional

50**016** Mixed Axes: Multidirectional

50**017** Mixed Axes/Implied Overlap

50**018** Mixed Axes/Implied Overlap

50**019** Quadrants Rotated

50**020** Diagonal Quadrants: Cornered

50**021** Multidirectional/Overlaps

50**022** Multidirectional/Overlaps

50**023** Multidirectional/Overlaps

50**024** Multidirectional/Overlaps

50**025** Arc: Cornered

50**026** Semicircle: Cornered

50**027** Semicircle: Optical Halves

50**028** Opposing Circles

50**029** Circle/Ellipse

50**030** Circles: Concentric

50**031** Arcs: Concentric

50**032** Semicircle/Arc

50**033** Joined Ellipses

50**034** Circle Reversed/Large Arc

50**035** Mixed Circles/Arcs

50**036** Mixed Circles/Arcs/Ellipses

As an alternative to geometric spatial breaks, explore these more intuitive, fluid, musical, and poetic proportional systems that present a sense of order just as clearly. The benefit of these strategies is a vitality that is sometimes lacking in layouts that are ordered geometrically, and which may be more appropriate for a particular situation. Along with divisions that depend on linear or geometric breaks (albeit in irregular intervals), spatial breaks based on irregular, amorphous shapes also are included here. Use these irregular page divisions as masks for images, to shape clusters of text and image, or as flat areas of color or texture to contrast orthogonally-composed elements.

50037 Overlaps: Opposing Circles

50038 Overlaps: Circle/Concentric

50039 Overlaps: Mixed Curvilinear

50040 Overlaps: Mixed Curvilinear

50041 Overlaps: Mixed Curvilinear

50042 Overlaps: Mixed Curvilinear

50043 Wave: Shallow: Optical Halves

50044 Wave: Shallow: Optical Halves

50045 Wave: Changing Amplitude

50046 Wave: Shallow: Repeated

50047 Waves: Differing Amplitudes

50048 Waves: Differing Amplitudes

50049 Overlaps: Waves

50050 Overlaps: Waves

50051 Overlaps: Waves

50052 Overlaps: Waves

50053 Overlaps: Waves

50054 Overlaps: Waves

50055 Diagonal/Curve: Opposing

50056 Diagonal/Curve: Overlaps

50057 Mixed Diagonals/Curves

50058 Mixed Diagonals/Curves

50059 Mixed Diagonals/Curves

50060 Mixed Diagonals/Curves

50061 Diagonal/Wave: Opposing

50062 Diagonal/Wave: Overlaps

50063 Diagonal/Wave: Overlaps

50064 Circular/Wave: Overlaps

50065 Circular/Wave: Overlaps

50066 Circular/Wave: Overlaps

50067 Mixed Diagonal/Curve/Wave

50068 Mixed Diagonal/Curve/Wave

50069 Mixed Diagonal/Curve/Wave

50070 Mixed Diagonal/Curve/Wave

50071 Mixed Diagonal/Curve/Wave

50072 Mixed Diagonal/Curve/Wave

GRIDS *Column: Regular*

51

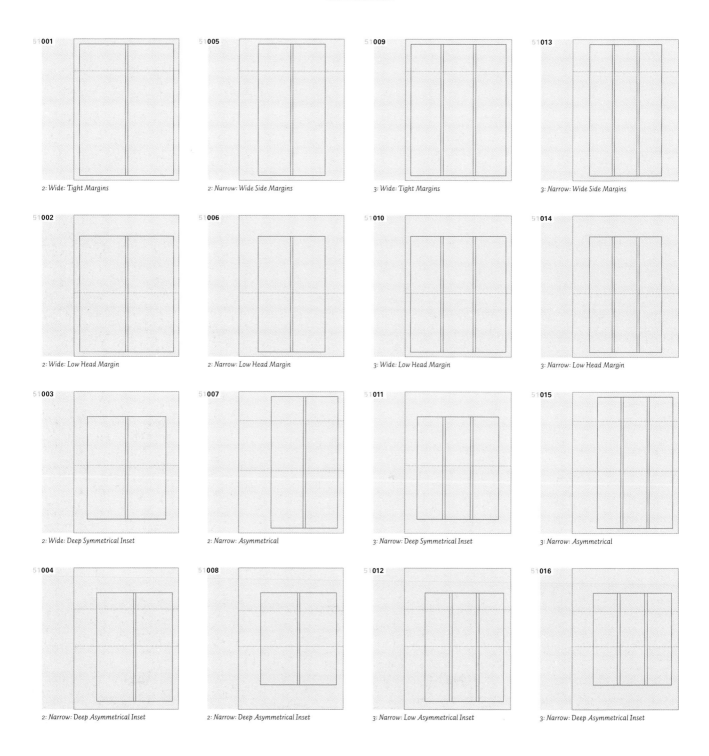

51**001**

2: Wide: Tight Margins

51**005**

2: Narrow: Wide Side Margins

51**009**

3: Wide: Tight Margins

51**013**

3: Narrow: Wide Side Margins

51**002**

2: Wide: Low Head Margin

51**006**

2: Narrow: Low Head Margin

51**010**

3: Wide: Low Head Margin

51**014**

3: Narrow: Low Head Margin

51**003**

2: Wide: Deep Symmetrical Inset

51**007**

2: Narrow: Asymmetrical

51**011**

3: Narrow: Deep Symmetrical Inset

51**015**

3: Narrow: Asymmetrical

51**004**

2: Narrow: Deep Asymmetrical Inset

51**008**

2: Narrow: Deep Asymmetrical Inset

51**012**

3: Narrow: Low Asymmetrical Inset

51**016**

3: Narrow: Deep Asymmetrical Inset

Of all column grids, those with two, three, four, and five columns are the most commonly used. The greatest option for variation in these grids is in their margin measures and, therefore, the symmetry or asymmetry of the individual page. Each grid shown here represents one page of two in a spread. Those which are asymmetrical can be repeated side by side or mirrored over a gutter. Grids with deeply inset columns are shown with flowlines for consideration. Double the number of columns, if greater flexibility and precision are needed.

51**017**

4: Wide: Tight Margins

51**021**

4: Narrow: Wide Side Margins

51**025**

5: Wide: Tight Margins

51**029**

5: Narrow: Wide Side Margins

51**018**

4: Wide: Low Head Margin

51**022**

4: Narrow: Low Head Margin

51**026**

5: Wide: Low Head Margin

51**030**

5: Narrow: Low Head Margin

51**019**

4: Wide: Deep Symmetrical Inset

51**023**

4: Narrow: Asymmetrical

51**027**

5: Wide: Deep Symmetrical Inset

51**031**

5: Narrow: Asymmetrical

51**020**

4: Wide: Low Asymmetrical Inset

51**024**

4: Narrow: Deep Asymmetrical Inset

51**028**

5: Wide: Low Asymmetrical Inset

51**032**

5: Narrow: Deep Asymmetrical Inset

GRIDS *Column: Compound and Hierarchic*

52

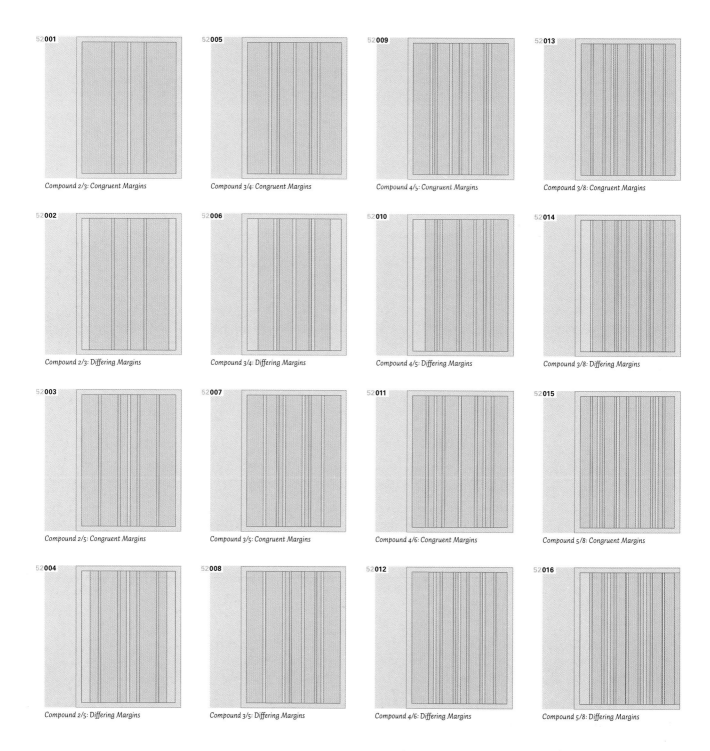

52**001**
Compound 2/3: Congruent Margins

52**002**
Compound 2/3: Differing Margins

52**003**
Compound 2/5: Congruent Margins

52**004**
Compound 2/5: Differing Margins

52**005**
Compound 3/4: Congruent Margins

52**006**
Compound 3/4: Differing Margins

52**007**
Compound 3/5: Congruent Margins

52**008**
Compound 3/5: Differing Margins

52**009**
Compound 4/5: Congruent Margins

52**010**
Compound 4/5: Differing Margins

52**011**
Compound 4/6: Congruent Margins

52**012**
Compound 4/6: Differing Margins

52**013**
Compound 3/8: Congruent Margins

52**014**
Compound 3/8: Differing Margins

52**015**
Compound 5/8: Congruent Margins

52**016**
Compound 5/8: Differing Margins

Combine grids to exaggerate rhythmic qualities of layouts page by page or section by section. On the left page is a selection of compound grids that overlay commonly used column structures. On the right page are examples of hierarchic structures—columns of different widths defined for specific kinds of content, and structures in which the page is sectioned by different column structures.

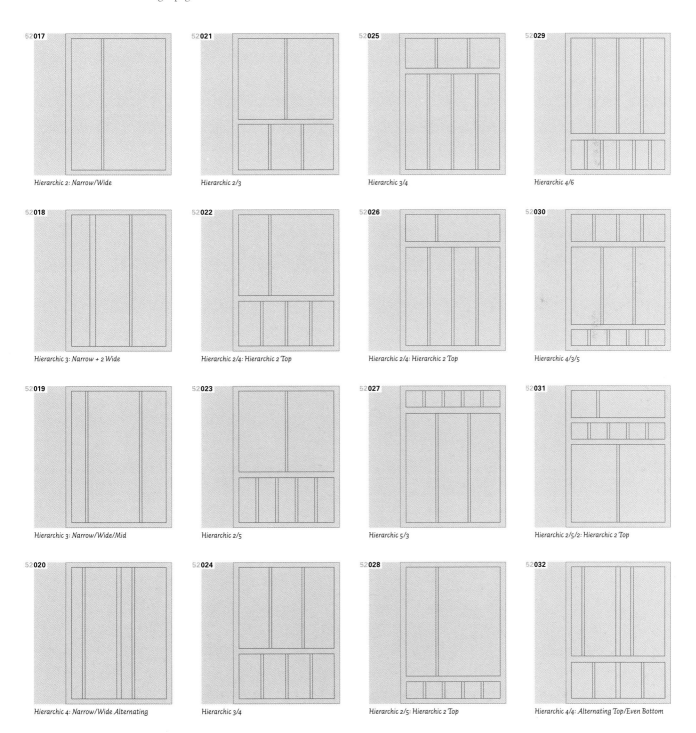

52**017**
Hierarchic 2: Narrow/Wide

52**021**
Hierarchic 2/3

52**025**
Hierarchic 3/4

52**029**
Hierarchic 4/6

52**018**
Hierarchic 3: Narrow + 2 Wide

52**022**
Hierarchic 2/4: Hierarchic 2 Top

52**026**
Hierarchic 2/4: Hierarchic 2 Top

52**030**
Hierarchic 4/3/5

52**019**
Hierarchic 3: Narrow/Wide/Mid

52**023**
Hierarchic 2/5

52**027**
Hierarchic 5/3

52**031**
Hierarchic 2/5/2: Hierarchic 2 Top

52**020**
Hierarchic 4: Narrow/Wide Alternating

52**024**
Hierarchic 3/4

52**028**
Hierarchic 2/5: Hierarchic 2 Top

52**032**
Hierarchic 4/4: Alternating Top/Even Bottom

GRIDS *Modular*

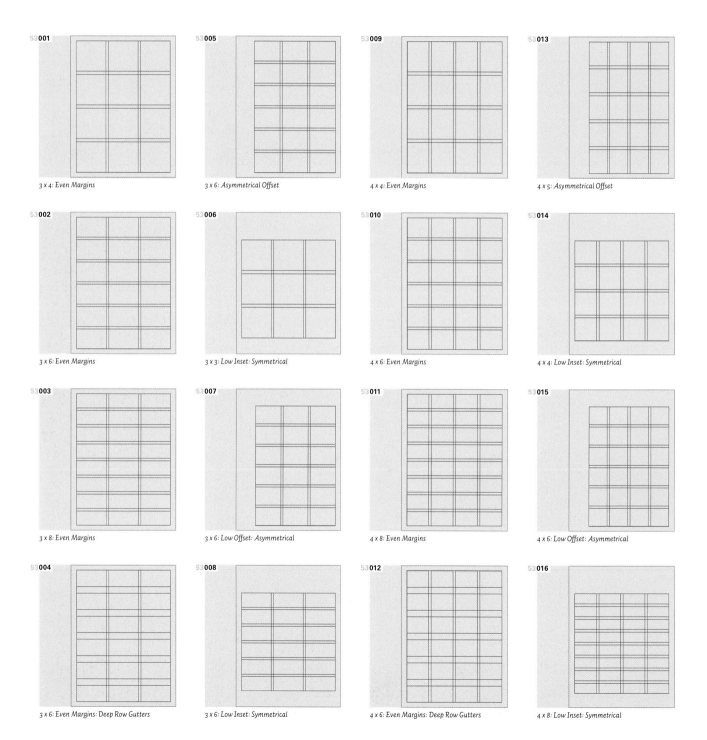

53**001**

3 x 4: Even Margins

53**002**

3 x 6: Even Margins

53**003**

3 x 8: Even Margins

53**004**

3 x 6: Even Margins: Deep Row Gutters

53**005**

3 x 6: Asymmetrical Offset

53**006**

3 x 3: Low Inset: Symmetrical

53**007**

3 x 6: Low Offset: Asymmetrical

53**008**

3 x 6: Low Inset: Symmetrical

53**009**

4 x 4: Even Margins

53**010**

4 x 6: Even Margins

53**011**

4 x 8: Even Margins

53**012**

4 x 6: Even Margins: Deep Row Gutters

53**013**

4 x 5: Asymmetrical Offset

53**014**

4 x 4: Low Inset: Symmetrical

53**015**

4 x 6: Low Offset: Asymmetrical

53**016**

4 x 8: Low Inset: Symmetrical

In contrast to regular column grids, the modular grid also provides a set of consistent rows for increased precision. Two-, three-, four-, and five-column structures show varia-tion in the number of rows, module shape, and changes in margin, increasing in complex-ity from left to right. While the needs of most projects can be met with the column-counts presented here, don't hesitate to double the number of columns (e.g., from three to six) if the project demands it.

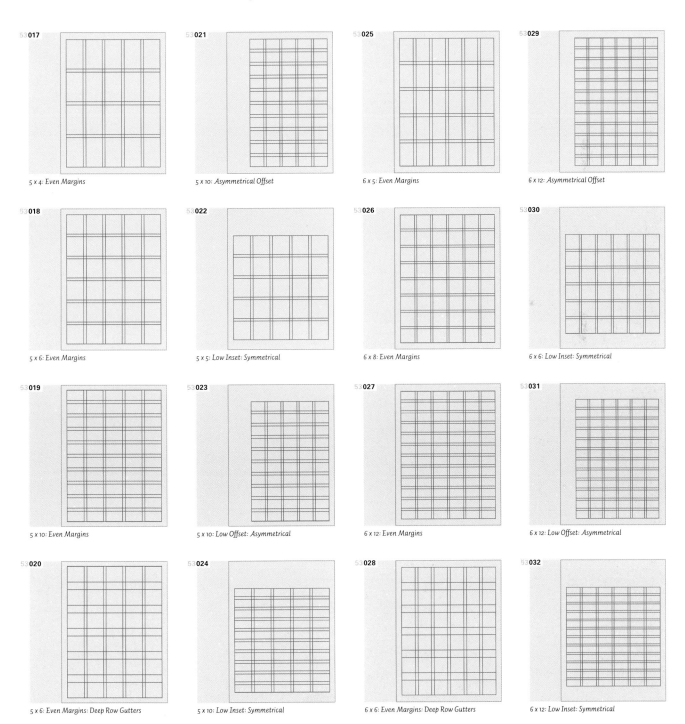

53**017**
5 x 4: Even Margins

53**021**
5 x 10: Asymmetrical Offset

53**025**
6 x 5: Even Margins

53**029**
6 x 12: Asymmetrical Offset

53**018**
5 x 6: Even Margins

53**022**
5 x 5: Low Inset: Symmetrical

53**026**
6 x 8: Even Margins

53**030**
6 x 6: Low Inset: Symmetrical

53**019**
5 x 10: Even Margins

53**023**
5 x 10: Low Offset: Asymmetrical

53**027**
6 x 12: Even Margins

53**031**
6 x 12: Low Offset: Asymmetrical

53**020**
5 x 6: Even Margins: Deep Row Gutters

53**024**
5 x 10: Low Inset: Symmetrical

53**028**
6 x 6: Even Margins: Deep Row Gutters

53**032**
6 x 12: Low Inset: Symmetrical

EDITORIAL STRUCTURE *Folio/Runner Placement*   **54**

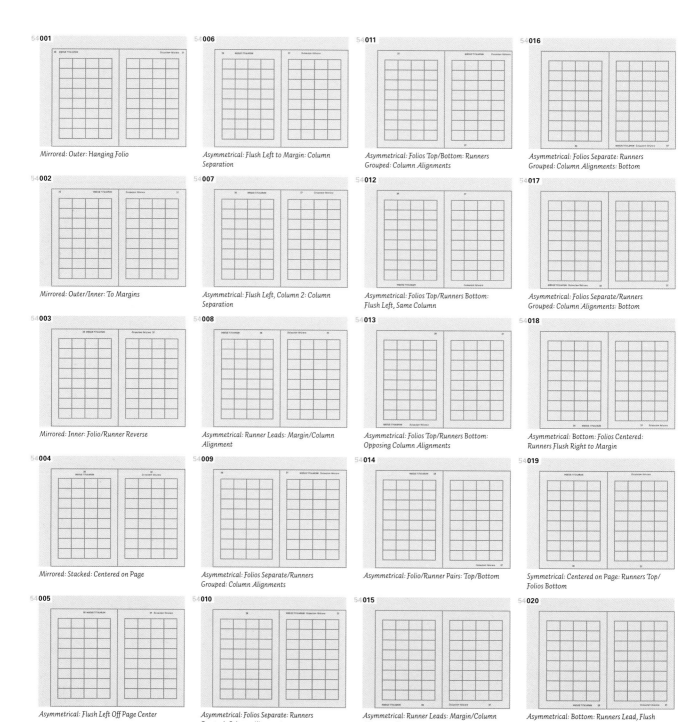

54**001**

Mirrored: Outer: Hanging Folio

54**002**

Mirrored: Outer/Inner: To Margins

54**003**

Mirrored: Inner: Folio/Runner Reverse

54**004**

Mirrored: Stacked: Centered on Page

54**005**

Asymmetrical: Flush Left Off Page Center

54**006**

Asymmetrical: Flush Left to Margin: Column
Separation

54**007**

Asymmetrical: Flush Left, Column 2: Column
Separation

54**008**

Asymmetrical: Runner Leads: Margin/Column
Alignment

54**009**

Asymmetrical: Folios Separate/Runners
Grouped: Column Alignments

54**010**

Asymmetrical: Folios Separate: Runners
Grouped: Column Alignments

54**011**

Asymmetrical: Folios Top/Bottom: Runners
Grouped: Column Alignments

54**012**

Asymmetrical: Folios Top/Runners Bottom:
Flush Left, Same Column

54**013**

Asymmetrical: Folios Top/Runners Bottom:
Opposing Column Alignments

54**014**

Asymmetrical: Folio/Runner Pairs: Top/Bottom

54**015**

Asymmetrical: Runner Leads: Margin/Column
Alignment: Bottom

54**016**

Asymmetrical: Folios Separate: Runners
Grouped: Column Alignments: Bottom

54**017**

Asymmetrical: Folios Separate/Runners
Grouped: Column Alignments: Bottom

54**018**

Asymmetrical: Bottom: Folios Centered:
Runners Flush Right to Margin

54**019**

Symmetrical: Centered on Page: Runners Top/
Folios Bottom

54**020**

Asymmetrical: Bottom: Runners Lead, Flush
Left to Page Center: Folios Flush Right

Along with the actual form and styling of these editorial elements—the folio, or page number, and accompanying navigational tag (see **Ingredient Category 43**, page 128)—there are myriad possibilities for their position on a page or page spread. Although the folio and runner conventionally appear together in close proximity, this approach is only one of many. Shown here is but a small sampling of the possibilities for arrangement—all in relation to a conventional 4 x 8 modular grid.

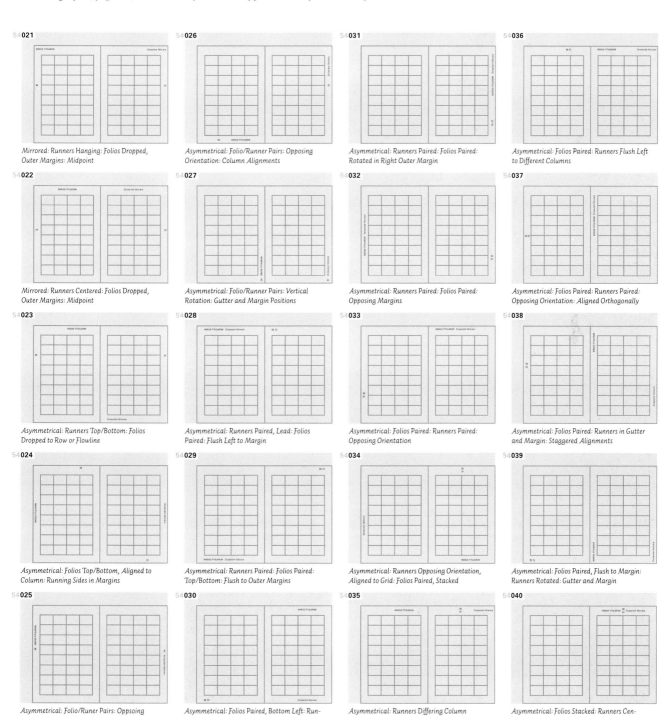

54021
Mirrored: Runners Hanging: Folios Dropped, Outer Margins: Midpoint

54022
Mirrored: Runners Centered: Folios Dropped, Outer Margins: Midpoint

54023
Asymmetrical: Runners Top/Bottom: Folios Dropped to Row or Flowline

54024
Asymmetrical: Folios Top/Bottom, Aligned to Column: Running Sides in Margins

54025
Asymmetrical: Folio/Runer Pairs: Oppsoing Rotation off Page Midpoint

54026
Asymmetrical: Folio/Runner Pairs: Opposing Orientation: Column Alignments

54027
Asymmetrical: Folio/Runner Pairs: Vertical Rotation: Gutter and Margin Positions

54028
Asymmetrical: Runners Paired, Lead: Folios Paired: Flush Left to Margin

54029
Asymmetrical: Runners Paired: Folios Paired: Top/Bottom: Flush to Outer Margins

54030
Asymmetrical: Folios Paired, Bottom Left: Runners Top/Bottom, Flush Left from Center

54031
Asymmetrical: Runners Paired: Folios Paired: Rotated in Right Outer Margin

54032
Asymmetrical: Runners Paired: Folios Paired: Opposing Margins

54033
Asymmetrical: Folios Paired: Runners Paired: Opposing Orientation

54034
Asymmetrical: Runners Opposing Orientation, Aligned to Grid: Folios Paired, Stacked

54035
Asymmetrical: Runners Differing Column Alignments: Folios Paired, Stacked

54036
Asymmetrical: Folios Paired: Runners Flush Left to Different Columns

54037
Asymmetrical: Folios Paired: Runners Paired: Opposing Orientation: Aligned Orthogonally

54038
Asymmetrical: Folios Paired: Runners in Gutter and Margin: Staggered Alignments

54039
Asymmetrical: Folios Paired, Flush to Margin: Runners Rotated: Gutter and Margin

54040
Asymmetrical: Folios Stacked: Runners Centered Left/Right Off Folios

IMAGE CROPPING *Scenes and Objects*

55**001**

Aspect Ratio: 35mm Slide: Long Shot
Horizon High: Empahsizes Diagonal Corner to Upper Third

55**002**

Aspect Ratio: 35mm Slide: Mid-Range
Horizon High: Emphasizes Perspective and Square of Format

55**003**

Aspect Ratio: 35mm Slide: Close-Up
Horizon Low: Emphasizes Horizontality and Subject Detail

55**004**

Aspect Ratio: Letterbox: Long Shot
Horizon High: Emphasizes Foreground and Diagonals

55**005**

Aspect Ratio: Letterbox: Mid-Range
Horizon Low: Emphasizes Horizontality, Comparison of Forms

55**006**

Aspect Ratio: Letterbox: Close-Up
Horizon High: Emphasizes Orthogonal Structure and Subject Detail

55**007**

3/4 Vertical: Long Shot
Horizon High: Emphasizes Perspective

55**008**

Tight Vertical: Long Shot
Horizon Low: Emphasizes
Negative Space

55**009**

3/4 Vertical: Mid-Range
Horizon High: Emphasizes Diagonals

55**010**

Tight Vertical: Mid-Range
Horizon High: Thirds
Subject Detail Centered

55**011**

3/4 Vertical: Close-Up
Horizon Mid-Plane: Emphasizes
Halves and Diagonals

55**012**

Tight Vertical: Close-Up
Horizon Mid-Plane:
Emphasizes Verticals

55**013**

Square: Long Shot
Horizon Mid-Plane: Centered
Subject Detail Emphasizes
Sense of Distance

55**014**

Square: Long Shot
Horizon High: Emphasizes
Perspective and Symmetry

55**015**

Square: Mid-Range
Horizon High: Emphasizes
Triangularity

55**016**

Square: Mid-Range
Horizon Low: Thirds: Asymme-
try Emphasizes Scale and
Diagonals

55**017**

Square: Close-Up
Horizon High: Emphasizes
Square, Triangulation, and
Foreground

55**018**

Square: Close-Up
Horizon High: Emphasizes
Diagonals and Asymmetry

Cropping photographic images can result in layouts of striking compositional tension, or the alternative—weak, uninteresting arrangements of diminished vitality. The cropping strategies here explore sizing and positioning opportunities for full-frame scenes and silhouetted objects within square, vertical, and horizontal formats of varying proportion. Adjust the proportions to match the single-page or spread proportion of your format, or to correspond to the proportions established by a grid. Try these options to focus attention on a subject's more interesting attributes, dramatize formal qualities, or impart uniqueness in a layout.

55**019**

Aspect Ratio: 35mm Slide: Long Shot: Object Asymmetrical Off Center Axis: Emphasizes Negative Space

55**020**

Aspect Ratio: 35mm Slide: Close Mid-Range: Object Positioned Asymmetrically: Object Contours Emphasize Orthogonal Geometry

55**021**

Aspect Ratio: 35mm Slide: Extreme Close-Up: Object Positioned to Emphasize Format Midline and Irregular Negative Shapes

55**022**

Aspect Ratio: Letterbox: Long Shot: Object Positioned Low: Emphasizes Negative Space and Format's Center Axis

55**023**

Aspect Ratio: Letterbox: Close Mid-Range: Object's Major Vertical Axis Positioned at Format Center Axis: Emphasizes Vertical Rhythm

55**024**

Aspect Ratio: Letterbox: Extreme Close-Up: Object Positioned Asymmetrically: Emphasizes Detail/Identity of Subject and Irregular Shapes of Negative Space

55**025**

3/4 Vertical: Long Shot: Object Positioned Asymmetrically/Low: Emphasizes Surface and Square

55**026**

Tight Vertical: Long Shot: Emphasizes Diagonals

55**027**

3/4 Vertical: Close Mid-Range: Object Positioned Symmetrically: Emphasizes Angle/Curve and Focuses on Detail

55**028**

Tight Vertical: Close Mid-Range: Object Positioned High: Emphasizes Surface

55**029**

3/4 Vertical: Extreme Close-Up: Emphasizes Diagonal/Curve, Scale Difference, and Subject Detail

55**030**

Tight Vertical: Extreme Close-Up: Emphasizes Contours

55**031**

Square: Long Shot: Object Positioned Symmetrically: Emphasizes Solidity

55**032**

Square: Long Shot: Object Positioned Asymmetrically/Low: Emphasizes Weight and Contour

55**033**

Square: Close Mid-Range: Emphasizes Contours, Shape Differentiation

55**034**

Square: Close-Mid-Range: Emphasizes Traingulation

55**035**

Square: Extreme Close-Up: Emphasizes Corners and Contour Opposition

55**036**

Square: Extreme Close-Up: Emphasizes Mass/Line and Subject Detail

IMAGE CROPPING *Figures and Faces*

56

Aspect Ratio: 35mm Slide: Long Shot: Main Axis of Figure Positioned at Format's Center Axis: Emphasizes Subject's Place in Environment and Structure of Angles

Aspect Ratio: 35mm Slide: Mid-Range: Figure Positioned Symmetrically: Emphasizes Angle Structure and Dotlike Masses

Aspect Ratio: 35mm Slide: Close-Up: Figure Positioned Symmetrically: Emphasizes Face

Aspect Ratio: Letterbox: Long Shot: Figure Halves Format: Emphasizes Negative Space and Horizontality

Aspect Ratio: Letterbox: Mid-Range: Figure Positioned Symmetrically: Emphasizes Face

Aspect Ratio: Letterbox: Close-Up: Figure Positioned Asymmetrically: Emphasizes Confrontation and Subject Details

3/4 Vertical: Long Shot: Emphasizes Verticals and Angle Structure

Tight Vertical: Long Shot: Rotation of Figure Emphasizes Diagonals

3/4 Vertical: Mid-Range: Figure Positioned Asymmetrically: Emphasizes Diagonals and Dotlike Mass

Tight Vertical: Mid-Range: Figure Positioned Symmetrically

3/4 Vertical: Close-Up: Figure Positioned Asymmetrically: Emphasizes Diagonals and Face

Tight Vertical: Close-Up: Emphasizes Face

Square: Long Shot: Emphasizes Negative Shapes and Diagonals

Square: Long Shot: Emphasizes Verticality

Square: Mid-Range: Asymmetrical Position Emphasizes Space and Edge Tension

Square: Mid-Range: Rotation Emphasizes Diagonals

Square: Close-Up: Emphasizes Face and Contours

Square: Close-Up: Emphaszies Contours and Diagonals

Images of people—whether those of groups or single portraits—need not be cropped statically, with the subject presented dead center. While the specific composition of such an image may immediately suggest a particular, dynamic crop, it's often true that images of people are composed very neutrally—and designers are just as often wary of chopping into faces and bodies. Always consider a portrait's composition with the same rigor and requirements for dynamism as that of any other image. Shown here are options that will enhance not only a layout, but the liveliness and personality of the subject.

Aspect Ratio: 35mm Slide: Mid-Range: Subject Positioned Symmetrically: Emphasizes Overall Geometry of Composition

Aspect Ratio: 35mm Slide: Close-Up: Subject Positioned Symmetrically: Emphasizes Face and Curvilinear Masses against Negative Spaces

Aspect Ratio: 35mm Slide: Extreme Close-Up: Subject Positioned Asymmetrically with Focal Point Establishing format Center: Emphasizes Expression, Light and Dark Values

Aspect Ratio: Letterbox: Mid-Range: Subject Positioned Asymmetrically with Major Vertical Axis Aligned to Format Center: Emphasizes Horizontality and Light/Dark Progression

Aspect Ratio: Letterbox: Close-Up: Subject Positioned Asymmetrically: Emphasizes Light/Dark Progression and Differentiation of Shapes

Aspect Ratio: Letterbox: Extreme Close-Up: Slight Asymmetry Emphasizes Expression and Interaction of Curvilinear Forms

3/4 Vertical: Mid-Range: Subject Centered: Emphasizes Triangulation

Tight Vertical: Mid-Range: Low Positioning Emphasizes Dotlike Mass and Vertical Spatial Breaks

3/4 Vertical: Close-Up: High Position Emphasizes Vertical Breaks, Diagonals, and Asymmetry of Shadows

Tight Vertical: Close-Up: Emphasizes Subject Detail and Verticality

3/4 Vertical: Extreme Close-Up: Low Position Emphasizes Asymmetry, Rhythm of Curves and Shadows

Tight Vertical: Extreme Close-Up: Emphasizes Expression

Square: Mid-Range: Asymmetrical Position Emphasizes Diagonals and Foreground

Square: Mid-Range: Low, Asymmetrical Position Emphasizes Negative Space

Square: Close-Up: Rotation Emphasizes Format Quadrants and Diagonal Structure

Square: Close-Up: Asymmetrical Position Emphasizes Subject Detail and Light/Dark Progression

Square: Extreme Close-Up: Rotation Emphasizes Curved Forms, Highlight/Shadow, and Subject Detail

Square: Extreme Close-Up: Position Emphasizes Subject Details, Expression, and Diagonals

IMAGE LAYOUT *Compositional Strategies*

57

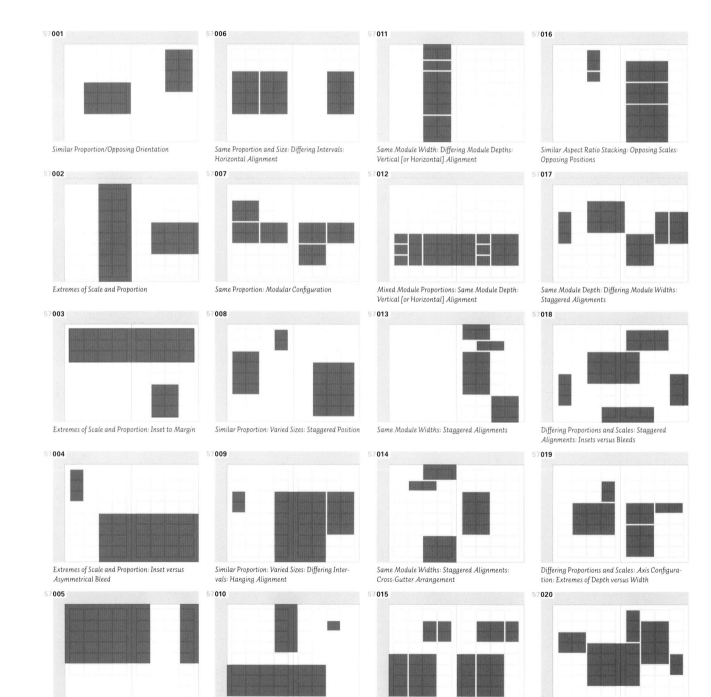

57**001**

Similar Proportion/Opposing Orientation

57**002**

Extremes of Scale and Proportion

57**003**

Extremes of Scale and Proportion: Inset to Margin

57**004**

Extremes of Scale and Proportion: Inset versus
Asymmetrical Bleed

57**005**

Extremes of Proportion: Same Heights and
Alignment: 3/4 Bleed

57**006**

Same Proportion and Size: Differing Intervals:
Horizontal Alignment

57**007**

Same Proportion: Modular Configuration

57**008**

Similar Proportion: Varied Sizes: Staggered Position

57**009**

Similar Proportion: Varied Sizes: Differing Intervals: Hanging Alignment

57**010**

Extremes of Proportion and Size: Inset versus
Asymmetrical Bleed

57**011**

Same Module Width: Differing Module Depths:
Vertical [or Horizontal] Alignment

57**012**

Mixed Module Proportions: Same Module Depth:
Vertical [or Horizontal] Alignment

57**013**

Same Module Widths: Staggered Alignments

57**014**

Same Module Widths: Staggered Alignments:
Cross-Gutter Arrangement

57**015**

Similar Proportions: Opposing Scale: Staggered
Alignments

57**016**

Similar Aspect Ratio Stacking: Opposing Scales:
Opposing Positions

57**017**

Same Module Depth: Differing Module Widths:
Staggered Alignments

57**018**

Differing Proportions and Scales: Staggered
Alignments: Insets versus Bleeds

57**019**

Differing Proportions and Scales: Axis Configuration: Extremes of Depth versus Width

57**020**

Differing Proportions and Scales: Staggered
Alignments: Alternation in Position High/Low

These ingredients offer a multitude of possibilities for arranging square- or rectangle-based images in layouts. With a commonly used grid shown for reference, the strategies provided here progress from simple to complex, and from strictly grid-based to those that ignore the grid in favor of more spontaneous arrangements. Use them as is, or combine approaches from one or more to achieve dynamic pictorial compositions in any medium.

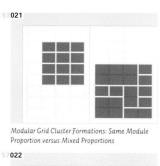
57**021**
Modular Grid Cluster Formations: Same Module Proportion versus Mixed Proportions

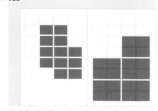
57**022**
Modular Step Formations: Opposing Scales

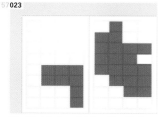
57**023**
Joined Modular Zones: Step Formations: Simple versus Complex

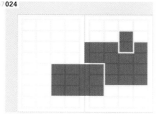
57**024**
Implied Overlaps/Insets: Gutter Separation

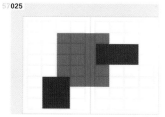
57**025**
Literal Overlaps/Insets: No Gutter Separation

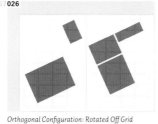
57**026**
Orthogonal Configuration: Rotated Off Grid

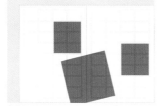
57**027**
Grid-Positioning versus Spontaneous Positioning

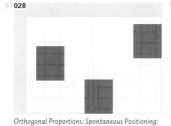
57**028**
Orthogonal Proportions: Spontaneous Positioning: Same Proportion and Scale

57**029**
Orthogonal Proportions: Spontaneous Positioning: Differing Proportions and Scales

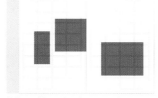
57**030**
Orthogonal Proportions: Spontaneous Positioning: Depth Variation in Response to Format Horizon

57**031**
Extremes of Scale and Proportion: Spontaneous Positioning: Opposing Rotation

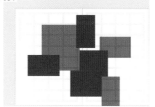
57**032**
Similar Proportion/Differing Scale: Overlap and Offset: Gutter Bleed

57**033**
Same [or Different] Proportion: Fan Configuration

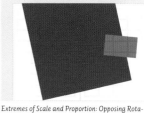
57**034**
Differing Proportions: Close Scale: Spontaneous Positioning: Collage Formation

57**035**
Extremes of Scale and Proportion: Orthogonal Orientation versus Rotation: Overlaps

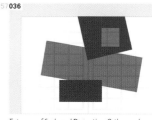
57**036**
Extremes of Scale and Proportion: Orthogonal Orientation versus Rotation: Overlaps and Inset

57**037**
Extremes of Scale and Proportion: Opposing Rotation: Overlap: Asymmetrical Bleed

57**038**
Clustering Formations: Same Proportion: Differing Scale: Insets versus Overlaps and Bleed

57**039**
Clustering Formations: Differing Proportions and Scales: Insets versus Overlaps and Bleed

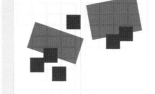
57**040**
Spontaneous Positioning: Rotation: Inset versus Exterior Bleeds

annual report spread

to prepare: flow text into columns
and style heads and subheads. lead the
text generously to enhance legibility

8x12 modular grid
{0.5" margin all around
except head {1.25"}
headline type: Univers 67
subheading: Univers 57
text face: Garamond 3 Oldstyle
bold caps

Project
RECIPES

A Full Menu of Graphic Concoctions for the Busy Designer's Every Need

1

APPETIZERS AND TAKEOUT

Such simple design applications as covers, ads, and website home pages—often the first taste of visual communication that viewers will confront—require the impact provided by strong imagery, color, and type, organized in simple, dynamic compositions. As a prelude to meatier content within, or as ephemeral, stand-alone visual snacks, they engage audiences at a glance with the promise of more to come.

Projects in This Section

COVER DESIGN
RESTAURANT MENU

SINGLE-PRODUCT PACKAGING
PHARMACEUTICALS

SIMPLE WEBSITE
HOME PAGE

IMAGE-DRIVEN AD
SINGLE-PAGE FORMAT

COVER DESIGN

RESTAURANT MENU
Japanese Restaurant

Messaging Menu

Convey a sense of the restaurant's cuisine through depiction of typical ingredients and preparation methods.

Communicate the cuisine's cultural context—geography, aesthetic heritage, and political history of Japan.

Visually support concepts related to the restaurant's name, which refers to the decorative art of folded paper.

Text Element Translations

Restaurant Name
The Origami House: Hibachi and Sushi Bar

Address
304 South Franklin Street

Supporting Information
Dinner Menu
Monday through Saturday, 6:00–11:00 p.m.

PICTO	
01001	*40*
01068	*41*
04013	*46*
04017	*47*
06005	*50*
14007	*66*
CHROMA	
20017	*80*
25021	*91*
TYPO	
37034	*117*
38029	*119*
SPATIAL	
49010	*142*
50004	*144*

FLAVOR PROFILE *Bold ● Simple ● Fun ● Symbolic ● Direct ●*
Formal Contrast ● Integrated ● Efficient

PICTO	
01058	*41*
01068	*41*
02020	*42*
03008	*44*
04020	*47*
05010	*48*
09018	*57*
10018	*58*
CHROMA	
20032	*80*
25021	*91*
TYPO	
37001	*116*
38023	*118*
SPATIAL	
49007	*142*
50038	*145*

FLAVOR PROFILE *Environmental ● Subtle Geometry ●*
Fluid ● Active Surface ● Architectural and Cultural References ●
Gestural ● Spontaneous

PICTO	
01016	*40*
01028	*40*
01068	*41*
09009	*56*
10031	*58*
17025	*72*
CHROMA	
25012	*90*
TYPO	
33007	*108*
37030	*117*
38009	*118*
SPATIAL	
49061	*143*

FLAVOR PROFILE *Geometric ● Handmade ● Organic ● Symbolic ●*
Rhythmic ● Detailed ● Emphasis on Land ● Type and Image Integrated

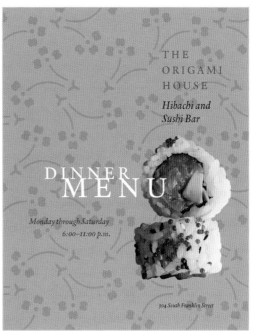

PICTO	
04001	*46*
06005	*50*
13001	*64*
CHROMA	
19013	*78*
19019	*78*
TYPO	
37006	*116*
38007	*118*
SPATIAL	
49032	*142*

FLAVOR PROFILE *Concrete Depiction ● Flat versus Dimensional ●*
Ornamental ● Detailed ● Elegant ● Emphasis on Food

PICTO
01064 41
01068 41
04017 47
10018 58
CHROMA
21019 82
TYPO
33001 108
33007 108
37030 117
38024 118
SPATIAL
49050 143
50005 144

FLAVOR PROFILE *Geometric ● Movement ● Ambiguous Space ●*
Playful ● Type as Image ● Dynamic ● Clean

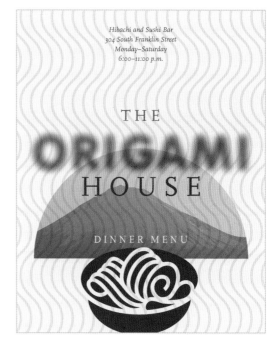

PICTO
01003 40
02053 42
04002 46
06023 51
15067 69
CHROMA
29002 98
TYPO
33031 109
37013 116
38002 118
SPATIAL
49025 142

FLAVOR PROFILE *Tension ● Movement ● Direct ● Iconic ●*
Stately ● Historical Color ● Hard/Soft Contrast

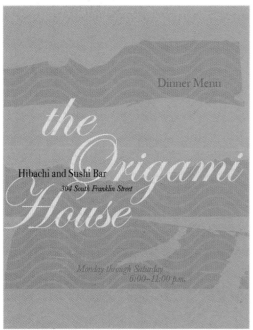

PICTO
01068 41
09015 56
15016 68
CHROMA
19028 78
29023 99
TYPO
37018 116
38040 119
SPATIAL
49009 142
50044 145

FLAVOR PROFILE *Allusive ● Organic ● Handmade ● Calligraphic ●*
Fluid ● Gestural ● Elegant ● Suggests Paper, Water, Land

PICTO
04012 46
04018 47
06026 51
CHROMA
19018 78
24010 88
TYPO
37030 117
38013 118
SPATIAL
49071 143

FLAVOR PROFILE *Architectural ● Dimensional ● Geometric ●*
Rhythmic ● Intricate ● Strong ● Layered ● Interactive Forms

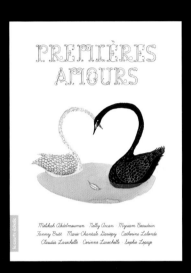

The delicate pencil and watercolor illustration of swans—whose slender necks create a symbolic heart shape—corroborates the romantic, ornamented title treatment and lilting script.
THOMAS CSANO
MONTREAL, QUEBEC | CANADA

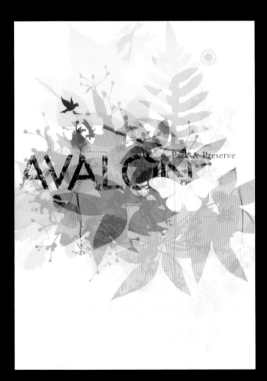

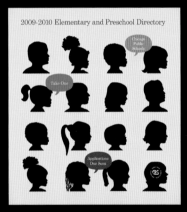

Stark black silhouettes are arranged in a four-unit grid on this school directory cover. This structure's regularity is relieved by the unique profile contours, asymmetrical placement of colorful callouts, and dynamic visual texture of the typeface.
KYM ABRAMS DESIGN CHICAGO, IL | UNITED STATES

The cover of this book for a nature preserve evokes the location's lush ecology with a luminous, layered collage of vividly colored plant and animal transparencies. The title nests itself among the leaves.
PAONE DESIGN ASSOCIATES
PHILADELPHIA, PA | UNITED STATES

The cover for an annual report (see spreads on page 193) focuses attention on an important financial figure with an asymmetrically configured shape that acts as a window for the image of a sky. A texture making up the large type, as well as crosshair elements and small, sharp text, contrast the neutral color field and bold geometric spatial breaks.

CREUNA OSLO │ NORWAY

The "discord" mentioned in the title of this CD cover is evoked in the misaligned meeting of the top and bottom halves of the diagonal line texture. The light, uniform strokes of all-uppercase type restate the pattern's linearity.

THINK STUDIO NEW YORK, NY │ UNITED STATES

This cover for a financial service firm's brochure uses a subtle visual metaphor to support the title concept; a rich palette of analogous and complementary colors underscores the concept's focus on the unique.

IDEAS ON PURPOSE NEW YORK, NY │ UNITED STATES

The designers of these covers for poetry books explore the allusive quality of form, situating a reserved titling treatment over sensuous, ornamental patterns. The swirling, decorative motifs provide a contemplative, literary quality, as well as evoke the fluid, metaphorical aspects of poetic writing. Austere, limited palettes bring warmth and contemporaneity.

PEOPLE DESIGN
GRAND RAPIDS, MI | UNITED STATES

The book covers in this series are unified through the use of a single serif type family and silhouetted, high-contrast images derived from treated photographs—as well as through a humble, textured, craft-paper cover stock.

THOMAS CSANO
MONTREAL, QUEBEC | CANADA

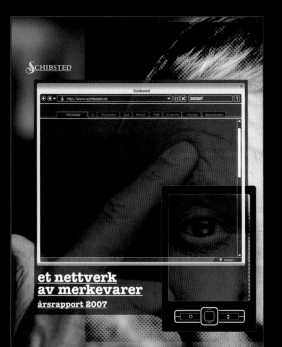

For the cover of this annual report, graphical depictions of browser interfaces overlap black-and-white photography (some of which is textured with a coarse dot screen) washed with color.

CREUNA OSLO | NORWAY

SINGLE-PRODUCT PACKAGING

PHARMACEUTICALS
Over-the-Counter Cold Remedy

Messaging Menu

Communicate the product's concept: a two-part remedy that provides relief and energy during the day, and comfortable restful sleep at night—suggested by the product's brand name, invented by combining the words relax *and* maximize.

Convey ideas of rest, energy, and health.

Suggest the efficacy of the product.

Text Element Translations

Product Brand Name
Relaximize Day and Night
Multisymptom 24-hour cold remedy

Tagline
Nondrowsy for daytime, helps you sleep through the night

Nondrowsy
for daytime,
helps you
sleep through
the night

RELAXIMIZE

DAY AND NIGHT

Multisymptom
24-hour
cold remedy

PICTO
14018 66
CHROMA
19001 78
19016 78
TYPO
37031 117
38025 119
38043 119
SPATIAL
49027 142

FLAVOR PROFILE *Complementary •
Direct • Abstract • Rhythmic • Ordered •
Energetic • Simple*

Multisymptom
24-hour cold remedy

NIGHT

RELAXIMIZE

DAY

Nondrowsy
for daytime,
helps you
sleep through
the night

PICTO
01028 40
01055 41
14018 66
CHROMA
19037 79
23028 87
TYPO
36028 115
38013 118
45014 132
SPATIAL
49025 142
50013 144

FLAVOR PROFILE *Diagonal Movement •
Transition • Direct • Strength • Reliability •
Ambiguous Space • Metaphorical*

Nondrowsy for
daytime, helps you sleep
through the night

Relaximize

Day and Night

Multisymptom
24-hour cold remedy

PICTO
01014 40
02089 43
15013 68
15043 68
CHROMA
19016 78
19025 78
TYPO
36027 115
38042 119
SPATIAL
49007 142
49018 142
50028 144

FLAVOR PROFILE *Transition • Integrated •
Complementary • Cool and Warm • Radial
Geometry • Time • Rhythmic*

Relaximize
Day
and Night

Multisymptom 24-hour cold remedy

Nondrowsy for daytime, helps
you sleep through the night

PICTO
01028 40
01035 40
02084 43
04019 47
05017 49
CHROMA
21045 83
TYPO
37029 117
38043 119
SPATIAL
49009 142

FLAVOR PROFILE *Allusive • Pictorial
Reference • Linear • Efficient • Direct*

Nondrowsy
for daytime,
helps you
sleep through
the night

MULTISYMPTOM
24-HOUR COLD REMEDY

RELAXIMIZE

D A Y A N D N I G H T

PICTO
01021 40
01028 40
02113 43
CHROMA
19049 79
20038 81
20066 81
TYPO
37043 117
38002 118
SPATIAL
49049 143

FLAVOR PROFILE *Juxtaposition of Abstract
and Iconic • Work • Relaxation • Contrast in
Energy • Strong*

Nondrowsy for daytime,
helps you sleep
through the night

Day and Night

Multisymptom
24-hour cold remedy

PICTO
01001 40
04020 47
12069 63
CHROMA
21033 83
25005 90
TYPO
34025 111
37043 117
38037 119
38039 119
SPATIAL
49008 142

FLAVOR PROFILE *Playful • Youthful •
Accessible • Montage • Vibrant • Contemporary •
Pill/Steel Equivalence*

Nondrowsy for daytime, helps you sleep through the night

R E L A X I

M I Z E D A Y

A N D N I G H T

MULTISYMPTOM 24-HOUR COLD REMEDY

PICTO
01057 41
08005 54
CHROMA
25010 90
TYPO
37029 117
38048 119
SPATIAL
49003 142

FLAVOR PROFILE *Stylized • Systematic •
Bold • Abstract • Effervescent • Energetic*

nondrowsy for
daytime, helps you sleep
through the night

Day and Night

relaximize

multisymptom
24-hour cold remedy

PICTO
01020 40
01021 40
04003 46
06005 50
06021 51
CHROMA
19038 79
25001 90
TYPO
34009 110
37027 117
38025 119
SPATIAL
49056 143
50007 144

FLAVOR PROFILE *Juxtaposition of Realism
and Stylization • Narrative • Dreamlike • Comfort •
Energy • Soft/Hard Contrast*

Nondrowsy for daytime, helps
you sleep through the night

RELAXIMIZE

DAY AND NIGHT

Multisymptom 24-hour cold remedy

PICTO
04001 46
CHROMA
21003 82
TYPO
37029 117
38038 119
SPATIAL
49008 142

FLAVOR PROFILE *Pictorial • Primary •
Vivid • Narrative • Everyday • Personal*

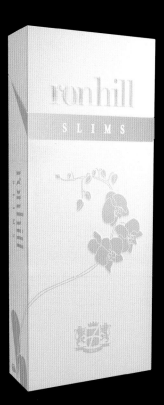

Neoclassical serif typefaces, with their pronounced stroke contrast, visually restate the thins and thicks of the iconic illustration, as well as impart a sense of luxury. The curling flower images position the product as refreshing and natural, while their compositional aspects suggest a cloud of smoke.

BRUKETA & ZINIC ZAGREB | CROATIA

In this cover for a songwriter's compilation CD, classic jazz-album typography is supported by a toned photograph; line and dot elements visually connect to the details in the image.

COMPASS 360 DESIGN
TORONTO, ONTARIO | CANADA

An economical label, as simple as it seems, nonetheless transforms this from a mere snack to an inviting experience through bold, sunny color, a friendly (almost schoolbook) slab serif, and cleverly subtle pictorial detail.

RED CANOE
DEER LODGE, TN | UNITED STATES

The tall, perky proportion of this juice packaging provides a tense, linear contrast to the collection of dotlike photographic forms. The images are lush and concrete, but organized to form a landscape, enhanced by illustrative elements that transform the scene into an engagingly surreal experience.

BRUKETA & ZINIC
ZAGREB | CROATIA

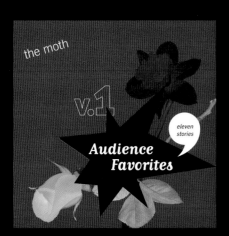

The dramatic complementary relationship of red-orange and blue-violet, enriched with black and an intense blue-green, acts as a compelling backdrop to the contrasting angular form and supporting, stylized flower images arranged in a loose, collage-like composition. The shapes, color, and abstracted floral forms allude to the dynamic experience of storytelling, the subject of this CD's package.

MARY DOMOWICZ
NEW YORK, NY | UNITED STATES

A subtle palette of blue hues—one intense, one desaturated and slightly darker in value—mutes the dramatic graphic quality of the abstract form language applied to this shopping bag. The logotype, a customized sans serif, contrasts the dots' mass with its sharp, heavy linearity.

SHINNOSKE, INC. OSAKA | JAPAN

SIMPLE WEBSITE

HOME PAGE
Financial Services Consultants

Messaging Menu

Communicate the client's primary service, banking and investment consulting.

Position the client as an advocate for their customers' lifestyle planning.

Convey the client's competency in their field of expertise.

*Differentiate the client through visual language that suggests
they are forward-thinking.*

Text Element Translations

Client Name
Fiske Market Consulting

Promotional Headlines
Investing from your perspective.
How do you see yourself living in the next twenty years? We see it, too.

Navigation Elements
Company Profile/Investor Services/Fund Portfolio/Client Area

PICTO	
01059	41
04001	46
04016	46
CHROMA	
19051	79
26001	92
TYPO	
36025	115
38005	118
46022	134
SPATIAL	
49007	142
52017	149
56004	156

FLAVOR PROFILE *Strong • Financial • Credible • Competent • Focused • Narrative • Planning versus Goal • Vibrant*

PICTO	
01068	41
04002	46
04005	46
05018	49
14022	66
CHROMA	
19051	79
26001	92
TYPO	
37025	117
38018	118
46044	135
SPATIAL	
53022	151
56006	156

FLAVOR PROFILE *Ordered • Mathematical • Rational • Linear • Dimensional • Fluidity • Responsive • Serious • Reliable*

PICTO	
04012	46
05004	48
CHROMA	
19057	79
26001	92
TYPO	
37001	116
38036	119
46045	135
SPATIAL	
52018	149

FLAVOR PROFILE *Distinctive • Neutral • Classical • Structured • Competent • Bookish • Textural • Reserved • Sophisticated*

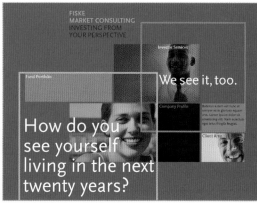

PICTO	
01052	41
04008	46
04017	47
CHROMA	
21028	83
26002	92
TYPO	
37025	117
38006	118
46049	135
SPATIAL	
53022	151
56006	156
56023	157

FLAVOR PROFILE *Simple • Organized • Direct • Mosaic • Part-to-Whole • Comprehensive • Progressive • Integrated*

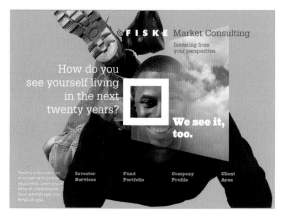

PICTO	
04001	46
06005	50
06019	51
06031	51
CHROMA	
29017	99
TYPO	
37040	117
38027	119
46047	135
SPATIAL	
52023	149

FLAVOR PROFILE *Personalized • Customer-Focused • Direct • Honest • Reliable • Clean • Metaphorical*

PICTO	
01054	41
01068	41
04001	46
06005	50
06009	50
06031	51
10001	58
CHROMA	
19018	78
26002	92
TYPO	
33031	109
37025	117
38025	119
46023	134
SPATIAL	
49056	143

FLAVOR PROFILE *Symbolic • Intangible • Aspirational • Concrete • Accessible • Youth into Retirement • Collage • Integrated*

A promotional website organizes closely cropped images and text in
a sliding, letter-boxed viewing area. Content is grouped according to
conceptual headings listed in the minimal navigation above the band.

PEOPLE DESIGN   GRAND RAPIDS, MI │ UNITED STATES

This elegant site groups thumbnail
grid navigation and text content
into a foreground box area, quietly
supported by muted color fields and
subtle patterns.

FORM   LONDON │ UNITED KINGDOM

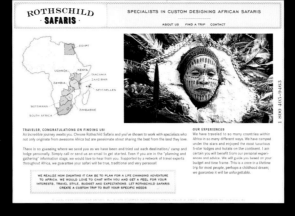

Relatively extensive informational text is cleanly organized on a hierarchic grid that provides distinct zones for branding, navigation, and imagery. Reversing the proportion of the geometric page breaks between zones adds movement. A selection of gothic sans serif and ornamental all-cap serif typefaces evokes the colonial period, as does the updated engraved line illustration of the map.

THINK STUDIO
NEW YORK, NY | UNITED STATES

The portfolio area of this design studio's website is accessed through a grid of intricate geometric patterns, each revealing a snapshot of a particular project case study upon rollover. The remaining navigation is clustered neatly to the left of the main texture grid.

BASE ART CO.
COLUMBUS, OHIO | UNITED STATES

This website for a manufacturer of hiking boots organizes images and navigation in a photographic scrapbook-style collage. Earthy colors and a background of tree bark reinforce the rustic message.

999 DESIGN
LONDON | UNITED KINGDOM

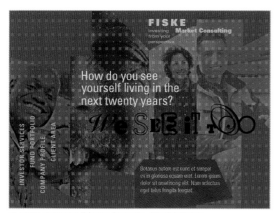

FLAVOR PROFILE *Eclectic • Geometric • Mixed Narratives •*
Presentational • Dimensional • Constructing • Fluid

FLAVOR PROFILE *Thematic • Romantic • Storybook • Dimensional •*
Interactive • Detailed • Dream versus Concrete • Metaphorical

FLAVOR PROFILE *Eclectic • Narrative • Symbolic • Delicate • Nostalgic •*
Comfortable • Reserved •

FLAVOR PROFILE *Contemporary • Clean • Professional •*
Subtle Ornamentation • Organized • Environmental Reference

FLAVOR PROFILE *Illustrative • Narrative • Gestural • Personal •*
Dimensional • Spontaneous • Playful

FLAVOR PROFILE *Efficient • Informational • Rigorous • Sophisticated •*
Neutral • Geometric • Systematic • Edgy • Technological

A free-form collage of photographic
elements allows users to navigate through
the content of this promotional website.

MAURICE REDMOND/FEUER
MUNICH | GERMANY

This website template articulates text
and inset images, along with an interactive
timeline, over a three-column hierarchic
grid; abstract forms derived from the
featured art activate the austere white
space of the background, their color used
to highlight navigational links.

FRANCESCA SCIANDRA
NEW YORK, NY | UNITED STATES

Text, images, and navigation, organized
in a hierarchic column grid, are supported
by a full-screen backdrop of sensuously
lit fabric in this site for an apparel manufacturer. The navigation is classically
typeset on a photographic clothing tag.

2FRESH ISTANBUL | TURKEY,
LONDON | UNITED KINGDOM

IMAGE-DRIVEN AD

SINGLE-PAGE FORMAT
Lifestyle Products

Messaging Menu

Identify the brand and purpose of the product.

Establish an understanding of the product's organic, botanical qualities.

Evoke the product's effectiveness as a result of advanced scientific manufacture.

Convey a sense of improved hygiene, health, and energy.

Communicate the product's potential to improve long-term health.

Text Element Translations

Client
Nutria Bath and Body System

Headline and Deck
Revive and Conquer! Don't simply clean, but catalyze—
with the science of organic botanicals.

Tagline
Science makes the difference.

Body copy is represented by dummy text
in this project.

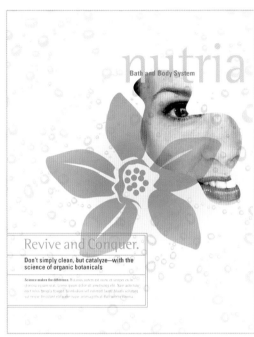

PICTO
02025 42
04001 46
06024 51
10011 58

CHROMA
19029 78
25010 90

TYPO
36028 115
38031 119

SPATIAL
49008 142
50003 144
56036 157

FLAVOR PROFILE *Iconic ● Botanical ● Scientific ● Authoritative ●*
Natural ● Clean ● Direct ● Refreshing

PICTO
01028 40
02005 42
09030 57

CHROMA
25010 90

TYPO
34024 110
36028 115
37025 117

SPATIAL
49040 143

FLAVOR PROFILE *Invigorating ● Clean ● Metaphorical ● Elemental ●*
Imaginative ● Organic ● Sensuous

PICTO
01028 40
01067 41
04001 46
06023 51
08020 55
10022 58

CHROMA
19029 78
25007 90

TYPO
36029 115
37025 117
38007 118
38038 119
39011 120

SPATIAL
49010 142
50040 145

FLAVOR PROFILE *Scientific ● Source versus Use ● Botanical ●*
Molecular ● Analytical ● High-End ● Personalized

PICTO
01025 40
01028 40
02033 42
06005 50
11042 61

CHROMA
20039 81
26008 92

TYPO
34048 111
36030 115
38008 118

SPATIAL
49005 142
50003 144
50045 145

FLAVOR PROFILE *Empowered ● Clean ● Aspirational ● Scientific ●*
Botanical ● Classical ● Strong ● Simple ● Health-Conscious

NUTRIA

Bath and Body System

Botanus autem est nunc et semper ex in gloriose equam erat. Lorem ipsum dolor sit ametlacing elit. Nam nelectus egestas fringilla fngiat mogaficat in dus coelis.

Science makes the difference

Vestibulum vel euismod lacus mauris volu tupat sui neque tincidunt elit sceler isque artem lsque isque artinfomgilla bogat magnificat in dus coelis. Lorem ipsum dolor sit amelsicing elit. Nam nelectus egestas fringila fngiat mogaficat in dus coelis.

Revive and
Conquer.
Don't simply clean, but catalyze—with the science of organic botanicals

FLAVOR PROFILE *Editorial • Classical • Victorian • Sensuous •*
Experiential • Detailed • Suggests Indulgence

PICTO	
04001	46
06005	50
13004	64
17009	72
CHROMA	
28001	96
29006	98
TYPO	
37047	117
38035	119
38040	119
40017	123
40030	123
SPATIAL	
49002	142
49011	142

revive and conquer.
don't simply clean, but catalyze—
with the science of organic botanicals

bath and body system

nutria

FLAVOR PROFILE *Joyous • Illustrative • Dimensional • Active •*
Healthy • Everyday • Youthful Lifestyle • Vibrant

PICTO	
01013	40
01018	40
02084	43
07022	53
18008	74
18013	74
CHROMA	
19002	78
25016	90
28002	96
TYPO	
37025	117
38029	119
38031	119
45025	133
SPATIAL	
50056	145

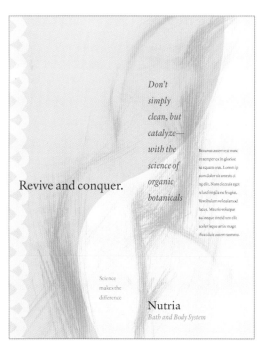

Don't simply clean, but catalyze— with the science of organic botanicals

Revive and conquer.

Botanus autem est nunc et semper ex in gloriose sa equam erat. Lorem ip sum dolor sit ameta ci ng elit. Nam clectus eger tclus fringila ex feugiat. Vestibulum vel euismod lacus. Mauris volutpat sui neque tincid um elit sceler isque artin magn ificat duis autem summa.

Science makes the difference

Nutria
Bath and Body System

FLAVOR PROFILE *Emphasis on Female Health • Energetic •*
Illustrative • Botanical Allusion • Personal • Handmade

PICTO	
01068	41
07002	52
17046	73
CHROMA	
19014	78
28002	96
TYPO	
37002	116
38007	118
44016	130
SPATIAL	
49012	142
50044	145

Revive and conquer.

Don't simply clean,
but catalyze—with the science
of organic botanicals

NUTRIA

bath and
body system

Botanus autem est nunc et semper ex in gloriose sa equam erat. Lorem ip sum dolor sit ametis ci ng elit. Nam clectus egt teius fringila ex feugiat.

Vestibulum vel euismod lacus. Mauris volutpat sui neque tincid unt elit sceler isque artix magn ificat duis autem summa.

Science makes the difference

FLAVOR PROFILE *Subtle • Gradual • Enhancing • Molecular •*
Modern Science versus Romantic Experience • Effective • Beauty

PICTO	
01018	40
01028	40
01057	41
04001	46
06005	50
06021	51
13048	65
14019	66
CHROMA	
21021	82
21043	83
TYPO	
37030	117
38041	119
44019	130
45024	133
SPATIAL	
49009	142
50043	145

The designer characterizes the family-friendly performance of an iconic symphonic work with a charming, simplified illustration style and stylized script titling elements. A rich, analogous color palette suggests the narrative's rural setting.

999 DESIGN LONDON | UNITED KINGDOM

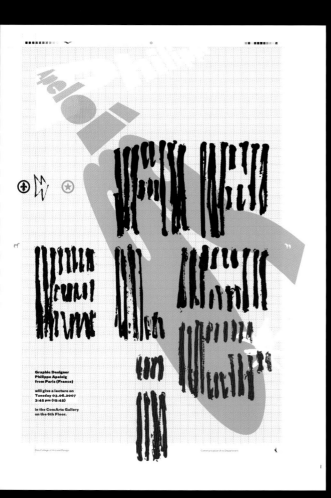

This poster for a lecture by typographic innovator Philippe Apeloig mixes hand-drawn icons with dimensional and abstract type treatments characteristic of his work. An intricate layout grid alludes to the designer's process and precision.

DURRE DESIGN RANCHO PALOS VERDE, CA | UNITED STATES

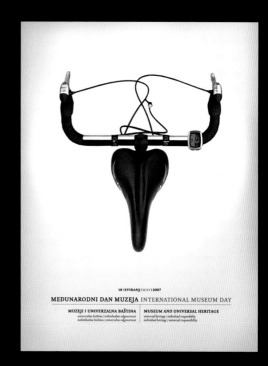

This poster ad promotes art's timelessness through an image that evokes the iconic messages of cave painting while riffing on an iconic, modern sculpture by Pablo Picasso. Careful control of visual contrast among elements introduces rhythm and tension

A swirling spiral of multicolored, woven texture leads the eye to its asymmetrically placed focal point—a block of information set all uppercase and organized by line elements.

TACTICAL MAGIC

MEMPHIS, TN | UNITED STATES

Complementary colors support the bold, iconic depiction in this poster. Careful attention to detail, such as can be seen in the dashed outline of the titling element, as well as in the positioning of darker elements, adds contrast and offsets the direct, symmtrical presentation of the image.

LSD MADRID | SPAIN

The grid used to organize product images within the pages of a jewelry catalogue (see page 193) appears in a clever arrangement of boxes on the catalog cover.

SUNG SOO SONG
NEW YORK, NY | UNITED STATES

Overprinting the same coarse dot-screen image in complementary red and green—usually associated with 3D images—evokes a disoriented state of mind in need of conceptual medication.

STEREOTYPE DESIGN

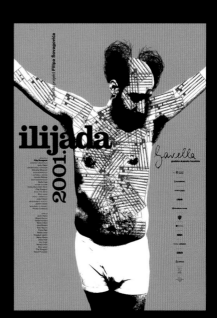

FIRST COURSES

These are savory transitions between the introductory messages of visual appetizers and the menu's main dish, or somewhat more complex projects of a serial or sequential nature. Type plays a greater role in flavoring these communications—storefront displays, editorial page spreads, and advertising campaigns—but imagery remains a strong component of the flavor profile.

SIMPLE EDITORIAL PAGES

NEWSLETTER/MAGAZINE FEATURE
Nonprofit Organization

Messaging Menu

Communicate the financial subject of the feature article.

Organize the editorial content with images and the newsletter's table of contents.

Refer to the client's core activities: building low-income housing, refurbishing neglected properties, and developing public green spaces and gardens.

Indicate the publication's seasonal period.

Text Element Translations

Article Headline

Welcome to the Jungle: Navigating the Nonprofit Venture Capital Market

Article Deck

In today's volatile economy, many venture capital firms are delaying investment until they see the prospect of a good return—often preventing early initiatives that could ensure such certainty.

Article Callout

"We have to look rational, but part of the equation is passion."
Walter Rosegarten, Venture Capitalist

Newsletter Masthead

Urban Hope Quarterly/October 2012 /Volume 5, Issue 02

Body copy and contents listing elements in this project are represented by dummy text.

FLAVOR PROFILE

Geometric • Ordered • Simple • Clean • Academic • Formal • Rigorous • Ecological • Urban • Journalistic

Welcome to the Jungle: Navigating the Nonprofit Venture Capital Market

In today's volatile economy, many venture capital firms are delaying investment until they see the prospect of a good return—often preventing early initiatives that could ensure such certainty.

"We have to look rational, but part of the equation is passion."
Walter Rosegarten, Venture Capitalist

PICTO
04017 47
04019 47
04029 47
06005 50

CHROMA
20047 81
20064 81

TYPO
37048 117
38017 118
40002 122
41001 124
42012 126
44017 130
46011 134

SPATIAL
49046 143
49048 143
51017 147
57002 158

FLAVOR PROFILE

Complex • Accessible • Layered • Graphing Reference • Iconic • Constructing • Organized • Financial Emphasis • Sophisticated • Formal

Welcome to the Jungle

Navigating the Nonprofit Venture Capital Market

In today's volatile economy, many venture capital firms are delaying investment until they see the prospect of a good return—often preventing early initiatives that could ensure such certainty.

"We have to look rational, but part of the equation is passion."
Walter Rosegarten, Venture Capitalist

PICTO
02090 43
02104 43
04017 47
04030 47
18049 75

CHROMA
21046 83

TYPO
37038 117
38034 119
41027 125
42008 126
44017 130
46010 134

SPATIAL
52011 148
57004 158

FLAVOR PROFILE

Dynamic Color • Dimensional • Physical • Icon Detailing • Organized • Industrial • Journalistic • Subtly Playful

In today's volatile economy, many venture capital firms are delaying investment until they see the prospect of a good return—often preventing early initiatives that could ensure such certainty.

Navigating the Nonprofit Venture Capital Market

We have to look rational, but part of the equation is passion.
Walter Rosegarten, Venture Capitalist

PICTO
02030 42
04012 46
04032 47

CHROMA
21022 82
21023 82

TYPO
37048 117
38025 119
39026 121
40002 122
40020 123
40029 123
41005 124
42019 127
46045 135

SPATIAL
53017 151
57003 158

These pages from an event invitation show a rich combination of illustrative elements—colorized photographs, ornamental patterns, and border treatments—supported by detailed typography that uses line rules, patterns, initial numerals, and colored text.

IDEAS ON PURPOSE
NEW YORK, NY | UNITED STATES

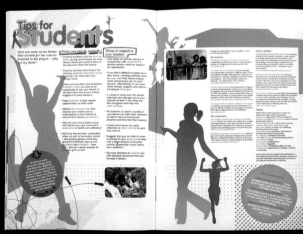

Using a common, stylized icon of the female form as a primary image in this brochure—for the cover, as part of a photographic illustration, and as the basis for charts—underscores statistical information and reinforces a projection of female worker identity.

KYM ABRAMS DESIGN
CHICAGO, IL | UNITED STATES

An exciting mix of such illustrative elements as vector silhouettes, scribbles, arrows, icons, and grids combines with a soft, neutral sans serif to create an engaging publication for students.

FORM LONDON | UNITED KINGDOM

Introduction

The word on the street & a simple version rule book

Dive Billiards is an up and coming quarterly Mag Zine with the means to promote and endure the ever so hard to find, decent dive bars with decent pool tables within the best part of New York City. We strive for a quality game and a quality priced beer without a crowd. Nothing beats free pool, free beer and playing a good game with your friends.

A scratch (cue ball in the pocket or off the table) is ball in the kitchen. There is no penalty for a table scratch (hitting no ball or hitting your opponents ball first, even if its hit an accident or on purpose). Everything must be called, every ball involved in a carom and every ball involved in a combo. You have to call each rail that you will hit.

Contents

The Editors Page
Jasen Rolfe & the quality game of pool.

Being only a few year resident of NYC new things come and go like crazy but some of them stick. After discovering pool again I figured out that it is actually a lot more entertaining to shoot some pool during your night of drinking.

Pool can be very competitive and difficult. If you strive to be a better pool player than keep reading. For me I go to the bar and drink and get completely wasted. When I go to the bar and play pool I dont get wasted. The game keeps you focused and excersizes your brain and eyes. It can actually be straining after lengths of time. However, the need for pool became a demand as I grew into a better player. Running the table at a bar is fun and you save money every time you win so no matter what there is always some kind of positive incentive.

Jasen D. Rolfe
Editor in Chief

info@thebambieffect.com

DIVE BILLIARDS INC.
357 Second Ave 2-F
New York, NY 10003
212.579.4473 P
212.434.9978 F
www.divebilliards.com

This quarterly newsletter mixes a variety of illustration styles—high-contrast photography, vector objects, and engraving—with contemporary sans serif faces and Victorian layout and text detailing to evoke the hip, yet timeless, character of the dive bar billiards enthusiast.

JASEN D. ROLFE LEXINGTON, MA | UNITED STATES

éire

words and images by joseph caserto

A vacation in Ireland helps me learn to look for beauty and inspiration in everyday surroundings.

My first trip out of the country after September 11th was my second journey to the Emerald Isle, birthplace of my Great-Grandfather, Bernard O'Connor. We left in October of 2002, by which time, I was in need of a break from the stress of living in New York as the new world-order unfolded. The news was full of reports on anthrax, bioterrorism, and (fictional) WMDs in Iraq, where war loomed imminent. Not at so

Starkly defined spatial divisions across the width of this magazine page spread establish a strong compositional geometry which the various elements alternately complement and contrast. The boundary between image and negative space is crossed by the deck, but repeated by the text block. The architectural qualities of the layout are contrasted by the roundness of the title form, yet the tree's arc is repeated in by the accented lowercase e. Diagonals differing line weights, and scale within the image are restated by the sizes, weights, and positioning of the typographic elements.

JOSEPH CASERTO
ART DIRECTION AND DESIGN
BROOKLYN, NY | UNITED STATES

FLAVOR PROFILE
Metaphorical ● Illustrative ●
Inviting ● Diverse ● Personal ●
Metaphorical ● Narrative ●
Hierarchic ● Navigable

WELCOME TO THE JUNGLE
Navigating the Nonprofit Venture Capital Market

In today's volatile economy, many venture capital firms are delaying investment until they see the prospect of a good return—often preventing early initiatives that could ensure such certainty.

We have to look rational, but part of the equation is passion. Walter Rosegarten *Venture Capitalist*

Urban Hope *Quarterly*
October 2012 Volume 4, Issue 10

In this issue

Early funding allowed Urban Hope to complete its first green space during startup, fulfilling its core mission and creating a strong track record from the very beginning.

PICTO	
04001	46
04019	47
06022	51
07009	52
07015	52
CHROMA	
20003	80
20025	80
20035	80
TYPO	
37048	117
38038	119
38043	119
40009	122
41029	125
42024	127
44017	130
44019	130
46026	135
SPATIAL	
49008	142
53026	151

FLAVOR PROFILE
Modular ● Precisely Organized ●
Dramatic Depth ● Textural ●
Gritty ● Businesslike ● Urban
Interactive ● Confrontational

In today's volatile economy, many venture capital firms are delaying investment until they see the prospect of a good return—often preventing early initiatives that could ensure such certainty

We have to look rational, but part of the equation is passion.

WELCOME TO THE JUNGLE

Navigating the Nonprofit Venture Capital Market

Urban Hope
Quarterly

OCTOBER 2012
Volume 4, Issue 10

In this issue

Early funding allowed Urban Hope to complete its first green space during startup, fulfilling its core mission and creating a strong track record from the very beginning.

PICTO	
04026	47
05022	49
17069	73
CHROMA	
19026	78
25002	90
TYPO	
33021	108
34028	111
37025	117
38007	118
38017	118
40005	122
41009	124
42004	126
44012	130
46012	134
SPATIAL	
49052	143
53026	151
55007	154
56021	157

FLAVOR PROFILE
Geometric ● Hierarchic ●
Journalistic ● Ecological ●
Urban ● Architectural ●
Businesslike

In today's volatile economy, many venture capital firms are delaying investment until they see the prospect of a good return—often preventing early initiatives that could ensure such certainty.

Lorem ex ipsum dolor sit amet, consec tetur ars adipi scing elitu. Cras aclect us arcu. Pelle due ntesque port titor ligula vita e quam mal escuto ada ut dignis sim lectus factuum somatis ardu etin se mateo, aivam us vitae auctor sem. Donec Lorem ex ipsum dolor sit amet, consec tetur ars adipi scing elitu. Cras aclect us arcu.

Doraxus autem est enim stela rutron facilatae sem et nihi. Mauris diam conec vol putate at ponuere id, euefend vel nunc. Nullam nulla lacus, rhoncus ut imnpuseo amet, tristique nec sat. Vivam us sit amet augue in bela elemen tem congue. Cras consec tet ut felis sed dui molestia at tinpor neque faclisis. Pellan nequ ani met months tristique senectus et tus sem uma an urda future aturpa is egestas. Nulla facilsi. Vestibul smarktoum sit auctor. Lorem ipsum dolor sit amet.

Welcome to the Jungle
Navigating the Nonprofit Venture Capital Market

Urban Hope Quarterly

IN THIS ISSUE

We have to look rational, but part of the equation is passion. Walter Rosegarten *Venture Capitalist*

Early funding allowed Urban Hope to complete its first green space during startup, fulfilling its core mission and creating a strong track record from the very beginning.

PICTO	
04001	46
04009	46
04032	47
06005	50
CHROMA	
21039	83
25002	90
TYPO	
37038	117
38017	118
38038	119
40009	122
41009	124
44002	130
44026	131
46013	134
SPATIAL	
52022	149
56003	156
56027	157
57006	158

Basic geometric shapes frame text columns, integrating them in the compositional spaces of dramatically cropped color photographs. Typographic callouts are treated with a linear pattern.

CREUNA OSLO | NORWAY

For a product catalog, jewelry is presented in varying layouts on a consistent grid structure, with page colors responding to the particular metal used in the work.

SUNG SOO SONG

NEW YORK, NY | UNITED STATES

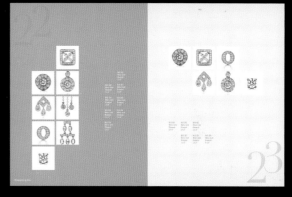

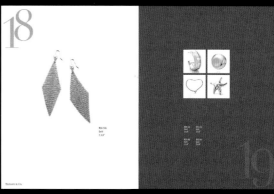

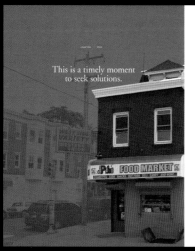

If Beverly Davis can get back on her feet, she wants to enroll her daughter Alyla in dance class or gymnastics.

This is a timely moment to seek solutions.

This sleek layout for a report related to urban poverty juxtaposes stately, almost bookish, typography—in a quiet mix of serif and sans serif faces—with selectively toned images in which focal points are silhouetted in vivid color.

IDEAS ON PURPOSE

NEW YORK, NY | UNITED STATES

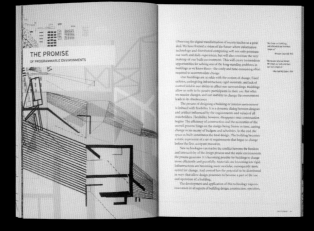

Geometric forms, abstracted from furniture, architecture, and science diagrams, compose the section-opener pages in this furniture brochure. Offsetting their cold linearity is the fact that they were drawn by hand. Overprinted colors in muted, complementary palettes enrich the chromatic experience. The typography alternates between hard-edged sans serif display and sharply elegant serif text.

PEOPLE DESIGN GRAND RAPIDS, MI | UNITED STATES

This annual report is unconventionally formatted as an accordion-fold booklet. One side presents upper-level messaging—an overview of business performance integrated with texture-treated slices of photography—while the other shows saturated, full-bleed photographs alternating with large typographic highlights. The financial tables are bound in as a saddle-stitched booklet, continuing the linear elements established in the other pages.

ANN IM SUNWOO
NEW YORK, NY | UNITED STATES

the overall visual unity provided by a
tight, eight-column grid and single
typeface family—in this case, a slightly
condensed sans serif with rounded terminals that is both strong and friendly.

CREUNA OSLO | NORWAY

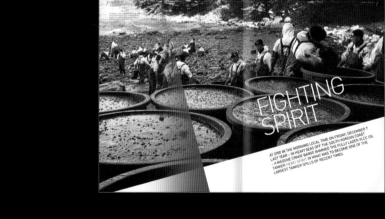

This season brochure for a dance company features
closely cropped black-and-white photographs of dancers,
overlaid with colored cutouts derived from the shapes
within the images. A neutral typographic structure
offsets the images' dynamism.

SURFACE FRANKFURT AM MEIN | GERMANY

RETAIL DISPLAY

STOREFRONT WINDOW PROMOTION
Home Decor and Housewares Store

Messaging Menu

Establish the nature of the client's business: retail home furnishings.

Communicate the range of product styles offered.

Appeal to style-conscious, upwardly mobile customers and interior designers.

Convey the aesthetic and production qualities of the furnishings.

Announce the featured sale on lighting.

Allude to the season of the promotion.

Text Element Translations

Client Logotype
The Home Store

Promotional Headline
*Essential Room Service: Fancy and Fine to
Mod and Minimal*

Deck
The Spring Collections Are Here

Sale Announcement
For a limited time: 30% off all lighting fixtures

Listing Elements
*Chairs / Sofa / Sectionals / Credenzas /
Ottomans / Divans / End Tables / Shelving /
Stools / Display Cases / Lamps / Sconces*

Dimensional • Kinetic •
Contemporary • Concrete •
Rich • Stylish • Eclectic •
Layered • Constructed •
Geometric • Detailed

PICTO	
02059	42
02064	42
04001	46
CHROMA	
28006	96
TYPO	
37003	116
37031	117
38038	119
38043	119
46041	135
SPATIAL	
49037	143

FLAVOR PROFILE
Eclectic • Ambiguous Space •
Seasonal • Fresh • Fun •
Decorative • Vibrant •
Contemporary • Pop

PICTO	
01016	40
01020	40
04009	46
04029	47
06005	50
10032	58
12026	62
13013	64
14004	66
CHROMA	
25029	91
28005	96
TYPO	
33025	109
33030	109
37029	117
38027	119
46048	135
SPATIAL	
49010	142
49040	143
49055	143

FLAVOR PROFILE
Pattern Against Solid •
Linear • Geometric •
Urban • Quirky •
Lifestyle • Objects and
Spaces • Dimensional •
Customizable

PICTO	
01019	40
01056	41
04011	46
04024	47
04030	47
06005	50
10022	58
13051	65
13052	65
13064	65
14011	66
14031	66
16126	71
CHROMA	
25002	90
TYPO	
36047	115
37030	117
38038	119
46022	134
SPATIAL	
52013	148

PICTO
08022 55
13042 65
13064 65
13067 65

CHROMA
25017 91
29023 99

TYPO
33009 108
37028 117
38042 119
38048 119

SPATIAL
49019 142
49035 142

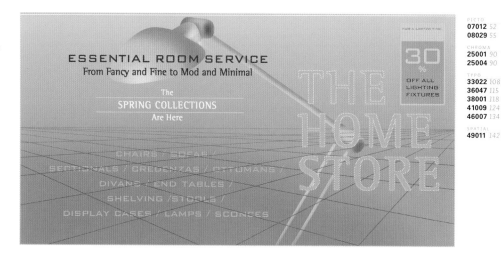

PICTO
07012 52
08029 55

CHROMA
25001 90
25004 90

TYPO
33022 108
36047 115
38001 118
41009 124
46007 134

SPATIAL
49011 142

PICTO
04032 47

CHROMA
22013 84
23027 87

TYPO
37030 117
38018 118
38042 119
41009 124
44017 130

SPATIAL
52011 148
56011 156
56028 157
57006 158

The graphic power of physical forms and materials—stone, glass, metal, textured paper—is evidenced by the bold environment created for this restaurant. A palette of neutrals is punctuated by a vivid orange wall, while the linearity of the wall pattern and seating areas gets a pop of contrast from giant, shiny dots: pendant lamps and grid-mounted mirrors.
KUHLMANN LEAVITT DESIGN
SAINT LOUIS, MO | UNITED STATES

In this exhibition design, compositional layering of photographic, textural, and physical elements creates dimensional, vignetted compositions. Considering multiple viewing angles, the effects of light and transparency, and color relationships between fabrication materials and the content of the display affords a design experience similar to that of a retail display or even a printed application.
ATELIER BRÜCKNER
STUTTGART | GERMANY

Branded construction barricades designed around various type-textured C forms provide visual relief from storefront renovation and create expectation for the future potential of the street-level display.
ADAMSMORIOKA
BEVERLY HILLS, CA | UNITED STATES

POSTER/AD CAMPAIGN

KIOSK OR SINGLE-PAGE FORMAT
Men's Fragrance

Messaging Menu

Introduce and visually brand an upscale Italian fragrance.

Convey the product's masculine focus.

Express notions of mystery and surrealism; evoke the sensuality of fragrance, creating a sensory experience.

Create provocative narratives, suggesting the taboo nature of diverse sexuality among men.

Equate the fragrance with an aspired-to lifestyle of adventure, intrigue, power, and pleasure.

Text Element Translations

Ad Headlines
It takes one to know one. (1)
Maybe you do, maybe you don't. (2)
One door closes, another opens. (3)

Product Brand and Positioning Statement
Mistero: There's a little mystery in every man

Tagline
The new fragrance for men who know better

Body copy is represented by dummy text in this project.

FLAVOR PROFILE

Smoky ● Fluid ●
Languorous ● Elegant ●
Sensuous ● Rich ●
Body-Conscious ●
Strong ● Nebulous

PICTO	
04007	46
09014	56
11040	61
CHROMA	
25013	90
25014	90
TYPO	
37025	117
38031	119
45005	132
45032	133
SPATIAL	
49001	142
50044	144
50045	145

FLAVOR PROFILE

Illustrative ● Sharp ●
Narrative ● Obscuring
and Revealing ●
Intrigue ● Power ●
Counterintuitive

PICTO	
01007	40
02014	42
02024	42
02027	42
02060	42
02090	43
02122	43
02125	43
07025	53
18010	74
18013	74
18039	75
CHROMA	
20013	80
23015	86
TYPO	
37026	117
38008	118
38038	119
45014	132
SPATIAL	
49008	142
50015	144

FLAVOR PROFILE

Sensuous ● Tactile
Ambiguous Space ●
Fluid ● Elegant ●
Powerful ● Hidden ●
Interior and Exterior
Life ● Emotional

PICTO	
04007	46
05026	49
06031	51
09030	57
CHROMA	
28010	96
28023	97
TYPO	
37039	117
38023	118
45024	133
SPATIAL	
49007	142
50044	145
56030	157

unify the four posters in this series; radically altering the
overprints of process colors differentiates each poster.

SHINNOSKE, INC.   OSAKA │ JAPAN

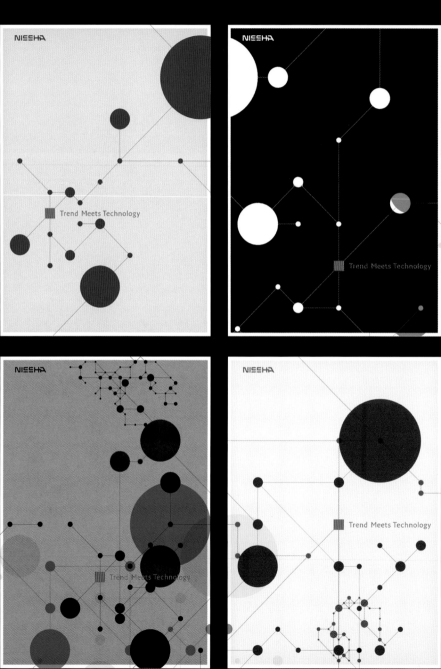

Each poster predicates the type arrangement on the photographic element, here reduced to nearly pure geometry and richly illuminated. A rhythmic mix of serifs and sans serifs alternates weights, cases, and spacing.

PAONE DESIGN ASSOCIATES
PHILADELPHIA, PA ｜ UNITED STATES

This ad campaign for children's furnishings creates surreal and dynamically composed environments with color coding; each ad mixes analogous values and temperatures of a predominant color, accented by tiny amounts of complements.

PEOPLE DESIGN

FLAVOR PROFILE

Iconic • Symbolic • Industrial • Urban • Edgy • Electronic • Pop-Culture Environment • Trendy • Dominating • Confrontational

PICTO	
02082	43
02084	43
02087	43
03019	45
08005	54
18031	75
18036	75
18037	75

CHROMA	
20006	80
21021	82

TYPO	
36044	115
37029	117
38006	118
38007	118
44026	131

SPATIAL	
49008	142
49010	142

FLAVOR PROFILE

Illustrative • Kinetic • Ambiguous Masculine Sexuality • Symbolic • Collage • Retro • Multilayered

PICTO	
05002	48
05012	48
17025	72

CHROMA	
25008	90
28014	96

TYPO	
37034	117
38016	118
45016	132

SPATIAL	
49033	142

FLAVOR PROFILE

Animal and Natural Allusions • Suggests the Irrational • Intimate • Seductive Gaze • Confrontation

PICTO	
04001	46
04023	47
06026	51
10006	58
10041	59
10043	59

CHROMA	
20018	80
25002	90

TYPO	
34036	111
37009	116

SPATIAL	
49015	142
56024	157

The deadpan quality of these ad headlines is echoed by cut-and-paste, photocopied imagery. Contributing to the dry sense of imperfection, the headlines are drawn in marker. A full-bleed texture softens the compositional geometry.

MAURICE REDMOND / FEUER
MUNICH | GERMANY

Much like an ad campaign, this series of educational book covers uses a graphic headline treatment to propose provocative questions related to social issues. The unified graphic language of vector illustrations and a soft, yet industrial, pseudo-stencil font is supported by a limited palette based on maps.

FORM LONDON | UNITED KINGDOM

High-contrast, posterized photography, supported by the dynamic texture of hand-generated ink spatter, works in tandem with neutral, all-uppercase text that has also been textured. The complementary colors vary in saturation and value to increase the poster's dimensionality.

MAURICE REDMOND/FEUER
MUNICH | GERMANY

A series of promotional flyers mixes textured, woodcut-like illustrations in varying combinations with a supporting abstract texture. An analogous color scheme in each flyer is accented by a complementary hue.

THOMAS CSANO
MONTREAL, QUEBEC | CANADA

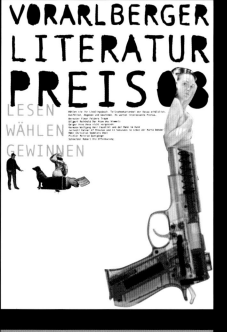

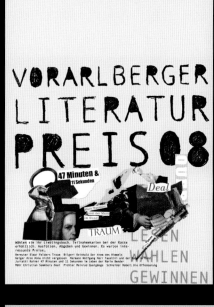

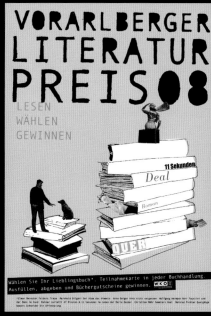

Charming, hand-drawn type treatments and quirky, primitively
cutout illustrations lend a friendly, inviting quality to these posters
for a culture festival. The designer rearranges similar elements to
unify the series while maintaining interest.

SÄGENVIER DESIGN KOMMUNIKATION

DORNBIRN │ AUSTRIA

LARGE PLATES AND ENTREES

Illustrated here are approaches to the meat and potatoes of
visual communication—casseroles of complex, informational
organization such as text-heavy editorial and web publishing,
and visual branding systems for multicomponent product packaging.
The audience has already whetted its appetite and is prepared to
dig in. Rich imagery and extensive typographic structure are folded
into stick-to-the-ribs layouts that will satisfy the hungriest viewer.

Projects in This Section

PACKAGING SYSTEM

LUXURY SWEETS
Artisanal Flavored Chocolates

Messaging Menu

Communicate the unique features of the product: unusually flavored, richly crafted chocolates.

Evoke the history and sensuality of chocolate.

Differentiate and express the individual flavor profiles of each product type.

Visually support the brand's mythological, narrative concept.

Allude to the geographical context of each product type.

Text Element Translations

Brand Name, Positioning, and Tagline
Celestia
Exotically spiced artisanal chocolates
Heavenly Different

Product Names and Descriptors
Vishnu (1)
Garam masala-infused milk chocolate with goat's milk praline chunks

Quetzalcoatl (2)
Jalapeño-infused white chocolate with turmeric-encrusted golden raisins

Artemis (3)
Rosemary-infused dark chocolate with almonds and braised apple slices

FLAVOR PROFILE *Sensuous • Exotic • Ornamental • Detailed • Finely-Crafted • Victorian • Sweet • Sumptuous • Narrative*

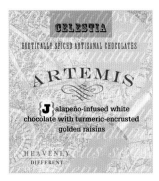

PICTO
04012 *46*
04029 *47*
05021 *49*
09014 *56*
17052 *73*

CHROMA
25012 *90*
29006 *98*

TYPO
35021 *112*
35022 *112*
37023 *116*
38001 *118*
38030 *119*
39008 *120*
48259 *139*
48280 *139*
48303 *139*

SPATIAL
49010 *142*

FLAVOR PROFILE *Sensuous • Organic • Tactile • Languid • Dreamlike • Restive • Quirky • Stylized*

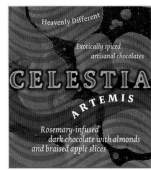

PICTO
04032 *47*
10010 *58*
15078 *69*

CHROMA
22042 *85*
25012 *90*

TYPO
33043 *109*
37001 *116*
45024 *133*
45032 *133*

SPATIAL
49007 *142*
50044 *145*

FLAVOR PROFILE *Cultural Context • Contemporary • Clean • Luxurious • Narrative • Concrete • Depiction • Flat versus Dimensional*

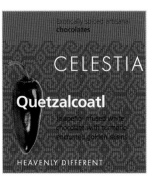

PICTO
04001 *46*
06005 *50*
13015 *64*
13064 *65*
13068 *65*

CHROMA
32003 *104*

TYPO
37031 *117*

SPATIAL
49008 *142*
49011 *142*

FLAVOR PROFILE *Mythic • Sculptural • Narrative • References • Cultural Aesthetics • Symbolic • Majestic • Magical • Rich*

PICTO
01041 *41*
01049 *41*
01060 *41*
04029 *47*
06005 *50*

CHROMA
25017 *91*
25019 *91*
25024 *91*

TYPO
37021 *116*

SPATIAL
49008 *142*

FLAVOR PROFILE *Abstract • Unexpected Color • Edgy • Innovative • Experimental • Hip or Trendy • Unconventional • Sophisticated • Bold • Exciting • Systematic*

PICTO
02027 42
02030 42
02031 42
CHROMA
19039 79
31010 102
TYPO
35046 113
37010 116
45020 133
SPATIAL
49008 142
50008 144

FLAVOR PROFILE *Delicate • Illustrative • Classical Styling • Old-World • Decorative • Sophisticated • Cultured • Reserved • Earthy • Handmade • Symbolic*

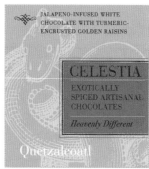

PICTO
07009 52
17009 72
CHROMA
30014 100
TYPO
37010 116
38006 118
48303 139
SPATIAL
49026 142
49027 142

FLAVOR PROFILE *Opulent • Classical • Formal • Crisp • Precision • Luxurious • Exclusivity • Unexpected Color • Environmental Context • Hint of Edginess • Artsy*

PICTO
04019 47
12003 62
12039 63
12044 63
17013 72
CHROMA
19039 79
19050 79
19053 79
TYPO
37020 116
38043 119
SPATIAL
49026 142

FLAVOR PROFILE *Layered • Contemporary • Energetic • Vibrant • Sensuous • Abstract • Fluid Rhythm • Formal*

PICTO
15070 69
15077 69
15085 69
CHROMA
19039 79
32011 104
TYPO
37035 117
SPATIAL
49009 142

A series of promotional tote bags for a fairy-tale festival supports a family of black-and-white creature illustrations with a rainbow of vivid hues. A contemporary serif, used for the type elements, visually relates to the thins and thicks in the drawings.

STUDIO CUCULIĆ ZAGREB | CROATIA

Electric hues and sharply stylized illustrations of insect pests convey the potency of these repellent sprays. Consistency among illustrative treatments, type styles and arrangement, positioning of the primary insect subject relative to the titling and background areas, and secondary hue identities provides immediate product family recognizability.

BRUKETA & ZINIC
ZAGREB | CROATIA

Wraparound labels of abstracted, dot-patterned photographs bring energy and a contemporary edge to this packaging system for a line of toiletries. The choice of a classical serif brings detail and organicism to the otherwise hard-edged presentation.

FRANCESCA SCIANDRA
NEW YORK, NY | UNITED STATES

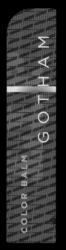

MASCARA

GOTHAM

GOTHAM
DYE

BRONZING
BLUSH

GOTHAM

COLOR BALM GOTHAM

COLOR BALM GOTHAM

For a funky, sophisticated cosmetics line, the designer evokes the energy and architecture of an urban environment with a variety of geometric patterns. A two-level palette brands the overall line and color codes products for day or evening. Added drama and contrast are supplied by the mix of typefaces: a sleek sans serif family and a chunky slab serif.

STIM VISUAL COMMUNICATION
BROOKLYN, NY │ UNITED STATES

The immediacy and variability of narrative inherent in public storytelling announce themselves in this vibrant packaging system for a set of archive CDs produced by a storytelling organization. A family of vivid primary hues underpins the packages; each cover's layout combines several elements whose subjects change from CD to CD, but whose visual treatments remain consistent. Formal attributes from within the images inform the selection of type styles to help unify the visual language.

MARY DOMOWICZ
NEW YORK, NY │ UNITED STATES

the moth

Blue
in the
Face

stories
about
smoke

the moth

Innocents
Abroad

stories
of strangers
in strange
lands

the moth
at the
U.S. Comedy
Arts Festival
in Aspen
2003

When Worlds
Collide

tales
from the
clash

slavonica

slavonica

Shopping bags for a delicatessen of regional Croatian specialties show a range of hand-drawn illustrations that evoke the area's rich heritage of textile design.

STUDIO CUCULIĆ ZAGREB │ CROATIA

A painterly composition of the continents on the cover of this CD, "Beats on Canvas," metaphorically links art making and drumming. Inside the case, a grid of paint daubs, an inscription on the reverse of a stretched canvas, and an array of paint-covered brushes (arranged to evoke long, vertical drips) continue the metaphor. The CD surface itself suggests a "paint-by-numbers" idea.

THOMAS CSANO MONTREAL, QUEBEC | CANADA

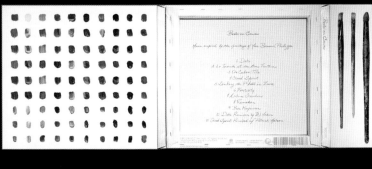

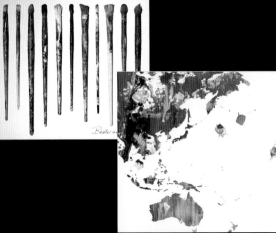

Brilliantly colored typographic pictorializations of each fruit wine's primary ingredient describe the products and how to enjoy them.

BRUKETA & ZINIC ZAGREB | CROATIA

COMPLEX WEBSITE

E-COMMERCE CATALOG PAGE
Eco-Conscious Apparel and Home Fashions

Messaging Menu

*Communicate the site's product offering: organic clothing—
produced using eco-friendly, sustainable production
methods—that doesn't sacrifice style.*

Evoke a sense of luxury and convey the materiality and workmanship of the products.

Convey the seasonality of the current collection.

*Provide catalog functionality for browsing products and exploring
selected items in greater detail.*

Text Element Translations

Client/Website Name
Sew Ready: Responsible Outfitters

Positioning Line
Organic apparel for the couture-conscious

User's Browsing Focus
Fall 2010 Collection / Womens / Evening Dresses / Silk

Navigation Elements
*Collections: Mens / Womens / Kids
Accessories
Home Fashions
About Sustainable Fashion
Company Profile
Shopping Cart / Checkout*

Product labels and description are represented
by dummy text in this project.

PICTO
01004 40
01016 40
01067 41
04001 46
04008 46
CHROMA
24009 88
TYPO
37013 116
38025 119
42011 126
46021 134
46050 135
SPATIAL
52017 149

FLAVOR PROFILE *Simple • Direct • Collage Browsing • Intuitive • Personal • Contemporary • Friendly • Fresh • Light*

PICTO
04001 46
04017 47
13028 64
17031 72
CHROMA
24014 88
28032 97
TYPO
33022 108
37019 116
46013 134
46043 135
46044 135
SPATIAL
53032 151

FLAVOR PROFILE *Modular • Organized • Thumbnail Grid Browsing • Layered • Embroidery Allusion • Well-Made • Detailed • Sophisticated*

PICTO
01006 40
01069 41
04001 46
04029 47
10061 59
CHROMA
24018 89
25002 90
TYPO
33025 109
37030 117
42029 127
45014 132
46039 135
SPATIAL
50009 144

FLAVOR PROFILE *Geometric • Collage Browsing • Kinetic Size Progression • Cutout • Weave Reference • Chic • Urban • Exclusive*

PICTO
04001 46
12004 62
17037 73
17061 73
17069 73
CHROMA
19063 79
21045 83
TYPO
36044 115
37028 117
38026 119
42003 126
46008 134
46036 135
SPATIAL
49010 142
51017 147

FLAVOR PROFILE *Textural • Page-Turn Browsing • Diversity • Look-Book/ Editorial Allusion • Tactile • Eclectic • Pop • Glamorous*

PICTO
04001 46
06005 50
14010 66
14115 67
15114 69
17031 72
17032 72
CHROMA
28032 97
TYPO
33022 108
37030 117
46044 135
46045 135
SPATIAL
52031 149

FLAVOR PROFILE *Simple • Geometric • Movable Strip Browsing • Weave Reference • Fabric Edges • Patterning*

PICTO
04001 46
CHROMA
22032 85
TYPO
37013 116
42009 126
46041 135
SPATIAL
49033 142
51017 147

FLAVOR PROFILE *Neutral • Minimal • Clean • Chic • Large Thumbnail Browsing • Informational • Direct • Reserved*

In this website, shifting planes of text, image, and pattern reveal greater complexities of content from screen to screen. The deep, saturated color and sleek sans serif typeface contribute to the sense of the client's competency.

STIM VISUAL COMMUNICATION
BROOKLYN, NY | UNITED STATES

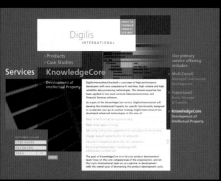

Sharp, vector-based, illustrative animations in the header combine with icons and geometric details to create a brightly modern site for a recreational club.

2FRESH ISTANBUL | TURKEY,

PICTO
04001 46
06005 50

CHROMA
20007 80
25031 91

TYPO
37001 116
42001 126
42009 126
46043 135

SPATIAL
52019 149

FLAVOR PROFILE *Collage • Button/Text Browsing • Subject Context •
Rich • Seasonal Color • Dimensional • Image/Navigation Form Similarity*

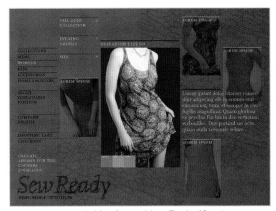

PICTO
02032 42
04001 46
04015 46
04030 47
05024 49
06005 50
09003 56

CHROMA
25012 90
28032 97

TYPO
33047 109
37039 117
38042 119
42019 127

SPATIAL
53030 151

FLAVOR PROFILE *Modular • Staggered, Large Thumbnail Browsing •
Ecological • Rich • Interaction with Nature • Collage • Illustrative • Textural*

PICTO
01014 40
02032 42
03016 44
04001 46
04011 46
05022 49
06005 50
07031 53

CHROMA
25009 90
25031 91

TYPO
33039 109
37013 116
42009 126
42027 127

SPATIAL
53032 151

FLAVOR PROFILE *Bold • Ordered • Pop • Kitschy Glamour • Street •
Fresh • Vivacious Energy • Large Thumbnail Browsing • Illustrative Detailing*

PICTO
04001 46
06005 50

CHROMA
20047 81
20070 81

TYPO
37031 117
38042 119
46018 134
46044 135

SPATIAL
53032 151

FLAVOR PROFILE *Modular • Thumbnail Grid Browsing • Ordered •
Neutral • Architectonic • Constructed • Utilitarian • Warm • Responsible*

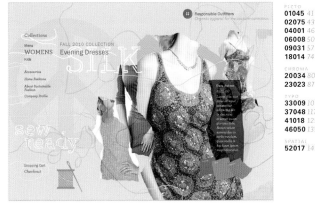

PICTO
01045 41
02075 43
04001 46
06008 50
09031 57
18014 74

CHROMA
20034 80
23023 87

TYPO
33009 108
37048 117
41018 125
46050 135

SPATIAL
52017 149

FLAVOR PROFILE *Collage Browsing • Intuitive • Fabric and Thread
Allusions • Textural • Populist • Responsible • Concrete versus Abstract*

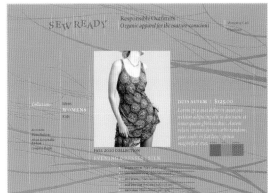

PICTO
01023 40
04001 46
06005 50
09011 56

CHROMA
23016 86

TYPO
33032 109
37048 117
42004 126
46017 134

SPATIAL
52013 148

FLAVOR PROFILE *Soft • Text/List Navigation • Rhythmic • Ecological •
Reserved • Formal • Sophisticated • Dimensional • Weather Allusion*

BOOK DESIGN

TRADE BOOK
Cultural/Historical Subject

Messaging Menu

Create a complex editorial layout structure for a coffee-table book titled
The Garden of Dark Delights:
Confronting Passion and Morality in the Vampire Legend.

Visually evoke legendary aspects of the vampire: undead state, sleeping in earth, shape-shifting, drinking of blood, superhuman movement, rising at night, death and decay, mysteriousness, the ethereal, animal sensuality, earthly pleasure, heightened sensory experience, sharpened teeth and nails, paleness, alienation, religious excommunication.

Suggest the spiritual context of the vampire with regard to religion and notions of good and evil.

Convey feelings of sensuality, pleasure, mystery, darkness, anxiety, horror, lust, sacrifice, and power.

Text Element Translations

Titling
Chapter 4
The Spiritual and the Secular: Embracing the Afterlife on Earth

Introductory Paragraph
Acknowledging the Victorian struggle between a desire for spiritual redemption and a newfound zeal for physical gratification, the figure of the vampire titillates with the suggestion that everlasting life—and worldly sensuality—need not be mutually exclusive pursuits.

Callout Head
Eternity in Heaven or Endless Living?
Comparing Symbolic Iconography

FLAVOR PROFILE *Classical •*
Renaissance • Historic • Aged • Sinister •
Formal • Manuscript • Artifact •
Treasure • Sensual • Metaphorical

PICTO
04001 46
04027 47
05007 48
07009 52
17033 72
17051 73
17052 73
CHROMA
29004 98
TYPO
37018 116
39031 121
40020 123
40029 123
41017 125
42013 126
43015 128
44028 131
48217 139
SPATIAL
51005 146
54004 152
55008 154
56006 156
57002 158

FLAVOR PROFILE *Contemporary •*
Iconic • Medieval References • Rich •
Jewel-like Color • Illustrative •
Dimensional • Emphasis on Symbolism

PICTO
04009 46
04023 47
07009 52
18002 74
18012 74
18034 75
CHROMA
21007 82
29003 98
TYPO
37043 117
38043 119
39026 121
40007 122
40029 123
41001 124
42013 126
43108 129
43155 129
44012 130
44026 131
SPATIAL
53015 150
54033 153
56021 157
57004 158

FLAVOR PROFILE *Timeless •*
Elegant • Ethereal • Narrative • Light •
Decorative • Elusive • Relatively
Neutral • Spiritual • Contemplative

PICTO
04002 46
04017 47
06005 50
06009 50
06023 51
07010 52
CHROMA
25014 90
25015 90
TYPO
37009 116
37013 116
40014 122
40021 123
41008 124
42009 126
43049 128
44017 130
44036 131
48306 139
SPATIAL
51015 146
54015 152
57027 159

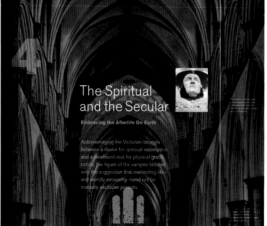

A six-column grid, used in a classical mirrored format, organizes a rich mix of text and illustrations for this book about sea travel. Gothic drop caps lead the paragraphs of serif-set text, while alternating page colors and textural details bring contrast and rhythm to the page sequence.

SUTHERN DESIGN
MADISON, NJ | UNITED STATES

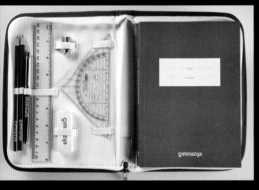

Actual objects—pencils, protractor, pencil sharpener, eraser, and ruler—become companion images to the printed photographs in this unusual monograph for a progressive school, bound inside a student's pencil case. Duotoned images, limited type style, and linear elements underscore the academic quality of the piece.

BRUKETA & ZINIC ZAGREB | CROATIA

This guide to the ancient city's secrets uses rich, yet restrained, color, delicate patterning, and exquisitely crafted text typography folded neatly into an intimate size. A light, sepia-toned photograph provides a sense of the city's historical weight.

RED CANOE DEER LODGE, TN | UNITED STATES

The text spreads in this book organize content on an eight-column grid, staggering text and images across the spread in a rhythmic bounce of proportions. This movement contrasts the focused, horizontal band that governs the chapter openers; both share a limited vocabulary of typeface, delicate floral color, and decorative geometric motifs.

JULIE SHIM
NEW YORK, NY | UNITED STATES

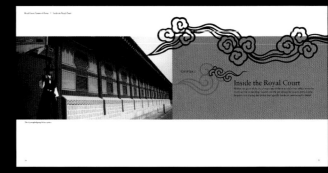

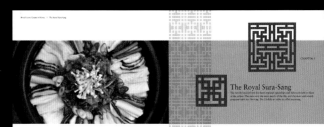

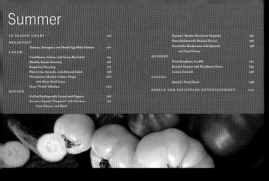

Summer

In the page spreads of a book for a nature preserve, precise and delicate typographic structure provides a quiet, analytical counterpoint to the vibrancy of color images. Section openers are graced with lush, layered collages of transparent plant silhouettes, while interior pages display super-saturated photographs of actual plants. Colored bands code the sections, corresponding to locations in the preserve.

PAONE DESIGN ASSOCIATES
PHILADELPHIA, PA | UNITED STATES

Simple and Satisfying Entertainment

Summertime invites us to share our table and experience the joy of eating communally. Sultry evenings let us drop from ideal perfection and ease into soaking for a crowd without stress or worry. After years of serving up food for family, friends, and sometimes nuts and cones, I have my system down.

1 Spend an hour doing morning prep work. Setting the table and doing prep early in the morning, or even the evening before people come, is a little time-management trick that makes entertaining more doable. Cut my veggies that need slicing or dicing for your recipes and refrigerate them. A spray of lemon juice keeps their color and flavor intact.

2 Don't fuss over a formal dinner setting. Summer tables are about fun-ivity. Choose colored recycled napkins and stack the utensils in colorful glasses. Put lemon and herbs in a bright yellow mug, your sprouts in salads blue, and your table looks like a party.

3 Serve interesting, nonalcoholic drinks in place of wines. Coconut water is a perfect, refreshing drink for hot weather. It is very hydrating, full of electrolytes, but free of the chemicals or cosmetic sugars of a sports drink, and it tastes fabulous. Mix with mint for an extra kick. Brewing some aromatic teas and then icing them in a pitcher with fresh herbs or fruit works well too. Delegate your friends to bring some drinks, but improvise. "No stress!"

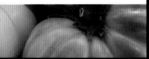

4 Place some snacks around the kitchen. Have some munchies ready for your guests like Spicy Mixed Nuts, Savory Cheese Bitterains, and Pumpkin Walnut Balls, for sure summer repells but arrivals and the early fortit get hungry. Credits can be bought presut and served with any of my dressings.

5 Make pace in your serving plates. Divide the composition of the meal amongst serving plates and bowls of different shapes and sizes. Proteins on one tray, salad in another bowl, dressing, nuts, and other sides in their own dishes. Look in it at a whole picture and make it pretty. A few flowers can decorate the platters. Let guests compile a plate that appeals to their senses.

6 Add an old-fashioned element. For a super simple but fun dessert, pass around a soda fountain-style whipped cream dispenser, and let guests squirt their own organic cream over fresh summer berries.

7 Don't rush. Eating in summer means there's no sense of time. People drift in when the cooking has begun and hang out by the stove or barbecue. The joy is that the preparation, cooking, and socializing are one and the same. You eat when the food is ready and even still, it can sit for forevermore! Piping hot isn't as important in August. Let it all be as it is. Everything about this season is casual.

Black Cod with Snow Peas

SERVES 4

If you aren't able to find black and white lemon as available as butterfish use whatever your favorite white fish.

4	(4-ounce) black cod fillets, about ½-inch thick, skin removed
¾	cup All-Purpose Marinade (pg. 49)
½	pound Chinese snow peas
¼	cup fresh organic orange juice
1	(1-inch) piece fresh ginger, peeled and diced
2	tablespoons unsalted butter
	Sea salt
	Freshly ground black pepper
1	tablespoon coconut or olive oil

1. Place fillets in a nonreactive container or large plastic bag and add half the marinade, reserving the other half. Seal container and refrigerate for about 30 minutes.

2. Meanwhile, bring a large pot of salted water to a boil. Add snow peas and cook for 30 seconds. Immediately drain under cold running water. Set aside.

3. To make sauce, place reserved marinade, orange juice, and ginger into a small saucepan over medium heat. Simmer until liquid begins to thicken, about 4 minutes. Remove from heat and discard ginger. Stir in butter. Season with salt and pepper. Cover to keep warm, and set aside.

4. Remove fillets from marinade and pat dry with paper towels. Season both sides with salt and pepper. Heat coconut oil in a large skillet. Sear fillets on each side until they are golden, being careful not to overcook, about 3 minutes on each side.

5. To serve, divide snow peas between four dinner plates, top with a fillet, and spoon a little sauce over the top. Serve any additional sauce on the side.

The straightforward, four-column structure and presentation of photographic imagery is enlivened through a mix of strongly-contrasted type styles, bold color fields, dramatic cropping, and visually interesting page breaks. Silhouetted images contrast those framed in rectangles, while smaller, overlapping insets and variations in positioning provide tremendous bounce across the spreads. Informational details set in color bring the rich chromatic quality of the images into the type.

BTD:NYC
NEW YORK, NY | UNITED STATES

68

Forest Pond and Pond Edge

The Forest Pond is an intimate yet elusive place to experience the riches of this diverse ecology...

"I went to the woods because I wished to live deliberately, to front only the essential facts of life, and see if I could not learn what it had to teach, and not, when I came to die, discover that I had not lived."
—Henry David Thoreau, Walden

Joe Pye Weed

Eupatorium purpureum

4

THE DESSERT TRAY

Purely Typographic Solutions

No less delectable than the rest of the menu, these typographic
treats explore the possibilities of letters and text alone—
whether sweet and light, strong and simple, or rich and textural.
The projects here present type's fascinating design potential
as a visual image unto itself, the perfect way to
round out a thoroughly enjoyable tasting of design dishes.

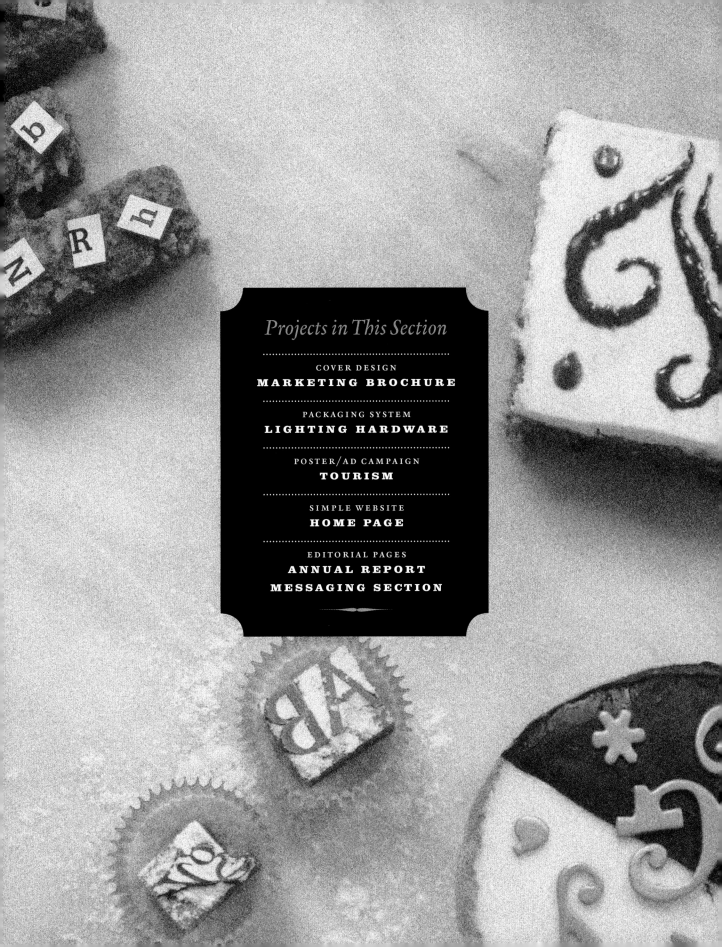

COVER DESIGN

MARKETING BROCHURE
Real Estate Marketing

Messaging Menu

Establish a connection between the heritage of a historic building, located close to New York City's Grand Central Terminal, and its contemporary renovation.

Convey the upscale nature of the property.

Evoke the energy of the urban environment and of the train station itself.

Promote the significance of the new architecture.

Invite prospective buyers to participate in a prestigious lifestyle.

Text Element Translations

Property Name
The Vanderbilt
At the Grand Central Complex
Luxury Condominiums

Address
120 Park Avenue South
At 41st Street

Tagline
Timeless style in the heart of the city

This series of financial books is "packaged" under a gigantic visual device—an ampersand cropped across the covers. Contrasting the continuity of the punctuation mark, the color of each cover changes, as does the linear, geometric pattern that creates the ampersand.

FORM LONDON | UNITED KINGDOM

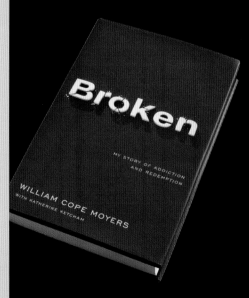

A rich red field creates a backdrop for the three-dimensional typographic treatment of the title on this book cover.

THINK STUDIO
NEW YORK, NY | UNITED STATES

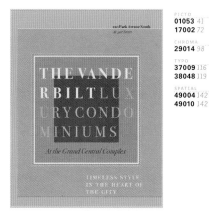

PICTO
01053 *41*
17002 *72*
CHROMA
29014 *98*
TYPO
37009 *116*
38048 *119*
SPATIAL
49004 *142*
49010 *142*

FLAVOR PROFILE *Classical • Exclusive •*
Majestic • Sharp • Historic • Precise • Timeless

PICTO
17052 *73*
CHROMA
21030 *83*
25002 *90*
TYPO
34002 *110*
37024 *116*
38046 *119*
39024 *121*
SPATIAL
49002 *142*
49049 *143*

FLAVOR PROFILE *Expressive • Gestural •*
Urban • Architectural Detail • Historic • Aesthetic
Quality • Decorative

PICTO
02089 *43*
18025 *74*
CHROMA
26016 *92*
TYPO
33016 *108*
37040 *117*
38038 *119*
SPATIAL
49011 *142*
49019 *142*

FLAVOR PROFILE *Iconic • Transit Heritage •*
Historic • Urban Culture • Detailed • Metaphorica •
Ambiguous Space

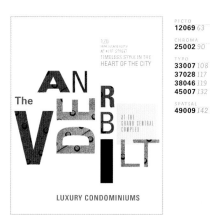

PICTO
12069 *63*
CHROMA
25002 *90*
TYPO
33007 *108*
37028 *117*
38046 *119*
45007 *132*
SPATIAL
49009 *142*

FLAVOR PROFILE *Bold • Architectural*
Allusion • Geometric • Progressive • Vibrant •
Cultured • Integrated

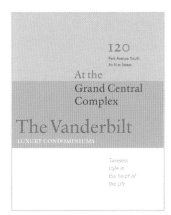

PICTO
NA
CHROMA
25015 *90*
TYPO
37002 *108*
37026 *117*
38017 *118*
38043 *119*
SPATIAL
49008 *142*
49049 *143*

FLAVOR PROFILE *Muted • Reserved •*
Elegant • Nostalgic • Geometric • Historic •
Contemplative

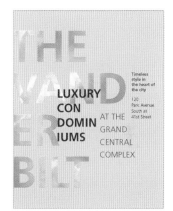

PICTO
10001 *58*
CHROMA
29023 *99*
TYPO
33007 *108*
37028 *117*
38024 *118*
38043 *119*
SPATIAL
49012 *142*
49033 *142*

FLAVOR PROFILE *Skyline Allusion • Visionary •*
Sophisticated • Pictorial Metaphor • Architectural •
Expansive • Aspirational

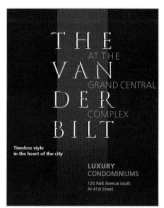

PICTO
NA
CHROMA
26002 *92*
TYPO
34035 *111*
35007 *112*
37028 *117*
38032 *119*
SPATIAL
49002 *142*
49011 *142*

FLAVOR PROFILE *Aggressive • Challenging •*
Majestic • Classical • Luxury • Confidence •
Urban Canyon Allusion • Privileged

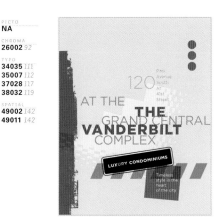

PICTO
01001 *40*
01015 *40*
01068 *41*
17037 *73*
17069 *73*
18046 *75*
CHROMA
19017 *78*
25002 *90*
TYPO
34034 *111*
37030 *117*
38007 *118*
38023 *118*
41009 *124*
SPATIAL
50021 *144*

FLAVOR PROFILE *Collage • City Allusions •*
Multilayered • Expressive • Artsy • Spontaneous

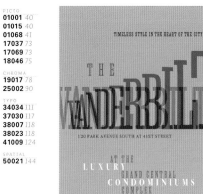

PICTO
01068 *41*
01069 *41*
CHROMA
19003 *78*
19067 *79*
TYPO
37023 *116*
38041 *119*
SPATIAL
49007 *142*
50004 *144*

FLAVOR PROFILE *Rhythmic • Columnar •*
Structural • Grandiose • Eclectic • Transit •
Rush-Hour • Movement

PACKAGING SYSTEM

LIGHTING HARDWARE
Energy-Efficient Lightbulbs

Messaging Menu

Clearly identify the product and visually position the brand as innovative; communicate the new technology of LED light production.

Express the notions of luminosity, energy conservation, and lasting usability, suggesting a beneficial, long-term effect on the environment.

Equate the product with a cost-conscious, responsible lifestyle.

Differentiate the color temperature of each product in the line.

Text Element Translations

Brand Name and Product Descriptor
Lumilast LED
Home Use Interior Light Bulbs

Product Features
60 Watt Equivalency
Featuring Chromoplex
Kelvin Temperature Simulation

Bulb Temperatures
2700 Warm White
4100 Cool White
5600 Neutral Daylight

Large-scale, elegant serif type against crisp, white backgrounds brings a refreshing, no-nonsense appeal to the packaging of these day-to-day bath products.
KYI SUN LEE NEW YORK, NY | UNITED STATES

PICTO	
18011	74
CHROMA	
20003	80
20025	80
20033	80
TYPO	
33016	108
37030	117
38042	119
SPATIAL	
49011	142

PICTO	
NA	
CHROMA	
21025	83
21027	83
32029	105
TYPO	
33043	109
34004	110
36032	115
SPATIAL	
49019	142

PICTO	
01028	40
CHROMA	
19051	79
27029	95
TYPO	
37009	116
38025	119
SPATIAL	
49020	142

FLAVOR PROFILE *Geometric • Concrete Depiction • Sharp • Clear • Efficient*

FLAVOR PROFILE *Radiant • Augmented Color • Hi-Tech • Vibrant • Geometric*

FLAVOR PROFILE *Austere • Economical • Efficient • Ordered • Systematic • Responsible*

PICTO	
NA	
CHROMA	
19040	79
21048	83
TYPO	
33021	108
34048	111
37028	117
38041	119
SPATIAL	
49056	143

PICTO	
01028	40
CHROMA	
32010	104
TYPO	
34024	110
37001	116
38031	119
SPATIAL	
49033	142

PICTO	
01069	41
15006	68
CHROMA	
19037	79
21027	83
32017	105
TYPO	
33010	108
37030	117
SPATIAL	
49072	143

FLAVOR PROFILE *Montage • Metaphorical Augmentation • Ecological • Responsible • Long-Term • Direct*

FLAVOR PROFILE *Organic • Luminous • Transition • Enlightened • Augmentation • Ecological • Illustrative Detailing • Humanistic*

FLAVOR PROFILE *Concrete • Grounded • Radiant • Straightforward • Utilitarian • Bold • Contemporary • Colorful*

POSTER CAMPAIGN

TOURISM
Government Agency

Messaging Menu

Express the mission of the client, a government agency concerned with the stewardship of natural environments.

Evoke the natural grandeur of the sites being promoted; convey the unique experience of the sites in winter.

Entice travelers to visit off-season.

Text Element Translations

Poster Headlines

The animals aren't the only ones in luxurious coats this season.
Acadia National Park (1)

Leave the hood and see some real bling…
Ice, ice, baby.
The Grand Canyon (2)

It's a white carpet without celebrities, but there's still plenty of flash.
Yellowstone National Park (3)

Client and Tagline
U.S. National Parks Service
See it in winter

This two-sided celebrity event poster wraps the first names of various famous personages front to back in a large scale, slab serif typeface set in a vivid process blue. The large text's varying color relationship to its background, along with transparent box elements and contrasting sans serif type elements, contribute to an edgy, yet elegant, layered dimensional quality.
PAARPILOTEN DÜSSELDORF | GERMANY

A study in textural scale, this performance poster pitches enormous, vertically emphatic script elements—themselves spliced into a secondary rhythm—against a textured, horizontal Roman headline, staggered, rotated text elements, and a delicate, linear pattern.
CASSRA STUDIO
TEHRAN | IRAN

FLAVOR PROFILE
Abstracted Space •
Colorful • Bold •
Layered • Weather
and Flag Allusions

PICTO
01057 41
14007 66
14008 66

CHROMA
21001 82
25028 91

TYPO
37028 117
38023 118
38031 119

SPATIAL
49008 142

FLAVOR PROFILE
1930s Americana •
Iconic • Streamline
Transportation •
Exploration • Crisp
Industrial • Abstract

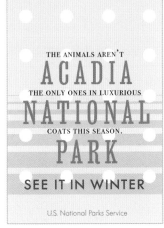

PICTO
01057 41
14008 66

CHROMA
29012 98
29015 98

TYPO
37023 116
37029 117
38032 119

SPATIAL
49025 142

FLAVOR PROFILE
Sense of Expectation •
Vertical Emphasis •
Grandeur • Focused •
Bigger than Life •
Dimensional • Cold

PICTO
NA

CHROMA
25028 91

TYPO
37028 117
38031 119
38048 119

SPATIAL
49027 142
49029 142

FLAVOR PROFILE
*Direct • Fresh •
Neutral • Emphasis
on Environment •
Contemporary •
Expansive • Under-
stated • Elegant*

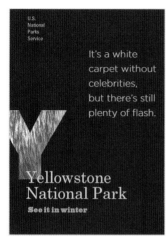

PICTO
04030 47
10017 58
10020 58
10038 59
CHROMA
23023 87
32006 104
TYPO
33007 108
37046 117
38017 118
38018 118
SPATIAL
49046 143

FLAVOR PROFILE
*Geometric • Iconic •
Pristine • Grandeur •
Experiential • Dynamic
Scale • Cinematic*

PICTO
01028 40
02009 42
02010 42
02011 42
CHROMA
19039 79
19049 79
25032 91
TYPO
33037 109
37030 117
38043 119
SPATIAL
49035 142

FLAVOR PROFILE
*Mid-Century Modern •
Nostalgic • Family
Activity • Ambiguous
Space • Iconic •
Emphasis on Train
Travel • Vernacular •
Stylized*

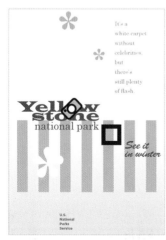

PICTO
01028 40
02093 43
03031 45
14005 66
CHROMA
26014 92
29017 99
TYPO
33016 108
37047 117
38027 119
SPATIAL
49040 143

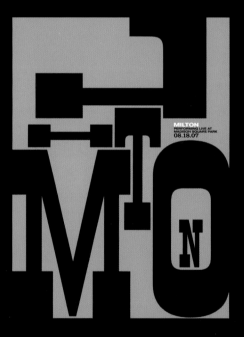

Old wood-type slab serif capitals are rearranged in playful configurations from poster to poster in this series to promote a band. Stark black-and-white text elements are set off by a different vibrant hue in each poster.

STEREOTYPE DESIGN
NEW YORK, NY | UNITED STATES

SIMPLE WEBSITE

HOME PAGE
Cultural Institution: Performing Arts

Messaging Menu

Communicate the concept of operatic performance, evoking its rich history and cultural significance.

Establish the organization's contemporary, nontraditional artistic direction.

Allude to the grand themes of opera and of the current season; introduce the performance currently on stage.

Convey the organization's context in a rural environment.

Text Element Translations

Client
The New Country Opera

Titling
Love, Death, and Everything in Between: The 2010 Season

Featured Content
On Stage Now: The Magic Flute
Wolfgang Amadeus Mozart
A surrealist adaptation set in the decade prior to World War I

Navigation Elements
Performance Calendar
Capital Campaign
People and Programs
Subscriptions

This home page uses modular grid elements, size changes, and sharp, angular rules to provide richness of detail; the shift of elements left and right, and the varied intervals of space around them, impart rhythm against the geometric solidity of the structure.

PAONE DESIGN ASSOCIATES
PHILADELPHIA, PA | UNITED STATES

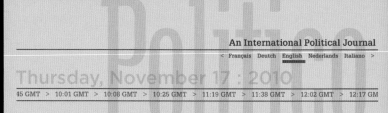

Updating and abstracting typographic language commonly associated with printed newspapers, this online political journal and blog captures the spirit of hard-nosed, credible journalism and nostalgia of the physical inspiration and translates it to speak to a current, techologically-savvy audience.

STIM VISUAL COMMUNICATION BROOKLYN, NY | UNITED STATE

PICTO	
14004	66
CHROMA	
19023	78
25013	90
TYPO	
34001	110
37045	117
46017	134
48001	138
48201	139
48292	139
SPATIAL	
49014	142
50043	145

FLAVOR PROFILE *Romantic • Sensuous • Musical • Rigorous • Ornamental • Ambiguous Space • Rhythmic • Classical*

PICTO	
02019	42
10028	58
CHROMA	
19070	78
24018	89
TYPO	
33007	108
33016	108
36023	114
37001	116
38040	119
46002	134
SPATIAL	
49056	143

FLAVOR PROFILE *Simple • Rural Environment • Rustic • Organic • Natural Color • Timeless • Decorative Detailing*

PICTO	
01002	40
02037	42
17028	72
17056	73
18013	74
18021	74
18034	75
CHROMA	
19032	78
19041	79
19049	79
TYPO	
33016	108
33037	109
36042	115
37001	116
38025	119
46050	135
SPATIAL	
49068	143

FLAVOR PROFILE *Vernacular • Eclectic • Geometric • Constructed • Narrative • Symbolic • Delicate • Nostalgic • Iconic • Collage • Symbolic*

PICTO	
NA	
CHROMA	
19006	78
29006	98
TYPO	
37022	116
38045	119
38046	119
39015	120
46008	134
48193	139
48208	139
48214	139
48265	139
48291	139
SPATIAL	
49046	143

FLAVOR PROFILE *Classical • Victorian • Eclectic • Rural Environment • Nostalgic • Romantic • Organic • Ornamental • Direct*

PICTO	
NA	
CHROMA	
24013	88
TYPO	
37026	117
38014	118
38018	118
38043	119
46020	134
48018	138
48089	138
48114	138
48181	139
SPATIAL	
49009	142
52018	149

FLAVOR PROFILE *Contemporary • Clean • Professional • Subtle Ornamentation • Organized • Efficient • Informational • Rigorous • Sophisticated • Neutral • Quiet*

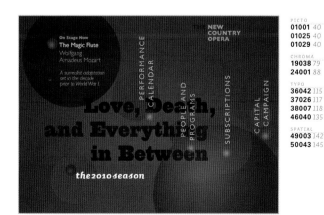

PICTO	
01001	40
01025	40
01029	40
CHROMA	
19038	79
24001	88
TYPO	
36042	115
37026	117
38007	118
46040	135
SPATIAL	
49003	142
50043	145

FLAVOR PROFILE *Eclectic • Geometric • Presentational • Thematic • Interactive • Informational • Systematic • Fluid*

Supported by an equally dramatic three-color palette, extremes of spatial proportion and scale among elements are enriched by a contrast in serif and sans serif faces, opposing structural logic, areas of bold simplicity, and a myriad of finely detailed informational elements.

ADAMSMORIOKA BEVERLY HILLS, CA | UNITED STATES

EDITORIAL PAGES

ANNUAL REPORT MESSAGING SECTION
Industrial Chemical Manufacturing

Messaging Menu

Communicate the client's core products and services: developing and distributing chemical compounds for industrial and technological manufacture.

Convey the general idea of chemistry

Establish the client's expertise and credibility within their field.

Visualize the page spread's primary message in an accessible, dynamic way.

Establish a sense of accomplishment and the client's aspirations.

Text Element Translations

Client/Project
Chemokore Industrial Group
2010 Annual Report

Spread Title
More than simple growth: A new formula for research and development efficiency

Deck
This past year saw the implementation of a dramatic new centrifuge system and informatics systems that not only shorten the development schedule by half, but open up new avenues of exploration

Diagram Head
Change in financial performance relative to development time

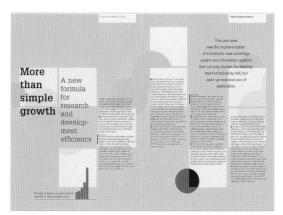

PICTO
01001 40
01004 40
18049 75
CHROMA
20037 81
26012 92
TYPO
36030 115
40003 122
40004 122
43055 128
44017 130
44018 130
45002 132
SPATIAL
53006 150
54005 152

FLAVOR PROFILE *Chemical • Bold • Abstract • Allusive • Complex • Diagrammatic • Scientific • Ambiguous Space • Kinetic*

PICTO
01001 40
01028 40
18050 75
CHROMA
20025 80
26011 92
TYPO
34048 111
36030 115
38030 119
40003 122
40009 122
40021 123
43057 128
44013 130
44028 131
48070 138
48146 138
SPATIAL
51009 146
54002 152

FLAVOR PROFILE *Classic Editorial Structure • Linear • Integrated • Progression • Efficient • Transformation • Molecular • Industrial*

PICTO
01018 40
01028 40
CHROMA
19004 78
26013 92
TYPO
33006 108
36032 115
37029 117
38014 118
40023 123
43119 129
43144 129
44021 130
44022 130
47001 136
SPATIAL
52008 148
54011 152

FLAVOR PROFILE *Systematic • Vibrant • Energetic • Innovative • Dimensional • Sequential • Chemically-Altered • Rotated Graph • Layered*

PICTO
01001 40
01067 41
CHROMA
20062 81
26012 92
TYPO
34032 111
37028 117
43016 128
43142 129
43153 129
44042 131
44049 131
SPATIAL
52008 148
54025 153

FLAVOR PROFILE *Symbolic • Abstract • Rotational Movement • Liquid • Psychedelic • Chemical • Augmentation • Complex Organization • Edgy*

PICTO
01004 40
18048 75
CHROMA
19049 79
23027 87
TYPO
37028 117
39011 120
40001 122
43013 128
44015 130
44047 131
SPATIAL
53026 151
54008 152

FLAVOR PROFILE *Geometric • Translucent • Ordered • Technological • Part-to-Whole Interaction • Innovative • Clean • Analytical • Competent*

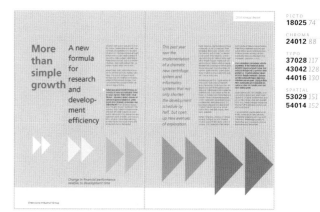

PICTO
18025 74
CHROMA
24012 88
TYPO
37028 117
43042 128
44016 130
SPATIAL
53029 151
54014 152

FLAVOR PROFILE *Precision • Analytical • Efficient • Metaphorical • Dynamic • Graph as Image • Rhythmic • Horizontal Emphasis • Dimensional*

Vivid orange sets off the text-heavy informational panels in this foldout brochure/poster enumerating the pop-culture history and places of interest within a city. A tight column structure is given movement through staggered-height boxes, and kitschy display caps add fun and texture.

DESIGNLIGA
MUNICH | GERMANY

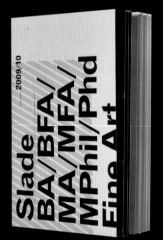

A chunky, grotesk sans serif, supported by near-primary colors and a diagonal line pattern, creates a bold, fresh, almost un-designed identity for an art school. Contrast is achieved through extreme scale and weight changes, along with carefully proportioned spatial intervals such as margins and paragraph separations.

PAARPILOTEN
DÜSSELDORF | GERMANY

AIDS AND POVERTY:
A GLOBAL CRISIS

Worldwide, millions afflicted with the disease are being helped
by drugs, but many in poor countries still go without.

By Bernard O'Connor

THERE IS NO DOUBT THAT AIDS RESEARCH HAS COME A LONG WAY. SINCE the disease was discovered, but there is still no cure. In the meantime, treatement relies heavily on the pharmacentical industry, which spends billions on research and development. Here in the United States, victims are living longer, healthier lives, because of drug therapy, but in other parts of the world, millions of AIDS patients simply cannot afford medication.

AIDS AND POVERTY:
A GLOBAL CRISIS

if it's even available to them. In order for everyone to get help, the world will need to pull together and come up with a solution. This is all placeholder text for this feature about something for you to read. It is set in Janson Text Roman, nine and one-quarter point, on 12 point leading. There are five Boroughs in New York City: Manhattan, Brooklyn, Queens, The Bronx, and Staten Island. Do you know which is the largest? If you answered Queens, you are correct. Manhattan is the most populated of the five.

In order to maintain even spacing between trains, we are being held in the station momentarily. Please be patient. We have a real signal ahead of us, but we will be moving shortly. Due to a train in the station with breaks in emergency, we are experiencing delays in service. As soon as this situation is resolved, we will proceed. Thank you for your patience.

THE WORLD PREPARES TO TAKE ACTION

If there are six people, and each has forty dollars, what is the total amount of money that the group has? There is a total of two hundred and forty dollars among the members of the group, which would be enough to enjoy a modest dinner at an inexpensive restaurant. For me to consider granting your request, I first must weigh all sides of the argument in an objective manner. I need to consider if it would be in your best interest, and in the best interest of the group. Finances will be a factor, and as you know, in these economic times, money is tight. Once I review the situation, I will make my decision, and give it to you.

High-speed train travel may be in America's future. Comonsm in Europe and Japan, our love for the automobile, and reliance on air travel, has prevented the development of a rail system that can handle this type of train, but that is changing. Travelers who might normally take shorter flights, 400 miles or less, would have the option to board a train, and avoid the hassle of getting to the airport early, waiting in long lines at security checks, and dealing with weather delays.

Digital technology seems to develop faster each minute, and consumers are continually faced with the dilemma of that great new product being obsolete before they even open the box. This is all placeholder text for this feature about something for you to read. It is set in Janson Text Roman, nine and one-quarter point, on 12 point leading. There are five Boroughs in New York City: Manhattan, Brooklyn, Queens,

The Bronx, and Staten Island. Do you know which is the largest? If you answered Queens, you are correct. Manhattan is the most populated. In order to maintain even spacing between trains, we are being held in the station momentarily. Please be patient. We have a red

signal ahead of us, but we will be moving shortly. Due to a train in the station with breaks in emergency, we are experiencing delays in service. As soon as the situation is resolved, we will proceed. Thank you for your patience. If there are six people, and each has forty dollars, what is the total amount of money that the group has? There is a total of two hundred and forty dollars among the members of the group, which would be enough to enjoy a modest dinner at an inexpensive restaurant. For me to consider granting your request, I first must weigh all sides of the argument in an objective manner. I need to consider if it would be in your best interest, and in the best economic times, money is tight. Once I review the situation, I will make my decision, and give it to you.

In order to maintain even spacing between trains, we are being held in the station momentarily. Please be patient. We have a red signal ahead of us, but we will be moving shortly. Due to a train in the station with breaks in emergency, we are experiencing delays in service. As soon as the situation is resolved, we will proceed. Thank you for your patience. If there are six people, and each has forty dollars, what is the total amount of money that the group has? There is a total of two hundred and forty dollars among the members of the group, which would be enough to enjoy a modest dinner at an inexpensive restaurant. For me to consider granting your request, I first must weigh all sides of the argument in an objective manner. I need to consider if it would be in your best interest, and in the best interest of the group. Finances will be a factor, and as you know, in these economic times, money is tight. Once I review the situation, I will make my decision, and give it to you.

High-speed train travel may be in America's future. Comonsm in Europe and Japan, our love for the automobile, and reliance on air travel, has prevented the development of a rail system that can handle this type of train, but that is changing. Travelers who might normally take shorter flights, 400 miles or less, would have the option to board a train, and avoid the hassle of getting to the airport early, waiting in long lines at

security checks, and dealing with weather delays. Digital technology seems to develop faster each minute, and consumers are continually faced with the dilemma of that great new product being obsolete before they even open the box. This is all placeholder text for this feature about something for you to read. It is set in Janson

Text Roman, nine and one-quarter point, on 12 point leading. There are five Boroughs in New York City: Manhattan, Brooklyn, Queens, The Bronx, and Staten Island. Do you know which is the largest? If you answered Queens, you are correct. Manhattan is the most populated. In order to maintain even spacing between trains, we are being held in the station momentarily. Please be patient and we all tightly until we say so.

We have a red signal ahead of us, but we will be moving shortly. Due to a train in the station with breaks in emergency, we are experiencing delays in service. As soon as the situation is resolved, we will proceed. Thank you for your patience. If there are six people, and each has forty dollars among the members of the group, which would be enough to enjoy a modest dinner at an inexpensive restaurant. There once was a little girl, who lived on a farm with her parents, sister, and brother. She had two kittens named Sam and Lucy. She would help her daddy feed them, and then get with him into the field, where everyone could see them happy. In order for everyone to get help, the world will need to pull together and come up with a solution. This is all placeholder text for this feature about something for you to read. It is set in Janson Text Roman.

HISTORIC BREAKTHROUGHS IN MEDICINE

For me to consider granting your request, I first must weigh all sides of the argument in an objective manner. I need to consider if it would be in your best interest, and in the best interest of the group. Finances will be a factor, and as you know, in these economic times, money is tight. Once I review the situation, I will make my decision, and give it to you.

If there are six people, and each has forty dollars, what is the total amount of money that the group has? There is a total of two hundred and forty dollars among the members of the group, which would be enough to enjoy a modest dinner at an inexpensive restaurant. In order to maintain even spacing between trains, we are being held in the station momentarily. Please be patient. We have a red signal ahead of us, but we will be

moving shortly. Due to a train in the station with breaks in emergency, we are experiencing delays in service. As soon as the situation is resolved, we will proceed. Thank you for your patience. High-speed train travel may be in America's future. Comonsm in Europe and Japan, our love for the automobile, and reliance on air travel, has prevented the development of a rail system that can handle this type of train, but that is changing.

Travelers who might normally take shorter flights, 400 miles or less, would have the option to board a train, and avoid the hassle of getting to the airport early, waiting in long lines at security checks, and dealing with weather delays. Digital technology seems to develop faster each minute, and consumers are continually faced

In America, being poor and contracting AIDS is tragic, of course, but in an impoverished nation with few resources, it is almost certain to be a death sentence.

with the dilemma of that great new product being obsolete before they even open the box. This is all placeholder text for this feature about something for you to read. It is set in Janson Text Roman, nine and one-quarter point, on 12 point leading. There are five Boroughs in New York City: Manhattan, Brooklyn, Queens, The Bronx, and Staten Island. Do you know which is the largest? If you answered Queens, you are correct. Manhattan is the most populated. In order to maintain even spacing between trains, we are being held in the station momentarily. Please be patient. We have a red signal ahead of us, but we will be moving shortly. Due to a train in the station with breaks in emergency, we are experiencing delays in service. As soon as the situation is resolved, we will proceed.

Thank you for your patience. If there are six people, and each has forty dollars, what is the total amount of money that the group has? There is a total of two hundred and forty dollars among the members of the group, which would be enough to enjoy a modest dinner at an inexpensive restaurant.

There once was a little girl, who lived on a farm with her parents, sister, and brother. She had two kittens named Sam and Lucy. She would help her daddy feed them, and then go with him into the field, where the would pick flowers for her mommy, and then bring them into the house as a surprise. Her mommy put them in a vase on the table, where everyone could see them while they ate dinner and were happy. Thank you for your patience. If there are six people, and each has forty dollars, what is the total amount of money that the

---

Typography need not be considered limited strictly to letters, numbers, and punctuation: the components of the alphabet—dots, lines, and planes—also count. In these editorial pages, the dot assumes a primary role not only as a structural and visual contrast to the linear word and text forms, but bcomes an evocation of the article's subject, being read both as blood and the molecules of a virus. Tremendous scale shifts and contrast between block and linear forms in the opener give way to a more rigid, tightly justified configuration on the jump spread. Expansive margins provide focus on the columns—as well as a pristine, credible, literary feel—and, in concert with carefully positioned callouts and text subheads, help relieve the texture of the primary reading area.

JOSEPH CASERTO
ART DIRECTION AND DESIGN
BROOKLYN, NY | UNITED STATES

Index *by Subject*

Note: Page numbers in grayscale indicate figures.

Directory of Contributors

2 FRESH
Pages 179, 218
Beybi Giz Plaza · Kat 26
Maslak 34396 Istanbul · Turkey

1 Liverpool Street
London EC2M 7QD · United Kingdom
www.2fresh.com

999 DESIGN
Pages 177, 183
91 Great Eastern Street
London EC2A 3HZ · United Kingdom
www.999design.com

ADAMSMORIOKA, INC.
Pages 199, 238
8484 Wilshire Blvd., Suite 600
Beverly Hills, CA 90211 · USA
www.adamsmorioka.com

ATELIER BRÜCKNER
Page 199
Krefelderstrasse 32
Stuttgart · Germany 70376
www.atelier-brueckner.de

BASE ART CO.
Page 177
17 Brickel Street
Columbus, OH 43215 · USA
www.baseartco.com

BRUKETA & ZINIC
Pages 172, 173, 183, 213, 215, 223
Zavrtnica 17
Zagreb · Croatia 10000
www.bruketa-zinic.com

BTD:NYC
Page 225
611 Broadway, Room 511
New York, NY 10012 · USA
www.btdnyc.com

**JOSEPH CASERTO
ART DIRECTION AND
DESIGN**
Pages 191, 241
238 7th Avenue, No. 4R
Brooklyn, NY 11215-3435 · USA
www.josephcaserto.com

CASSRA STUDIO
Page 232
Unit 11, No.5 · 4th Golestan Alley ·
Golestan Street · Marzdaran Blvd.
Tehran · Iran
www.cassraabedini.com

**COMPASS 360 DESIGN
AND ADVERTISING**
Page 172
11 Davies Avenue, Suite 200
Toronto, Ontario · Canada M4M 249
www.compass360.com

CREUNA
Pages 168, 169, 193, 195
Karenslyst Allé 9B
0278 Oslo · Norway
www.creuna.no

THOMAS CSANO
Pages 167, 169, 206, 215
3655 Boulevard St. Laurent · No. 202
Montréal, Quebec · Canada H2X 2V6
www.thomascsano.com

DESIGNLIGA
Pages 20, 240
Erzgiessereistrasse 4
Munich, Bavaria · Germany 80335
www.designliga.com

MARY DOMOWICZ
Pages 173, 214
New York, NY · USA
www.domowicz.com

DURRE DESIGN
Page 183
26440 Birchfield Avenue
Rancho Palos Verde, CA 90275 · USA
www.durredesign.com

FORM
Pages 176, 190, 205, 228
47 Tabernacle Street
London EC2A 4AA · United Kingdom
www.form.uk.com

GROW CREATIVE
Page 20
107 SE Washington St., Suite 251
Portland, Oregon 97214 · USA
www.grow-creative.com

IDEAS ON PURPOSE
Pages 190, 193
307 Seventh Avenue, Suite 701
New York, NY 10001 · USA
www.ideasonpurpose.com

KYM ABRAMS DESIGN
Pages 167, 190
213 West Institute Place, Suite 608
Chicago, IL 60610 · USA
www.kad.com

**KUHLMANN LEAVITT
DESIGN**
Page 199
7810 Forsyth Boulevard, 2 West
Saint Louis, MO 63105 · USA
www.kuhlmannleavitt.com

KYI SUN LEE
Page 230
480 Second Avenue, No. 27F
New York, NY 10016 · USA
www.kyisunlee.com

LSD SPACE
Page 184
San Andreas 36, 2° 6
28004 Madrid · Spain
www.lsdspace.com

PAARPILOTEN
Pages 232, 240
Wasserstrasse 2
40213 Düsseldorf · Germany
www.paarpiloten.com

**PAONE DESIGN
ASSOCIATES**
Pages 16, 167, 203, 225, 236
240 South Twentieth Street
Philadelphia, PA 19043 · USA
www.paonedesign.com

PEOPLE DESIGN
Pages 21, 169, 176, 194, 203
648 Monroe Ave. NW, Suite 212
Grand Rapids, MI 49503 · USA
www.peopledesign.com

RED CANOE
Pages 172, 224
347 Clear Creek Trail
Deer Lodge, TN 37726 · USA
www.redcanoe.com

**MAURICE REDMOND/
FEUER**
Pages 179, 205, 206
Herzogstrasse 32
80803 Munich · Germany
www.mauriceredmond.com

JASEN D. ROLFE
Page 191
1 Loring Road
Lexington, MA 02421 · USA
www.thebambieffect.com

**SÄGENVIER DESIGN-
KOMMUNIKATION**
Page 207
Sägerstrasse 4
6850 Dornbirn · Austria
www.saegenvier.at

**FRANCESCA
SCIANDRA**
Pages 179, 213
38 Hope Street
Providence, RI 02903 · USA
www.fsciandra.com

JULIE SHIM
Page 224
211 West 58th Street · No. 8
New York, NY 10019 · USA

SHINNOSKE, INC.
Pages 173, 202
2-1-8 Tsuriganecho, Chuoku,
6th Floor
Osaka 540-0035 · Japan
www.shinn.co.jp

STEIN ØVRE
Page 21
Grensefaret 23C
1341 Slependen · Norway
www.steinovre.com

**STEREOTYPE
DESIGN**
Pages 185, 235
39 Jane Street, No. 4A
New York, NY 10014 · USA
www.stereotype-design.com

**STIM: VISUAL
COMMUNICATION**
Pages 31, 215, 218, 236
238 South 3rd Street, No. 4
Brooklyn, NY 11211 · USA
info@visual-stim.com

STUDIO CUCULIĆ
Pages 185, 213, 214
Bukovačka 218 A
Zagreb · Croatia 10000
www.studio-cuculic.hr

SUNG SOO SONG
Pages 185, 193
820 Avenue A
Bayonne, NJ 07002 · USA
designurban@hotmail.com

SURFACE
Page 195
Peterstrasse 4
60433 Frankfurt am Main ·
Germany
www.surface.de

SUTHERN DESIGN
Page 223
37 Alexander Avenue
Madison, NJ 07940 · USA
sutherndesign@gmail.com

ANN IM SUNWOO
Page 194
214 East 24th Street, No. 6
New York, NY 10010
swik0929@gmail.com

TACTICAL MAGIC LLC
Page 184
1460 Madison Avenue
Memphis, TN 38104 · USA
www.tacticalmagic.com

THINK STUDIO, NYC
Pages 168, 177, 228
16 Beaver Street
New York, NY 10004 · USA
www.thinkstudionyc.com

Acknowledgments

Patience, in the design process as well as in the kitchen,
is said to be a virtue. If that's true, I must acknowledge
the tremendous virtue of everyone around me throughout
this book's unusually arduous development process:
first, the editorial and design team at Rockport Publishers
(Emily, Betsy, Regina, and Winnie); my long-suffering
partner, Sean; and last, my friends and parents.

As always, I owe a debt of gratitude to the designers and
studios who contributed their work to be featured as
examples; I am once again honored by such professionals
taking time from their busy work schedules to collect and
prepare their projects. A special thanks is due Jasen Rolfe
and Jess Underwood, student assistants who helped with
image production during the more challenging phases.

I would like to dedicate this book to all my students, past
and future, as well as all aspiring design chefs, in the hope
that it will prove useful and enjoyable to read.